ETHICS AND SOCIAL SCIENCE RESEARCH

ETHICS AND SOCIAL SCIENCE RESEARCH

Paul Davidson Reynolds
University of Minnesota

Prentice-Hall, Inc., Englewood Cliffs, New Jersey 07632

Library of Congress Cataloging in Publication Data

Reynolds, Paul Davidson.
 Ethics and social science research.

 (Prentice-Hall methods and theories in the social
sciences series)
 Bibliography.
 Includes indexes.
 1. Social sciences—Research—Moral and religious
aspects. I. Title. II. Series.
H62.R469   300'.72   81-15893
ISBN 0-13-290965-0   AACR2

Prentice-Hall Methods and Theories in the Social Sciences Series
Herbert L. Costner, Neil J. Smelser, *Editors*

Printed in the United States of America

10   9   8   7   6   5   4   3   2   1

Editorial/production supervision: Maureen Connelly
Manufacturing buyer: John Hall

ISBN 0-13-290965-0

Prentice-Hall International, Inc., *London*
Prentice-Hall of Australia Pty. Limited, *Sydney*
Prentice-Hall of Canada, Ltd., *Toronto*
Prentice-Hall of India Private Limited, *New Delhi*
Prentice-Hall of Japan, Inc., *Tokyo*
Prentice-Hall of Southeast Asia Pt. Ltd., *Singapore*
Whitehall Books Limited, *Wellington, New Zealand*

Written in the hope that future generations
will respect social science research
and profit from its contributions.

CONTENTS

LIST OF EXHIBITS

PREFACE

This book is designed to provide the knowledge and a strategy to facilitate the analysis of moral problems in social science research and applications to practical affairs. The perspectives and approaches of this book are found in the codes of ethics developed by associations representing social scientists (see Appendices), but the relationship between analysis and application is more explicit in the following discussions. Codes of ethics are useful for extreme or trivial cases in which the solutions are obvious; the resolution of intermediate problems—the true dilemmas—requires something more. It is hoped that this book can be of help.

One precaution: Chapter 6 reviews the mechanisms for controlling investigators engaged in research with human participants; these mechanisms include federal rules and procedures and standards embodied in the legal system. While these rules and procedures were current at the time the book was written, they are changing constantly; for any complex or delicate problem, the reader should obtain the most recent information. The official responsible for the Institutional Review Board and liaison with the Department of Health and Human Services (DHHS) should be able to provide timely assistance.

I am very grateful to others for their help. As this work is a condensed and reorganized version of my *Ethical Dilemmas and Social Science Research* (San Francisco, Calif.: Jossey-Bass, Inc., Publishers, 1979), including the use of Exhibits 3, 6, and 12 (appearing in this book as Exhibits 1-2, 2-1, and 1-1), it would not have been possible without the permission of Jossey-Bass, Inc. Thanks are also extended to the American Anthropological Association, American Political Science Association, American Psychological Association, and the American Sociological Association for allowing their respective codes of ethics to be published in the appendices. Finally, it is time to once again show appreciation to Mrs. Helen Keefe for her excellent and efficient work in typing the manuscript.

CHAPTER ONE
BASIC ISSUES: STRATEGIES FOR RESOLUTION

An adult male, seeking a sexual experience, visits a public restroom in a remote area of a city park. Upon entering, he notices two other adult males; through nonverbal signals he arranges to participate in a sexual act with one while the other serves as a lookout. Over a year later the same man is interviewed by the "lookout" (now disguised). This man has participated in a study that indicates that brief impersonal, homosexual contacts are a regular occurrence for men who otherwise appear typical for their community (Humphreys, 1970).

Immediately after leaving a station, subway passengers notice a man swooning and falling to the floor of the car with blood trickling from his mouth. After several seconds, a bystander stoops to help the fallen person. Someone moves to pull the emergency cord, but he is restrained by another "passenger." The "stricken" man is helped to his feet and leaves the car at the next station. This staged emergency is part of a study that indicates that help is usually provided (80 percent or more of all incidents), that the helper is likely to be male, and that help is more likely if the problem appears to be medical (rather than alcoholic) and not serious (the presence of blood reduces the number of responses) (Piliavin & Piliavin, 1972).

Residents of a typical neighborhood receive the accustomed police response to calls for service, although the frequency of patrols (officers cruising in squad cars) is twice the normal rate (which they do not seem to notice). Residents of an adjoining neighborhood receive equally efficient responses when they request police assistance, although there are *no* patrols in their area (which they do not seem to notice). Both neighborhoods are part of a study of the effect of police patrols on crime rates, being conducted without their knowledge. No difference is found in rates of crime and citizen attitudes toward crime or the police as a result of these variations; following the study, the regular patrol patterns are reestablished (Kelling et al., 1974).

Do these make your blood boil? Some of them may. Though outraged indignation is less common than an instinctive feeling that something is inappropriate, unjust, or not right—people shouldn't do such things. A distinctive feature of all research that involves human participants is a possibility for moral abiguity. Such concerns, common in social and biomedical studies, usually raise the following questions.

> *Is that (the research) the right thing to do?*
> Should sociologists be spying on homosexuals?
> Should psychologists create fake emergencies?
> Should investigators take the risk that crime may increase?
> *Is it (the research) good for society?*
> Is it important to know more about atypical sexual behavior?
> Is it important to have more information about altruism (helping behavior)?
> Is it important to know if police patrols reduce crime?
> *Are they (the investigators) good people?*
> Should anyone deceive another about his or her true purpose?
> Should anyone pretend to need help and create anxiety in others?
> Should anyone risk the criminal victimization of others?

Such questions may be asked by social scientists before or during a research project or moral observers (participants, citizens, journalists, other social scientists) after research is completed. The questions are not necessarily independent. An investigator may be convinced he is a "good person" if the research is considered good for society; research that benefits participants may be seen as good for society *and* the right thing to do. Equally important, similar types of analysis may be employed in resolving each question.

One strategy to ensure that research is ethically correct is to develop a set of guiding rules or principles (the very word "ethical" implies that explicit standards exist). Almost every major association of social scientists (except for economists) in the United States has developed a code of ethics for research, frequently after a great deal of controversy. However, several features of scientific research and professional societies make it quite difficult to establish a fixed code of ethics; not only are investigators constantly developing new research procedures not covered in existing codes, they are also selecting new phenomena for study. Moreover, the norms and standards of society are constantly changing. The diversity of phenomena and research procedures at any one time is great enough that an explicit, precise code covering all possible research procedures would be complex, voluminous, and prohibitively expensive to develop. Existing codes are therefore very general, consisting of several printed pages, and their application to specific activities is often ambiguous.

The alternative, the focus of this book, is to consider the strategies one might employ to develop a personal judgment about the moral character of a research activity. Three such strategies have been used to resolve moral questions:

- Concern for individual rights, particularly participants' rights to self-determination (the extent to which individuals are able to control their own destiny) by allowing them an opportunity to give their informed consent to become involved in research.
- Consideration of the advantages and disadvantages of research for the greater society, organized in the form of a cost-benefit (sometimes called risk-benefit) or utilitarian analysis.
- Evaluation of interpersonal relationships; the extent to which the individuals involved (investigators related to participants; participants related to participants) treat each other as people "should."

The first two strategies were developed to resolve somewhat different, more general, issues: specifically, to justify a political state and to evaluate public programs and legislation. The third strategy, which deals with ideal interpersonal relationships, has been a moral or ethical issue for a long time. Strategies developed for resolving these general issues are also used, often instinctively, to resolve concerns related to research; they are the philosophical basis for the codes of ethics developed by associations representing social scientists.

But strategies for analysis are useful only if directed toward specific questions. Such questions can provide a guide for organizating a moral analysis; those to be used in the moral analysis of research are as follows:

Effects on Rights	1. What rights of various parties associated with the research activity—participants, investigators, society at large—may be affected?
Program/Project Effects	2. What are the costs and benefits of the research program and this project?
Participant Effects	3. What are the costs (or risks) and benefits for the participants?
Distribution of Effects	4. What is the expected distribution of the costs and benefits?
Respect for Rights, Welfare	5. How has respect for the rights and welfare of the participants been demonstrated?
Personal Treatment	6. To what extent does the personal treatment of the participants by the investigator(s) approach the ideal?
Acceptability to Social Scientists	7. Which social scientist role definitions, if any, would be consistent with the major features of the moral analysis?

The order of the questions is one of convenience; treating all issues in arriving at a final judgment is more important than the sequence. The identifying labels, to the left of the questions, will be used for reference in discussions of specific types of research.

The remainder of this chapter will review these three orientations for resolving moral dilemmas: respect for individual rights, evaluation of effects, and the personal treatment of others. This should provide a fuller understanding of how these strategies relate to research analysis and important issues.

RIGHTS AND RESEARCH

Two of the questions selected to guide the moral analysis of research are directly related to concerns for rights:

Effects on Rights	1. What rights of various parties associated with the research activity—participants, investigators, society at large—may be affected?
Respect for Rights, Welfare	5. How has respect for the rights and welfare of the participants been demonstrated?

Resolution of the first issue requires an understanding of the nature and types of rights that have developed within society, which is largely a matter of definition. But the resolution of the second is somewhat more complicated; for it is frequently not possible to ensure that all the rights of all participants will be respected (or observed), and it is necessary to demonstrate respect by asking participants to forego some rights. An appreciation of the conditions under which individuals may give up rights requires an understanding of the justifications for them; both will be discussed.

The basic concept of a "right" is something to which an individual may have a "just claim"; all rights are negative or positive (MacCallum, 1967). *Negative rights* are those in which individuals have a right not to be interfered with; they can expect to do "something" without hindrance from others (persons, groups, or governments). "Something" would include the familiar rights of speech, worship, movement (travel), pursuit of happiness (economic well-being), freedom from physical assault, privacy, and the like. Further, if another were to hinder the exercise of such rights, as in preventing freedom of speech (by disrupting a peaceful political meeting), the government would be expected to come to the defense of such rights. *Positive rights* are those in which others have an obligation to help or assist an individual to exercise such a right. A right to a fair and timely criminal trial implies that others (typical citizens) have an obligation to participate; they can be legally compelled to serve as a witness or juror. In advanced societies, rights have been changing status in the recent past; the right to physical health has been changing from a negative right (where government action prevents interference or discrimination in an individual's attempt to obtain medical care) to a positive right (where government action provides adequate medical care for all).

Two general strategies are associated with justifications for rights. One is based on a religious or philosophical belief in what "should" be the status of individuals, and the other is based on legal arrangements that reflect experiences with political systems. If a right (such as freedom from physical assault) is found in many different societies and has persisted for some time, this may be used as evidence (1) that a right reflects God's (either Christian, Jewish, Muslim, or other) intentions, or (2) that it exists in the absence of organized societies or formalized legal systems (that is sometimes referred to as "natural law") (Olafson, 1961). Another approach, social contract analysis, emphasizes the type of political structure that rational, thoughtful adults would develop if they were to create one for the first time, in the absence of any existing constitutions or models that could serve as a guide. It is generally concluded that such individuals would be willing to forego certain decisions and allow them to be made by a "government" (such as controlling violence or negotiating with other political states) in return for individual autonomy in certain areas of their own lives (speech, travel, assembly, religion, and the like) and the efficient, effective administration of society.[1]

A quite different justification of individual rights is given by those who are committed to the development and maintenance of the political system; this justification appears in the legal history of modern societies.[2] Rather than being based on an analysis of the natural order, religious principles, or idealized origins of society, this argument states that unless some constraints are placed upon those who rule society (kings, presidents, or other sovereigns), they will abuse ordinary citizens whenever there is a clear advantage. Historical evidence shows that such abuse was (and is) a common occurrence. Hence, the "special contract" that specifies the privileges and obligations of rulers and citizens also specifies individual citizens' rights; this device constrains those in positions of political or government influence (Gough, 1957; Pound, 1957). Such a device is present in the Magna Charta (A.D. 1215), one of the first legal documents that specified restrictions (defined as the rights of the citizens) upon the English king and his administrators. It is also an important feature of the Constitution of the United States, particularly the issues raised in the Bill of Rights, the first ten amendments to the Constitution. Those approving the Constitution were so cautious that they ordered any right not specifi-

---

[1] Such speculation on the origin of political structures is more properly called "social compact analysis" (as in the Mayflower Compact) rather than social contract analysis (Gough, 1957). While the notion that groups of individuals engaged in parliamentary debates to create a fully developed political plan is no longer considered an accurate reflection of the origin of modern societies, it does lead to some interesting analyses (Rawls, 1971). These include the conclusion that the individuals designing the political structure might be more careful regarding the treatment of the disadvantaged since they cannot predict their own future position in society (whether or not they would be capable or disadvantaged); they may wish to organize society in such a way to maximize the benefits (or minimize the risks) for the disadvantaged. This contrasts with the present form of all societies, where there are substantial differences in the benefits and privileges accorded to the capable and the disadvantaged.

[2] It is quite possible that rights developed and defined on the basis of religious or other analyses are eventually incorporated into the legal system as binding upon citizens and rulers alike; nonetheless, the argument that rights come from nature or God is quite different from the one that considers them part of a contract between two categories of individuals.

cally transferred to the government to be retained by the people (Tenth Amendment).

An emphasis upon individual rights leads directly to an attempt to specify these rights; but to compile a list of rights that is unambiguous, complete, consistent, and acceptable to all is not only complicated, it is—in most instances—impossible. The biggest single problem is putting together a consistent set of general rights; except for some philosophical presentations, there is always more than one right under consideration. When more than one right is involved, situations inevitably develop where the simultaneous exercise of two rights by one individual may be difficult. For example, the right to an efficient government administration would involve a periodic census of the citizens; a right to individual privacy might necessarily involve not responding to a census. More frequently, the rights of two different individuals are incompatible (one person's right to freedom of speech conflicts with another's right not to be slandered or defamed). The usual solution is to create a list of rights and a mechanism for resolving such conflicts; the courts are a major source of such resolutions, although legislation may be adopted for recurring cases.

Some of the rights that have been suggested or established for individuals involved in research—citizens, participants, investigators (either natural persons or the state)—are presented in Exhibit 1-1. Most of the rights are negative rights (the state prevents infringement upon the right), a few are positive (the state takes actions to ensure their observance). Many rights have both qualities, depending upon the nature of the situation. For example, governments help people satisfy a "right to education," but only provide full financial support through secondary schools (high school); only the right not to be discriminated against receives government attention thereafter. In a similar fashion, governments will provide substantially greater assistance for rectifying a serious physical assault than for a minor physical or verbal attack.

Most rights specifically associated with social science research reflect general rights accorded all citizens. Perhaps most common are the rights not to be deceived, to privacy, and to be treated with dignity and respect; the potential for permanent physical harm is usually remote. Of substantial importance to investigators is the "freedom of research"; while not yet subjected to a Supreme Court interpretation, it is expected that the right to study any phenomenon would be upheld as an extension of the negative right of freedom of the press (Robertson, 1978). On the other hand, the right to use any procedure for research—regardless of its consequences for the participants—would clearly not be upheld, for some types of research could produce severe damage, perhaps even death. Further, the right to study a phenomenon does not include the right to receive public financial support for the research; such assistance is not a positive right.

Foregoing Rights: Informed Consent

While there are many advantages to specifying rights that all citizens automatically acquire by virtue of participation in society, there is one major problem: how to deal with those situations where individuals may wish to give up a right. For

EXHIBIT 1-1 Rights of Parties-at-Interest Involved in Research

PARTIES-AT-INTEREST	NEGATIVE RIGHTS (State prevents infringement)	POSITIVE RIGHTS (State helps to achieve)
All citizens	Self-determination	Extreme restrictions (when criminal abuse)[1]
	Life (freedom from assault)	Health (freedom from disease)
	Privacy	Extreme cases (when criminal abuse)[1]
	Dignity	
	Respect	
	Freedom of thought	Extreme cases (when criminal abuse)[1]
	Freedom of travel	Extreme cases (when criminal abuse)[1]
	Property	Freedom from fraud (when criminal abuse)[1]
	Freedom from deception	Due process (criminal matters)
	Due process (civil matters)	
	Equality of treatment	
	Benefits of scientific knowledge	Expansion of knowledge, as a public resource
		Efficient public administration
		Effective public administration
Research participants	Self-determination	
	Freedom from personal physical abuse, mental strain, anguish	
	Privacy	
	Dignity and respect	
Investigators (individuals)	Recognition for contributions	
	Contributions as personal property (patents, copyrights, etc.)	
	NOT LEGALLY RECOGNIZED:	
	Maintain confidentiality of sources and content of research data	
Investigators (governments)		Descriptive data for policy analysis
		Research on effective programs
		Research on efficient programs
Future generations	Ambiguous at this time	

[1] Serious infringements are considered criminal abuses.

7

example, persons may wish to forego a claim to private property for other advantages such as a cash sale or pledging property as collateral for a loan. They may wish to exchange the right to a wide range of interpersonal relationships for a single, intense, intimate relationship, as in a marriage "contract" (implied, if not explicit). They may wish to give up the right to unrestricted, spontaneous freedom of movement in exchange for accepting the obligations of an organizational position—that is, a job.

Widely recognized as a recurrent issue, procedures have been developed to allow individuals to forego most (but not all) rights under certain conditions. This is generally referred to as providing *informed consent*; it is widely applied in research if there is the possibility that participants may experience stress, discomfort, or be asked for sensitive information. The major restriction upon rights that may be given up is the exclusion of those related to severe, permanent, physical damage (death or mayhem). It is argued that the state (representing all the people) has a right to healthy, productive citizens; and if individuals agreed to sustain permanent, substantial physical damage, they would not only be depriving society of productive members, they may require others to provide them with care and assistance.

The first legal specifications of informed consent in research participation were contained in the Nuremberg Code (Appendix 1); here standards were developed for judging physician-investigators accused of mistreatment of Nazi prisoners (Jews, political dissidents, mental defectives, and the like) in biomedical research. Some biomedical experiments simulated high-altitude (low-pressure) environments, which were varied to study the limits of human tolerance—that is, to the point of death. In studies of frostbite treatments, human subjects were stripped and forced into the cold until their body parts froze. In others, healthy adults were infected with lethal diseases in order to maintain a supply of the disease culture for future research (Katz, 1972). These experiments have several features in common: knowledge of the research objectives and procedures would have little effect upon the biomedical phenomenon under investigation; the negative effects for the participants were severe and resulted in death for many; and there was substantial reasons to assume that the prisoners were not free to determine their involvement. Under such conditions, the use of informed consent would have provided substantial protection for the rights of participants.

Four legal standards are involved in informed consent to participate in research: (1) the capacity to make a rational, mature judgment; (2) freedom from coercion or undue influence; (3) information about what is to occur; and (4) comprehension of the possible effects (Annas et al., 1977). If the research will provide direct benefits to the participants, the ability to comprehend the possible effects may be deemphasized; this may occur in clinical research in which a new therapy or procedure (such as marriage counseling) is tested and in which patients expect to benefit from the procedure.

While compliance with the spirit of informed consent is a valuable objective for scientific research, several major problems occur in its universal application. The first is a fundamental feature of much research, particularly experimental: the inability to predict the consequences for the participants. In fact, the reason experiments are conducted is to determine the consequences; if the outcomes were predictable, there would be no reason to conduct the research. Hence, the best investigators can do is to estimate the range and intensity of possible consequences; complete information may not be available.

A second problem is much more fundamental, for it defeats the very objectives of research. For many phenomena, both social and biomedical, knowledge of the purpose and expectations of the research can have a substantial effect upon the outcome. Specifically, if people are led to expect benefits from a new form of therapy (psychotherapy, counseling, chemical, or otherwise), they will often show improvement regardless of the actual effects; this is referred to as the *placebo effect* (Bok, 1974; Honigfeld, 1964). In many studies of cognition and mental processes, complete information will encourage participants to become aware of processes that are normally subconscious; when these processes become explicit, they are often dramatically affected. Substantial ingenuity has gone into finding ways of meeting the spirit of informed consent without divulging information that will defeat the scientific objectives (this will be discussed further in the next chapter).

A third problem is administrative in nature. To apply a full, formal informed consent procedure to participants in some studies may be so impracticable or costly as to prevent the completion of the research. For example, insisting that all research participants provide their informed consent would make it impossible to conduct research on anonymous census data, photographs of crowds, or even movies or TV programs; in these cases the participants may be anonymous, unidentifiable, and difficult to contact. It is hard to argue that the use of such public data infringes upon participants' rights. There are other situations, again where the research is fairly innocuous, where a full, complete informed consent procedure may be more complicated than the actual research. Many survey questionnaires cannot be fully explained before an interview; respondents are better informed if they receive a brief description and know they may refuse to answer specific questions they consider private or embarrassing. (Asking questions is seldom a cause of embarrassment.)

A fourth problem with the informed consent mechanism, as a device for allowing individuals to forego rights, is that it requires rational, alert participants. When individuals are not able to make their own decisions, it becomes substantially more difficult to determine how to protect their rights. For example, research conducted with children or those who are mentally deficient is frequent in social science; determining what such individuals would agree to if they were able to comprehend and evaluate their experience is a major problem (their legal guardians often make the decisions). In more extreme cases, those who are physically alive but not capable of thought or communication present special problems, although fetuses or comatose medical patients are not usually participants in social science research. Finally, it is impossible to query those who are expected to be major benefactors of scientific research; unborn future generations are beyond contact.

Perhaps the major problem with the informed consent procedure is that it is not a sufficient single device for demonstrating respect for the rights and welfare of the participants; other ways include ensuring that the data remain anonymous and confidential and following up participants to determine and correct negative effects. In short, one advantage of a full, formal informed consent procedure is that it shifts some of the responsibility for the effects of research to the participants, since they voluntarily agree to become involved after receiving full information. However, even though participants may share responsibility for detriments to their welfare, investigators remain accountable. They are expected to check on the participants following a research experience to ensure that no negative effects go untreated. A major limitation of informed consent is that it can never relieve investigators of all responsibility for the participants.

There have been attempts to extend the notions of rights to other entities such as groups and animals. Those concerned with the status of and discrimination against social aggregates (e.g., minorities and women) have suggested that they be given special treatment because they comprise a social category, regardless of their individual attributes. These are sometimes referred to as "group rights" (Fiss, 1976). Despite some attempts to prohibit research that entails "social risk" (risk to the reputation of a social category or aggregate), it seems clear they will not be recognized in the law (Shils, 1973). The recent *Bakke* case involved the question of whether admission to a medical school should be based on social classification or individual attributes (such as aptitude for study); individual rights were recognized over group rights by the Supreme Court (Van Alstyne, 1978).

Even though animals are extensively used in research and may experience pain, the religious or philosophical arguments for animal rights (Singer, 1975) have not dealt with the major justification for human rights: the protection of those capable of developing political constitutions from abuse from societal rulers. Since they are not capable of developing political contracts, animals may continue to be legally defined as property (*The New York Times,* 1977), although such "property" should be spared unnecessary pain and provided with healthy, sanitary living conditions when involved in research (National Institutes of Health, 1968; Appendix 4, Principles 10d, e).

In conclusion, there are three important aspects of individual rights that are significant to the moral status of research involving human participants. First, a number of different rights involve both participants and investigators; the scope of individual rights is constantly increasing. Second, rights vary in terms of legitimation; some have a well-defined legal status and substantial government resources are devoted to their maintenance; others are considered to be highly desirable though not yet established in the law; and still others are controversial or promoted by special segments of society. Finally, the primary basis for informed consent is its importance as a mechanism for respecting the self-determination of individuals in foregoing rights. However, it is clear that informed consent is not an all-purpose solution for protecting rights, and other procedures may be required to demonstrate respect for participants or allow investigators to achieve scientific objectives.

UTILITARIAN (COST-BENEFIT) ANALYSIS

Three of the questions for guiding the moral analysis of research compare the potential benefits of research with the costs.

Program/Project Effects	2. What are the costs and benefits of the research program and this project?
Participant Effects	3. What are the costs (or risks) and benefits for the participants?
Distribution of Effects	4. What is the expected distribution of the costs and benefits?

In contrast to concern for individual rights, where the major solution involves identification of rights affected by the research and the extent to which they are respected, the utilitarian analysis is much more ambiguous and open. Despite complaints that a utilitarian approach to the moral analysis of research may lead to the callous treatment of participants, it is virtually impossible to avoid, for research is only one of many activities where resources and attention may be directed. Such resources are usually public and never unlimited; choices must be made.

Choosing what is best for an entire social system is a recurring problem in all social systems, regardless of political form (democratic, monarchy, or totalitarian) or size (nations, governments, businesses, or families). Such decisions may involve new social programs, new legislation, new investment opportunities, or choosing a vacation. Originally developed by Jeremy Bentham (1789) and John Stuart Mill (1863), who were simultaneously legislators, lawyers, and political philosophers, utilitarian, or cost-benefit, analysis is the major strategy that has been developed and refined for such problems. Its outlines are simple. First, a systematic attempt to estimate the total benefits and total costs for all affected by a decision is made. Then, if the benefits outweigh the costs, a course of action is initiated. Otherwise, if total costs outweigh total benefits, nothing is one.

For example, a secondary school may consider the development of specialized educational programs for different students: an enriched program for those with a high aptitude for academic work, a regular program for typical students, and a special program for those not well suited to ordinary academic instruction. Under a cost-benefit analysis, the major benefits would be an increase in the total amount learned by all groups as the more talented cover more material, the less talented are assured of understanding the basics, and neither group disrupts the instruction of typical students. Furthermore, forming classes of students with comparable aptitudes enhances the possibility for more satisfying peer interactions. Major costs would involve money (the additional expense of developing and maintaining three different courses of instruction), social stigmas (being categorized as either "brains" or "slow learners"), and the stereotypes that may develop if particular groups are dominated by culturally distinct students (few minority students might be found in advanced classes).

A review of this inventory of costs and benefits emphasizes one of the major problems with precise implementation of the utilitarian strategy; it is generally impossible to develop a common measure to allow one number to represent all the costs and a comparable number to represent all the benefits, despite the valiant efforts of economists to translate everything into dollars. For example, to develop a number that represented pleasant interaction with classmates that is comparable to a number that may represent potential negative stereotypes for a cultural group is virtually impossible. Yet such quantification is required for a direct comparison between costs and benefits. This difficulty is the reason for a less precise final step in the analysis; the comparisons of costs and benefits are often subjective in nature, and the conclusion is usually an informed judgment. Even so, a major advantage of this strategy is that it systematically reviews all benefits and costs and reduces the chance of overlooking some major considerations.

Utilitarianism is most acceptable as a strategy when all individuals share equally in the costs and benefits. For example, a community may conclude that it is cheaper if all contribute to the construction and maintenance of a water system; the cost for each household may be lower and the quality of the water may be higher under such a joint arrangement. In contrast, there may be situations where the costs are distributed unequally. In order to build a dam to provide a reliable water supply, some individuals may be required to give up their homes or farmland and thus pay a very high cost for the good of the community. In contrast, there may be situations where a few individuals receive considerable benefits although all members share some small costs, such as the recipients of government-financed organ (kidney) transplants. Similar situations occur in research, where a few individuals are asked to bear great risks (astronauts) in order to provide benefits to all (national pride in space achievements).

Determining an equitable or just allocation of costs and benefits is called the *distributive justice problem.* It is of particular relevance when disadvantaged individuals—prisoners, mental patients, minorities—are involved in research that is expected to provide benefits to all segments of society or, even more controversial, the advantaged members (such as those that can afford high-priced medical care). Studies on the safety of drugs to control mental disorders, new instructional techniques to improve school performance, or the effectiveness of contraceptives (birth control practices) might be tested on disadvantaged individuals. This has led to the suggestion that any new technique or innovation first be utilized with advantaged members of society (Veatch, 1978) to ensure that the disadvantaged are not misused for the benefit of the more advantaged. This was inadvertently done in a study of the effects of a simulated prison environment on upper-middle-class college students (Zimbardo, 1973); the major benefactors of the applications of the results were real prisoners. Analysis becomes more complex when the research participants themselves may benefit (as with a new therapy for mental disorders or an innovative teaching procedure), as well as society as a whole.

The distributive justice problem reflects what is perhaps the major difference between these two strategies:

Utilitarian analysis is designed to facilitate decisions about activities that may affect the entire society, with an emphasis upon the total effects, both positive and negative.

Concern for individual rights arose to prevent infringements that are, from the perspective of the individual, capricious and unjust, yet are promoted as "best for society."

Such differences may enter subtly, as when planners estimate the value of human life in calculating the expected benefits of expensive safety devices for highways or nuclear power plants; assigning a monetary value to human life suggests that the "right to life" is not so inalienable or basic. The usual solution is to try to ensure that those bearing great costs are not capriciously and deliberately chosen for such treatment by a malevolent government (accident victims are usually not pre-selected) or that they are compensated for any unusually high costs they may bear to promote the common good (financial payments to those who lose their homes to a new highway). Those who voluntarily bear great costs (risks) preserve their right to self-determination; such is the value of informed consent.

In making research decisions, the utilitarian analysis may be utilized at three different levels:

1. Should a program of research directed toward a general intellectual problem be implemented?
2. Is a particular project the best way to further a program of research?
3. Should an individual participate in a specific research activity?

While most of the attention with regard to the moral status of research is directed toward the third issue, the effects on individual participants, the first and second are equally important in balancing the benefits of the research against the costs. Each decision involves different analyses of costs and benefits and each is made by persons in different situations.

Research programs may develop in two quite different ways. Perhaps the oldest and most common procedure is for scientists and investigators, acting alone or in casual coalitions, to select an issue for attention and then develop a series of projects designed to assist in their resolution. The alternative is to have a government, usually a federal agency, officially select a social problem for attention and support research projects aimed at the predetermined objective. Projects conducted by inside or outside investigators. In either case, a general program of research is the intellectual device that organizes the results of a variety of specific projects.

Once the general objectives are established, either formally within the government or informally among scientists, the moral acceptability of specific research projects becomes a major issue. For example, there is a continuing concern regarding the relative impact of genetic background (heredity) and developmental experience (environment) upon various individual characteristics, such as intelligence, mental disorders, athletic potential, academic aptitude, and the like. Focusing upon intelligence, one strategy would be to develop an experiment in which more or less intelligent adult men and women would be identified; these research subjects would then be asked to accept sexual partners selected by the investigators to produce combinations of high, mixed, and low potential for intelligent children; they would bear the children; and these children would, in turn, be raised in different settings designed to foster high and low intelligence. The result would allow estimates of the relative contribution of genetic background and early experience upon intelligence.

Despite the importance of this issue for both science and society, such a project is morally unacceptable. Aside from telling adults who they would share parenthood with, it would require the deliberate creation of children with low intelligence. However, such studies can be done and have been done with animals such as rats; both factors are found to have an effect on animal intelligence (Jensen, 1969).

Rather than abandon attempts to answer the question for humans, an alternative is to examine those individuals who have different degrees of similarity in their genetic and developmental backgrounds. This involves identifying and measuring a variety of different individuals: unrelated persons, half-siblings, full siblings, parents and children, children and grandparents, fraternal and identical twins (reared together or apart). Both the context in which the individuals developed and their intelligence can be examined with respect to similarity; the experiment is created by natural processes. If such is the case, the investigators are not responsible for the meeting and mating of adults to produce offspring or the context in which the individuals grow up. While the results of such a study are not as precise nor as satisfactory as a controlled experiment, they do provide some evidence and allow progress to be made without creating a moral dilemma for the investigators.

It is at this level of analysis—designing specific projects and determining the nature of participants—that the distribution of effects among members of society should be considered. Relevant to the analysis is the extent to which participants receive direct benefits and represent any special subgroups or segments of the population (welfare mothers, prisoners, or typical adults); also relevant are the mechanisms for disseminating the results and their effect on practical affairs. For the vast majority of social science research, the ultimate effects upon any social or cultural group are trivial or nonexistent (the results are buried in the professional literature), so this is not a major issue. However, studies will occasionally be used to support political action; unfortunately, it is usually impossible to predict either what groups will become aware of research findings and attempt to use them to justify their recommendations or how the results will be interpreted. In the absence of the ability to predict the effects of research results for different groups or segments of society, the major concern is usually with the direct effects on the participants.

The third type of decision for which a cost-benefit, or utilitarian, analysis is appropriate concerns the participation of a specific individual. If the research involves systematic data collection and all participants have the same research experiences (as in field observation or survey research), then analysis is simplified. However, if the project involves an experiment and the research experiences of participants differ, then several different analyses may be necessary. Some of the beneficial and detrimental effects for participants are reviewed in Exhibit 1-2; they are divided into several major categories: temporary personal effects; permanent personal effects; effects mediated by society; effects upon rights specified by society; and effects for all individuals as members of society. Some of the specific effects of different research activities will be reviewed in later chapters.

These are the effects—beneficial and detrimental—that would be mentioned in an informed consent procedure. However, rather than attempt to cover them all, an informed consent procedure should include only those of direct relevance to the participants and their expectations; perhaps only those substantially greater than the risks of daily life.

To the extent that research is a public activity (and most scientific research is publicly supported), it is quite appropriate to evaluate its worth utilizing a cost-benefit analysis. This highlights the expected balance of costs and benefits for society and participants at three different levels: research program, research project, and paricipant involvement. In some cases, there is concern over the distribution of effects, particularly when those in disadvantaged situations may experience risks for the benefit of those in more advantaged situations. When the costs to be borne by participants are greater than expected in everyday life, provision of informed consent becomes more significant; it is the major mechanism for resolving conflicts between utilitarian solutions and guaranteed individual rights.

PERSONAL MORALITY

When research involves human participants, it may be considered in terms of the relationship between two people, reflected in the following issue:

Personal Treatment   6. To what extent has the personal treatment of the participants by the investigator(s) approached the ideal?

There is considerable diversity in the extent to which the investigator-participant relationship is seen as basically personal; some of the orientations adopted by social scientists are explored below. But aspects of a personal relationship enter into all research with human participants; the extent to which individuals can feel good about themselves is usually related to their personal treatment of others.

The focus of concern in personal morality is the treatment of other people; the image of two friends is often involved, and the principles of friendship are frequently extended to relationships with all others, even total strangers in different cultures. Major attention is given to behavior that may have a direct and significant effect upon another (such as recklessness that may result in injury). There is also concern for acts that may have no direct effect (others may not even know they occurred) and are still considered "wrong." For example, prying into the pri-

EXHIBIT 1-2 Effects on Individual Research Participants

MAJOR CATEGORY OF EFFECTS	TYPE OF EFFECT	
	BENEFICIAL	DETRIMENTAL
Temporary Personal		
Direct	Biomedical Psychological Social context	Biomedical Psychological Social context
Economic situational	Cash payments Use of facilities, privileges Professional services	Personal expenses Denial of facilities, privileges Additional professional services Time taken from other activities
Miscellaneous	Novel, interesting experience Altruistic satisfaction	Resentment of treatment as "object"
Permanent personal		
Direct	Biomedical Psychological Social relations Educational	Biomedical Psychological Social relations
Miscellaneous		
Mediated by society	Benefits of new programs based upon the research Benefits to a social category, which includes the participant, based upon the research	Harm from new norms that are established or enhanced by research Appropriate to treat individuals as objects Legitimation of deceit Discrimination or harm to a social category, to which the participant belongs, based upon the research

EXHIBIT 1-2 (continued)

MAJOR CATEGORY OF EFFECTS.	TYPE OF EFFECT	
	BENEFICIAL	DETRIMENTAL
"Rights" specified by society	Right to scientific progress Right to share in scientific benefits Right to efficient and effective government	Infringement upon rights of: Privacy Self-determination Liberty Not to be deceived[1] To be left alone[1] Benefits of science when assigned to a control group
Society in general	Increase in objective, empirically based knowledge (science) Potential increase of capacity to control biomedical, psychological, and social phenomena	Financial costs of research Time of trained professionals Potential costs and disruption associated with restructuring society in response to research findings Cost of reorganizing society so those with the responsibility for control of phenomena, previously considered uncontrollable, can be trusted to act in the best interest of society Reduced sense of individual autonomy or personhood as more phenomena are considered controllable

[1] Ambiguous legal status; mentioned by some commentators.

vate affairs of another is considered inappropriate even if the offended party is unaware of the activity. Moral significance is extended to promises made to another, even if the "promisee" does not know of a violation; witness the special attention given to deathbed pledges, which the deceased can never confirm.

Ambivalence about the appropriate treatment of others and one's own moral worth is substantially reduced if some principle or strategy exists for guiding personal behavior or activities. Three major approaches have been developed to answer the question, "Am I a good person?" They include adherence to a set of rules, evaluation of the outcome of the actions, and instinctive judgments.

Following a set of rules (the denotative strategy) is one of the best-known solutions to this problem; the Golden Rule and the Ten Commandments are two such examples. One of the most complete analyses is that of Kant (1785); he advocated principles that would meet three criteria—universal application (all people could follow them), treatment of individuals as ends rather than means, and acceptability to all members of society (that is, all individuals, acting independently, would develop the same personal guidelines). An alternative strategy is to engage in a utilitarian analysis and adopt those principles that would consistently benefit society. Despite the continuing problems in developing precise, complete, and consistent rules (there are frequently conflicts between different rules as conditions change), rigid adherence to rules is still advocated by some: "We must do no wrong—even if by doing wrong suffering would be reduced and the sum of happiness increased" (Fried, 1978, p. 2).

The analysis of an immediate situation in which a moral choice is required (the telelogical strategy) is the major alternative to a rigid adherence to a set of "rules for life." Several strategies are suggested for such decisions; "situation ethics" emphasizes a "mature compassion for humanity' and considers that the "ends justify the means more than anything else" (Fletcher, 1966, 1967). Utilitarianism may be applied to such choices; the person makes a conscientious attempt to compare the costs and benefits of alternative actions and selects the one expected to provide the greatest benefits to those affected. While useful for major decisions, a detailed, complete analysis of every personal choice could be quite time-consuming; acceptance of rules or the adoption of habits for most routine activities substantially reduces the investment required in making decisions.

A third strategy is to rely completely upon one's instinctive, subjective judgment about the correct thing to do (Prichard, 1912). To determine the morally appropriate choice, an individual would have to completely immerse herself or himself in the situation and all its constraints, alternatives, and obligations. While this is useful for a single individual attempting to determine the most appropriate solution to his or her own moral dilemmas, it prevents others from verifying or, perhaps, understanding the basis for the decisions.

Different strategies for developing rules to live by have different implications for appropriate action. If the emphasis is upon promoting the best interests of society (or humanity as a whole), actions not known to others may be tolerated. For example, the secret surveillance of citizens (wiretapping, reading their mail) may be seen as acceptable for national security purposes. In contrast, analysis emphasizing the immediate effects of behavior in a particular situation may de-emphasize considerations of a more general nature—what others might think or the impact on society. Violation of a deathbed promise (undermining a societal norm) may be seen as justified to promote personal survival. The implications of reliance on instinct to solve moral problems is harder to predict, but most persons would probably emphasize the direct effects for their immediate associates rather than general consequences for society.

SOCIAL SCIENTISTS IN SOCIETY

There is a wide range of conceptions of the appropriate role of social scientists in society, and the diversity is at least as great as in other professional groups. Such variety is crucial to the moral analysis of research; different perspectives on this issue lead to different emphasis in such analysis. Hence, a final question for consideration:

Acceptability to   7. Which social scientist role definitions, if any,
Social Scientists   would be consistent with the major features of
                             the moral analysis?

The problem represents a specific application of a more general issue: the relationship between obligations to society as an aggregate of persons versus obligations to others as distinct individuals. Much of the controversy over the moral status of societal endeavors is related to this issue, for there is often agreement upon the specific nature of the costs and benefits or the rights and welfare of the individuals involved.

Some of the most serious complications that develop in societal endeavors (of which research is one) arise when individuals accept obligations to act in behalf of the greater society (as do judges, administrators, scientific investigators, or even executioners) and take actions in this capacity that may be inconsistent with standards for interpersonal behavior. For example, it may be determined that when an individual deliberately and sadistically takes the life of another, it will be best for society if the murderer is executed. But the decision to take the life of a person (even a murderer) violates the moral standards for personal relationships (such as forgiveness and mercy); yet the judge and the executioners in the judicial system must carry out such activities or be considered negligent. Little wonder they often wear a costume that symbolizes their societal position (robes, uniforms, hoods) to remind others that they are not acting in an ordinary capacity. In a similar fashion, investigators may feel that assembling and analyzing information about the private and personal actions of others will develop knowledge to benefit society as a whole, even though it requires violating norms for interpersonal relationships.

There continues to be substantial variation among social scientists regarding their own views of their role in society and how research may contribute to satisfying responsibilities or obligations. At least three can be identified:

Societal Agent: Investigators are considered to be agents of society and to be responsible for developing new knowledge that will provide general benefits for all.

Social Reformer: Investigators are considered to be responsible for improving society, either by contributing to the welfare of the disadvantaged, by eliminating or controlling those that may abuse social privileges or influence, or by making direct improvements that will serve all citizens.

Model Citizen: Social scientists are considered to be responsible for setting standards for others to emulate in their daily lives as teachers, counselors, or investigators; therefore their treatment of others (students, clients, research participants, and so on) should be exemplary.

Social scientists may emphasize one or more of these perspectives as their situations or interests change. Further, all are seen as relevant for most social scientists; and even those who pursue research as agents of society may not be willing to violate all norms of interpersonal behavior to achieve a scientific objective. Variation in emphasis upon these perspectives contributes to the uniqueness of each social scientist.

A STRATEGY FOR ANALYZING
RESEARCH ACTIVITY

Three orientations for resolving moral dilemmas—respect for individual rights (defined by society), evaluation of the effects (costs-benefits), and the personal treatment of others—are relevant to research involving human participants. While one approach for evaluating the moral nature of research activities is to develop a set of rules (as reflected in the ethical codes adopted by professional associations), there is considerable difficulty and ambiguity in using such rules due to the diversity, complexity, and unpredictability of research. An alternative is to develop a set of questions to guide the review of each project, accepting the fact that the final decision will be one of personal judgment.

Seven questions have been chosen to reflect the central features of the three different approaches to moral dilemmas. They are:

Effects on Rights	1. What rights of various parties associated with the research activity—participants, investigators, society at large—may be affected?
Program/Project Effects	2. What are the costs and benefits of the research program and this project?
Participant Effects	3. What are the costs (or risks) and benefits for the participants?
Distribution of Effects	4. What is the expected distribution of the costs and benefits?

Respect for Rights, Welfare	5. How has respect for the rights and welfare of the participants been demonstrated?
Personal Treatment	6. To what extent has the personal treatment of the participants by the investigator(s) approach the ideal?
Acceptability to Social Scientists	7. Which social scientist role definition, if any, would be consistent with the major features of the moral analysis?

These seven questions can only help to ensure that major issues relevant to a moral decision have been reviewed. The final conclusion regarding the moral appropriateness of any research activity is ultimately a personal, intuitive judgment.

The next three chapters will analyze different types of research and are organized around these questions. Chapter 2 emphasizes experimental research, in which the investigator deliberately creates a new situation or environment for the participants and assumes increased responsibility for any effects (good or bad) they may experience. Such experiences may be conducted in both controlled (or laboratory) and natural (or field) settings. Chapter 3 reviews projects designed to provide overt descriptions, where the participants are fully aware of the research activity (as in surveys, personality testing, field observation, and the like). Chapter 4 shifts the focus to covert research in which participants are unaware they are contributing to a scientific endeavor (surreptitious natural experiments, participant observation, use of unobtrusive measures, or secondary analysis of census or official records). Several types of research that raise additional complications—such as research with social systems (organizations, families, and the like) and cross-cultural research—are discussed in Chapter 5.

As social scientists begin to explore more sensitive, important phenomena and as the results of their efforts are given more serious attention by policy makers and the general public, their research has become more of a public issue. The major response to this concern has been to develop mechanisms to control the investigators; such procedures are designed to ensure that the moral character of research is acceptable to the majority of typical citizens. For many investigators, these control mechanisms provide the major incentive for conducting a moral analysis of their own research. Three such mechanisms are reviewed in Chapter 6: codes of ethics developed within professional associations, the federally required review of research (requiring a prior review by institutional review boards for some, not all, research), and the legal constraints. Finally, Chapter 7 considers the responsibilities of investigators for the practical application of scientific knowledge and how they might affect its implementation.

There are no perfect solutions to the significant problems that confront social scientists, no answers that all will consider morally acceptable. The confidence to make a decision and take action usually comes from an exploration of the alternatives and the knowledge that the decisions may be ambiguous and difficult. In moral analysis, each person is his or her own ultimate authority; each must live with his or her own conscience.

CHAPTER TWO
OVERT EXPERIMENTS

Experiments are primarily conducted to contribute to explanations, one of the two basic objectives associated with science. (The other, description, is the focus of the next chapter.) The simplest form of an experiment involves the random assignment of similar individuals into two categories; each is then provided with a different experience to determine if this variation has an effect upon a behavior, attitude, or personal characteristic. Such experiments are based on a strong confidence that any differences between categories are caused by the variables manipulated or controlled by the investigators. But, just as the investigator has high confidence he or she has caused the differences by controlling the participants' experiences, he or she also assumes responsibility for all effects (good or bad) upon the participants' rights and welfare.

This lack of ambiguity about responsibility for effects simplifies the demonstration of moral analysis of research activity. Two general types of experiments represent extreme cases of investigator influence. The first are conducted in highly controlled (usually laboratory) settings; virtually all aspects of the participants' physical and social environment (including the size of the room, temperature, lighting, social contact, tasks, and the like) are managed—as in the typical social-psychological experiment. Field experiments provide a contrast; in these, participants (individuals or social units) are chosen to be typical of natural populations. One feature of their context may be changed—such as a guaranteed minimum income, a health insurance plan, or police patrol services—to determine its effect upon other features of their lives. In such studies, investigators control fewer aspects of the situation, although they may influence the choice of participants and the nature of their special experiences. Some of the general features of each and examples of moral analysis will be reviewed below.

CONTROLLED (LABORATORY) SETTINGS

Example of Analysis: Obedience to Authority

A problem of both scientific and practical significance is the determination of the extent to which a "norm of habitual obedience" may persist among ordinary individuals. Stated as a research question, it may be phrased as follows: "Is it possible to observe the conditions under which an individual will fail to obey the instructions of a person in a position of authority?" Not only may such knowledge have implications for the administration of organizations (both private and public), but it may also facilitate understanding of how organizations with questionable ends—ends that seem inconsistent with widely shared objectives and values—are able to function. Examples of "ordinary" people agreeing to the requests of superiors in "legitimate" organizations to facilitate "bad ends" are commonplace. The most dramatic examples occur in wartime, such as the civilian massacres in Vietnam and the Nazi bureaucracy's routine and systematic extermination of over six million individuals (a considerable organizational feat, monstrous as it was). Contemporary examples of extreme violence by radical political groups, dictators, or invading armies are much too common.

Such consideration led to the creation of a research procedure that allowed systematic variation of the factors encouraging acquiescence to a person in authority, a person who requested—for seemingly reasonable ends—the commission of acts counter to the norms of everyday life. This is the "obedience to authority" research program that contributed to an open and extensive discussion of the ethical aspects of social science research involving human participants.[1] Out of a concern for the ability of the Nazi government to develop smoothly functioning "death camps," a research situation was developed to simulate the conflict an ordinary person would encounter in a similar situation—a conflict between the desire to comply with the apparently legitimate requests of a person in authority and an assumed reluctance to inflict pain upon an innocent party.

The initial plan was to develop a research situation that would provide for a range of responses beyond that elicited from most individuals, in order to examine the effect of various factors (characteristics of participants, physical setting, experimenter, and the like) on obedience to authority. Each of the participants (ordinary

---

[1] See the following for discussions of this research program: Milgram, 1963, 1964, 1965, 1968, 1972, 1974, 1977; Baumrind, 1964; Erickson, 1968; Etzioni, 1968; Kaufman, 1967; Orne and Holland, 1968; Patten, 1977a, 1977b; Ring, Wallston, and Corey, 1970.

individuals who were solicited through newspaper ads) would arrive at the research setting and encounter another participant (actually a confederate in the employ of the investigator). After being told that the project was concerned with learning processes, one participant was chosen to serve as the "teacher" and the other as the "pupil." A rigged "random" procedure resulted in the confederate always being assigned the role of "pupil."

After signing informed consent forms, in which both agreed to continue the procedure to the end, the "teacher" was asked to read a sequence of four word-pairs ("blue—moon") to the "pupil." Testing of memory retention was based on correctly identifying the second word of each pair ("moon") after the first ("blue") was read to the participant; there were thirty such sets of four word-pairs. Each time the "pupil" made a mistake (nonresponses were to be considered mistakes), the "teacher" was to (1) increase the level of an electric shock and (2) administer a shock to the "pupil." The shock levels ranged from 15 volts (level 1) to 450 (level 30); at level 20 (300 volts) a label on the equipment warned "Extreme Intensity Shock"; at level 24 (360 volts), a label warned "Danger: Severe Shock"; over levels 28 to 30 (420 to 450 volts) a label indicated "XXX"—in red. The "pupil," usually played by the same confederate in the employ of the investigator, never actually received any shocks: he consistently made mistakes or failed to respond and faked pained reactions to the "shocks" following a standardized script.

The major dependent variable (the event to be measured), was the refusal of the "teachers" to follow the instructions of the person in authority, the experimenter. He encouraged the "teacher" to administer increasingly severe shocks to the "pupil," who would continue to make mistakes or fail to respond. This encouragement took the form of a series of standardized statements: "You must go on," "The experiment requires you to go on," or "I'll take responsibility." Expectations that the "teachers" would refuse to continue were consistent with the judgments of psychiatrists, college students, and middle-class adults, all of whom predicted that most participants would defy the experimenter before completing one-third of the shock scale, a mean shock level of 120 to 150 volts (Milgram, 1974, p. 29).

The actual results were quite different. In most conditions a substantial number of participants were obedient and continued to provide quite painful and dangerous shocks to the "pupil" in compliance with the instructions of the experimenter. The results of nineteen different experimental conditions are summarized in Exhibit 2-1; depending upon the circumstances, from none to 92.5% of the "teacher"-participants (ordinary young and middle-aged adults) were obedient and provided the shocks at the maximum level for the "pupil"-confederates. Conditions where the majority of the "teachers" were defiant and refused to administer further shocks include: factors conflicting with the authority of the experimenter; the personal presence or touching of the "pupil"; an experimenter instructing the "teacher" to stop; an ordinary person (not an experimenter) providing instructions to shock the "pupil"; conflicting instructions from two experimenters; or a "peer" refusing to cooperate (actually another confederate). The tendency to comply with

EXHIBIT 2-1   Major Results of the Obedience to Authority Research Program

PERCENTAGE ADMINISTERING MAX. SHOCK[1]	MEAN SHOCK LEVEL[2]	EXP. NO.[3]	EXPERIMENTAL CONDITION
Original Condition			
30.00	17.88	4	Touch-proximity (n = 40) "Teacher" must hold "pupil's" hand on metal plate to complete circuit and operate equipment simultaneously
40.00	20.80	3	Proximity (n = 40) "Teacher" and "pupil" in same room
62.50	24.53	2	Voice-feedback (n = 40) "Teacher" hears "pupil" protest over intercom
65.00	27.0	1	Remote (n = 40) "Teacher" hears "pupil" bang on wall in protest
Revised Procedure			
.00	10.00	12	"Pupil" demands to be shocked (n = 20) Experimenter instructs "teacher" not to go on
.00	10.00	14	Experimenter serves as "pupil" (n = 20) Ordinary man instructs "teacher" to go on
.00	10.00	15	Two experimenters give conflicting instructions (n = 20) Ordinary man serves as "pupil"
2.50	5.50	11	"Teacher" chooses shock level (n = 40) "Pupil" protests coordinated to shock level
10.00	16.45	17	Two peers rebel (n = 40) "Teacher" task subdivided into three activities, subject "shocks"
20.00	16.25	13	Ordinary man gives orders (n = 20) Experimenter leaves; "ordinary man," an accomplice, suggests increasing shock levels as own idea
20.50	18.2	7	Experimenter absent (n = 40) Orders to "teacher" received over telephone
40.00	21.40	9	"Pupil" does not give full informed consent (n = 40) Insists on right to terminate at will prior to becoming involved
47.50	20.95	10	Research conducted in commercial building (n = 40) All other conditions on campus of major university
50.00	22.20	6	Variation in personnel (n = 40) Different experimenter-"pupil" team

EXHIBIT 2-1   (continued)

PERCENTAGE ADMINISTERING MAX. SHOCK[1]	MEAN SHOCK LEVEL[2]	EXP. NO.[3]	EXPERIMENTAL CONDITION
65.00	24.55	5	Voice-feedback condition: male subjects ($n = 40$)
65.00	24.73	8	Voice-feedback condition: female subjects ($n = 40$)
65.00	23.50	16	Two experimenters ($n = 20$) One served as "pupil"
68.75	24.90	13a	Subject as bystander ($n = 16$) "Ordinary man" assumes right to administer shocks on own initiative
92.50	26.65	18	Peer administers shock ($n = 40$) Subject maintains records on "pupil's" performance

[1] Refers to the percentage that administer shocks at the 450-volt level ("Danger," "Severe Shock," and "XXX" labels on equipment). In all but one condition, Exp. No. 12, this reflects obedience to the instructions of another; in Exp. No. 12, the experimenter instructs the "teacher" to terminate the study; he is always compliant.

[2] Equipment involved 30 levels of shock, labeled from 15 to 450 volts at 15-volt intervals. The shock level, in volts, can be computed by multiplying the level by 15; for example, level 10 was 150 volts.

[3] Indicates the number of the experiment as described in Milgram (1974).

Source: Descriptions based on Milgram (1974). Numbers in parentheses indicate the number of participants in each condition, a total of 636. Except in Exp. No. 8, all participants were male, chosen to represent different ages in the following proportions: 20-29, 20 percent; 30-39, 40 percent; and 40-49, 40 percent. Occupational categories were represented as follows: skilled and unskilled workers; 40 percent; white color, sales, and business, 40 percent; and professionals, 20 percent.

authority and provide the punishment was increased when the "pupil" was in a more remote situation or when the "teacher" was acting as an accessory to the activity, doing clerical work and not operating the equipment.

The first major finding from this research program was the ease with which typical individuals—men and women who were decent citizens—can be encouraged to inflict pain upon another. (Despite the fact that the "pupil," usually the same passive, pleasant, rotund man in his fifties, mentions a heart condition and, midway up the shock scale, requests that the study be stopped.) There is no question that the context of this situation and the presence of the experimenter had a profound effect upon the responses of these ordinary individuals, all of whom had a strong tendency to obey authority.

The second major finding was the high levels of stress experienced by the "teachers" (or subjects); the "pupil," who was never actually shocked, experienced no real stress.

Subjects were observed to sweat, tremble, stutter, bite their lips, groan, and dig their fingernails into their flesh. These were characteristic rather than exceptional responses to the experiment.

26

One sign of tension was the regular occurrence of nervous laughing fits. Fourteen of the forty subjects showed definite signs of nervous laughter and smiling. The laughter seemed entirely out of place, even bizarre. Full-blown, uncontrollable seizures were observed for three subjects. On one occasion we observed a seizure so violently convulsive that it was necessary to call a halt to the experiment. The subject . . . was seriously embarrassed by his untoward and uncontrollable behavior. In postexperimental interviews subjects took pains to point out that they were not sadistic types and that the laughter did not mean they enjoyed shocking the victim (Milgram, 1963, p. 375).

In short, there was substantial evidence that the stress for the participants, usually those who were obedient and administered the full range of shocks, was extreme. Such stress was acknowledged by both the participants and the investigator associated with the research.

The third major finding was the unexpected facility the participants had for denying responsibility for their actions, thus protecting themselves from a "guilt experience" (Milgram, 1964, 1974). Participants found numerous ways of rejecting their responsibility for their actions—they were only following orders, they were part of a system they could not influence, and so on; or they assumed a position of moral superiority over the authority figure who "caused" their behavior. In short, cognitive or psychic mechanisms prevented the participants from experiencing significant levels of guilt, an important research finding.

The potency of this last finding was not apparent when the initial study was completed and a number of procedures were implemented to minimize and measure the potential impact of guilt. Immediately following the postexperimental interview, the subjects were given a complete description of all procedures and had a friendly encounter with the unharmed pupil. Further, there was a follow-up questionnaire for all participants and a psychiatric interview with some a year after they had participated in the research. Questionnaire responses indicated that both obedient and defiant "teachers" were strongly supportive of the research (Milgram, 1964, p. 849). Ninety-two percent of the participants returned the questionnaire, and only 1.3 percent expressed regret about participating; 15 percent were neutral about participating; and 84 percent were glad to have participated. Eighty percent "felt that more experiments of this sort should be carried out," and 74 percent indicated they had learned something of personal importance. The report of the psychiatrist who interviewed forty participants twelve months after the study indicated that: "No evidence was found of any traumatic reactions. A few accepted responsibility for their actions and described their distress when faced with their willingness to inflict pain on another human being. They felt that as a result of the experiment they had learned something valuable about themselves (Errera, 1972, p. 400).

Effects on Rights.   The right of investigators to explore any topic of personal interest is consistent with the investigation of factors that affect conformity to requests from authority. The right of typical citizens to expect social scientists to explore significant, critical topics seems to have been fulfilled by this research program; if fully understood and properly applied, the implications of this research could have substantial benefits for future generations. While none of the major positive rights (life, liberty, privacy and so forth) of the participants was abridged, there was clearly some infringement upon a claim to an honest, truthful presentation of the situation and freedom from stress, guilt, or a possible reduction in self-esteem.

Research Program/Project Effects.   Substantial benefits could accrue from a precise knowledge of the conditions under which individuals will be compliant to those in authority. Not only would such knowledge allow for an understanding of the conditions that would lead to efficient and conflict-free operation of organizations, but it would also help predict when substantial noncompliance could be expected and when influences from other sources might have a major effect, leading individuals to be ambivalent about compliance with organizational directives. Given the importance of organizations and persons in positions of authority in advanced societies, thorough knowledge of these phenomena could be quite useful. The major negative effects might be related to the location of the knowledge rather than to the knowledge itself; it might be considered an instrument of those in positions of influence for the manipulation of organizational members, but this goes beyond the question of effects to that of application. The information could also be utilized by average individuals to modify the influence of those in authority.

This particular project explored the conditions that produce obedience to, and defiance of, authority by individuals under very special conditions—those where the behavior may produce effects counter to most social norms, such as inflicting pain upon another. While this is not the usual type of situation in which authority is exercised—in most situations there is consensus between superiors and subordinates about the goals in question—it may be considered an important limiting case. If authority can be successfully exercised in this type of situation, it would suggest that very few situations exist in which authority would be systematically resisted by subordinates. While the experiment had no obvious positive benefits for the participants, except an increase in self-knowledge, there could be a substantial positive benefit to society—and the participants—if the knowledge gained helps to ensure that those in positions of authority will be responsive to major social values and norms.

Participant Effects.   There were no systematic, major positive effects for the six to seven hundred participants in this research program. There may have been benefits in terms of receiving cash (a relatively modest $4.00 to $4.50), participating in an interesting experience, contributing to scientific knowledge, or gaining self-knowledge, but compared to some studies (where considerable counseling, substantial money, or significant health care is provided), these cannot be considered major. The major negative effects were the loss of time in participation, the stress experienced by a substantial proportion of "teachers" (extreme in some cases), and possible guilt over their behavior. One of the findings, however, was that certain cognitive mechanisms tend to prevent full development of self-blame.

Distribution of Effects. The bulk of the participants in the research projects were young to middle-aged adult males from the New Haven, Connecticut, area and belonged to the working and middle class (based upon occupational characteristics). The burdens of the research were not shared by women (except for one study), younger or older citizens, those with very low or very high social status, or those living in other parts of the United States. While there were few direct benefits to the research participants, all other social categories may benefit from the general knowledge that resulted from this series of studies. While the burdens of the research experience were not equally shared by individuals in all social categories, the distribution of burdens was clearly not unjust, if it was unjust at all.

Respects for Rights, Welfare. Several aspects of the routine treatment accorded the participatnts reflected respect for their rights and welfare. With regard to the stress they may have experienced during the experiment, their activity was closely monitored, and when necessary, the procedure was terminated. Concern about stress and guilt led to the extensive postexperimental interview and the friendly reconciliation with the "pupil." To determine if these efforts were successful, the follow-up questionnaire and interviews were used. While fully aware that participants would be deceived about the true nature of the research, the researchers discussed both the nature of the study and the reason for the deception with the participants after the experiment. Evidence from the participants' responses on the questionnaire indicated that these efforts were successful in removing most resentment and guilt.

Personal Treatment. Treatment of the participants, on an interpersonal level, presumably was comparable to that of ordinary interactions—i.e., it was courteous and straightforward. There were two major deceptions, regarding the purpose of the research and the actual degree of pain experienced by the "pupil." Immediately following the experience, both illusions were revealed to the participants. While deception is a common occurrence in daily life (in advertising, political statements, and the like), extended attempts to reveal and explain such deceptions are not. In that sense, and in the postexperimental concern for the participants' well-being, the personal treatment seems to approach the ideal. On the other hand, it has been argued that once deceived by a psychologist, the participants' distrust has been activated and can never be fully eliminated.

Acceptability to Social Scientists. Despite the dramatic findings of this research and the respect shown for the participants, the central fact remains that they were deceived and subjected to stress (considerable in some cases); many temporarily experienced reduced self-esteem. Social scientists who consider their *primary* obligation to be promoting the well-being of all individuals and the reputation of their discipline through good interpersonal relations may find this study unnecessary and unacceptable. Social scientists who consider their primary obligation to be the development of useful knowledge of important social and human phenomena may consider this program of research to be a contribution; it is morally acceptable as long as the appropriate respect was shown for the participants' rights and welfare. Social scientists who consider their primary objective to be the improvement of society or the human condition through direct action may have no strong moral judgment regarding this type of research.

Effects of Typical Experiments

The research on obedience to authority is dramatic and distinctive both for the importance of the phenomena it investigated and for its impact on participants. Participants in typical laboratory experiments may realize a number of positive effects, such as involvement in an interesting activity, altruistic satisfaction at contributing to science, new and valuable self-knowledge, knowledge about research procedures, or cash payments, academic credits, special privileges, and the like. Negative effects may include being deceived, physical discomfort, psychological stress, or unpleasant self-knowledge; participants seldom need to fear permanent damage or a major change in their social status or prestige. A complete cost-benefit analysis would take into account the frequency with which these effects occur and participants' reactions to them.

In estimating the occurrence of negative effects, most attention has focused upon the risks associated with research projects rather than the actual effects for participants; the conclusions have not been based upon negative experiences reported by the participants themselves. One strategy has been to review a sample of research published in leading journals and to estimate the extent to which it reflects "unethical practices"; emphasis has been given to deception, particularly in social psychology experiments. Several studies suggest that as much as one-third of all published social psychology studies incorporate deception in their "instruments" (personality tests, attitude measures, problems or tasks, and so forth), or in the information given to participants about other participants, the purpose of the research, or the participants' own behavior (Menges, 1973; Seeman, 1969; Stricker, 1967). But the nature and significance of the deceptions in these studies are based upon the judgment of those reviewing the journal articles; there is no way of knowing the extent to which deception has occurred in unpublished research or the extent to which the participants considered themselves "deceived" or misused at the conclusion of the research (after a debriefing).

Another strategy has been to interview investigators about the expected risks for participants in projects they have proposed or completed. A study of a national sample of projects submitted to Institutional Review Boards (human subject committees) asked the principal investigators to comment on the project (Institute for Social Research, 1976). Research was categorized according to "behavioral intervention," or the amount of controlled influence upon the participants, perhaps for their own benefit (as a new type of counseling technique), perhaps not (but as a contribution to science). Investigators estimated the probability that various types of positive and negative effects for the participants may have occurred; these are presented in Exhibit 2-2. Note that this does not reflect the actual occurrence of the effects, but an estimate of their likelihood of occurring. For example, investigators conducting 60 percent of the projects estimated that the

EXHIBIT 2-2   Effects in Experimental Research: Investigator's Estimates[1]

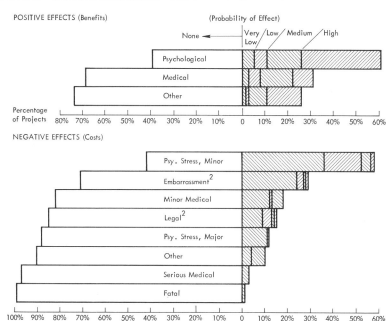

EXHIBIT 2-2   Effects in Experimental Research: Investigator's Estimates[1]

NOTES: 1) From Institute of Social Research, 1976, Table IV. 8, pg. 121. Percentages refer to investigator's ratings of projects, e.g. 1% of 136 projects were seen to have a very low risk of fatal effects for participants.
2) Risks are related to possible breaches of confidentiality.

probability of a positive psychological effect (benefit) was greater than zero (very low, low, medium, or high); conversely, investigators conducting 1 percent of the projects thought the risk of participant death was very low, and those responsible for the other 99 percent considered no fatal risk to be present.

In contrast to these estimates—which indicate a rather low potential for any serious risks—the reports of actual negative effects were almost nonexistent. From investigators reporting on 2,052 projects (62 percent of a biomedical nature), only three reported instances of subject embarrassment or harm due to a breach of confidentiality; other trival or temporarily disabling effects not predictable as part of the research therapy or procedure were reported for 3 percent of the projects (average of two participants each for each project where negative effects were reported) (Institute for Social Research, 1976, pp. 26-27). But as the majority of the projects were biomedical research, it is unlikely that these unexpected negative effects were experienced by participants in social science research.[2] It has been very difficult to

[2] A study of the effects on participants in biomedical research, also based upon the investigators's reports, found that the risk for the participants (or the proportion experiencing negative effects) in nontherapeutic research (where there were no direct benefits) was slightly less than the risk of accidents in daily life; and the risk for participants in therapeutic research was less than the risk in ordinary medical care (Cardon, Dommel, & Trumble, 1976).

locate participants who have experienced long-term negative effects, although one example, in which one individual resented being deceived ten years after the study occurred, has been cited by a commentator on research ethics (Baumrind, 1975, p. 57).

Despite the lack of evidence to suggest permanent negative effects for participants are a common experience, there is reason to believe that research participation may often involve temporary stress, physical discomfort, or deception. What are the reactions of participants to such experiences? It has been found that undergraduates are more negative toward a poorly administered study (one with unclear instructions, one directed by an experimenter who is late, incompetent, or disrespectful) than toward concealed purposes, deception, or possible electric shock (Epstein, Sudefeld, & Silverstein, 1973). When asked to evaluate a wide range of possible experimental "discomforts," college students rate few at the extreme end of a five-point discomfort scale ("maximum tolerable" electric shock is least preferred); and they do not appear to resent requests for personal information about, for example, past sexual experiences (Farr & Seaver, 1975). When comparing possible experimental experiences with events occurring in daily life, the students rated only physical discomfort as potentially more severe; they considered psychological stress and invasions of privacy equivalent to daily life experiences, such as taking an exam (Meglino, 1976a, 1976b). In summary, the typical participant in social psychology experiments—a college student—considers the negative features of research to be much less severe than most investigators; psychologists are two to three times more likely than students to condemn studies as unethical (Sullivan & Deiker, 1973).

There is little question that highly controlled experiments may involve some degree of deception (it is almost impossible to know when the "whole truth" has been conveyed to another), minor degrees of psychological or physical stress, and requests for private information. The occasions on which these constitute dramatic, significant infringements upon the rights and welfare of the participants appear to be infrequent; the obedience to authority program represents an atypical, extreme case. However, the moral ambiguity of deceiving participants has led to a concerned effort to develop alternatives that will be morally acceptable and still allow the achievement of scientific objectives.

Alternatives to Informed Consent

Just as there is no question that illusions and incomplete information infringe upon participants' rights to an honest and complete presentation regarding the research experience, there is also no question that complete information about the research may have a substantial effect upon some phenomena. For example, if participants are aware they are in a study of verbal conditioning (in which they are given positive verbal feedback following the mention of certain words or topics in order to increase the frequency of such words or topics), the positive reinforcement will have little or no effect; the phenomena will have disappeared (Resnick & Schwartz, 1973). This dilemma has led to serious attention to alternatives to using full, complete informed consent or deception. Three such alternatives have been: (1) avoiding the use of deception in research, (2) developing alternative mechanisms for obtaining informed consent, and (3) minimizing the negative effects of the deception itself.

Alternatives to experimental research involving deception include surveys or natural experiments (where the variation in conditions is the result of natural processes, not the experimenter's manipulation) or the use of role playing. Non-experimental research, such as surveys, lead to ambiguity about causal inferences, particularly the phenomena that are responsive to a variety of subtle, interrelated, difficult-to-measure variables; natural experiments may lead to confidence regarding causality, but are often so rare or unpredictable that it is difficult to make timely progress on scientific issues. These problems led to the use of experimental research designs in the first place. Role-playing situations involve carefully developed stories or scenarios and asking participants what they would do if confronted with the situations—that is, participants adopt the role of a central character. These experiments may vary in the extent to which they provide participants with complete information and opportunities to give thoughtful attention to a decision. Role-playing situations are substitutes for actual staged dilemmas in which participants may believe their actions have real consequences; such created situations are a major form of deception in social psychology studies.

Despite the good intentions of those promoting this strategy, a substantial amount of evidence suggests that role playing does not provide an adequate substitute for the reactions and behavior of participants in situations they have defined as real. Considerable evidence shows that attitudes and behavior are, as a general rule, not well correlated (Deutscher, 1973; Liska, 1975; Wicker, 1969), particularly for those actions seen as socially sensitive (La Pierre, 1935). Second, there are a number of examples where expectations about behavior have been dramatically different from the actual behavior. For example, no group of individuals—undergraduates, middle-aged adults, or psychiatrists—who predicted reactions to the obedience to authority situation expected any shocks above the 300-volt level (Milgram, 1974; p. 29); in fact, a substantial percentage of comparable participants faced with the actual research situation administered shocks at the maximum level of 450 volts (see Exhibit 2-1). On the other hand, it has been reported that a careful simulation of the same research, where the "script" was read to participants but there was no expectation that a pupil would be shocked, produced simulated obedience equivalent to that in the "full-dress" study, although "teacher" stress was reduced and denial of responsibility were not present (Mixon, 1972). A growing and complex discussion (see the symposium edited by Hendrick, 1977), has developed around the phenomena for which "role playing" is considered to provide responses that justify confidence in predictions about reactions in natural (non-experimental) settings. Role playing is clearly suited to a wider range of situations than can be "created" to provide a realistic context for participants.

But role playing itself may not avoid ethical controversy; the written material may be questioned. Based upon a content analysis of pornographic material found in "adult" bookstores, two major themes were found in depictions of sexual assaults upon women: the victims' experiences of pain and their involuntary orgasms. College students of both genders were asked to read different descriptions of sexual assaults and rate the extent to which they found them sexually stimulating. While both genders found mutually consenting sexual descriptions most stimulating, they also found descriptions of a female victim experiencing an involuntary orgasm exciting (more so for men and less so for women when the victim experienced pain) (Malamouth, Heim, & Feshbach, 1980). Involuntary orgasms by women are known to be both unrealistic and impossible; controversy developed over whether or not this would lead impressionable college students to believe this fantasy and whether it would have detrimental effects on their future sexual relations (Sherif, 1980). This was countered by the suggestion that with proper post-experimental discussions, male participants would realize the inaccuracy of this portrayal and the inappropriate nature of their response (Malamouth, Feshbach, & Heim, 1980).

Another solution to this dilemma has been to develop alternative procedures for providing informed consent; one procedure uses individuals comparable to the participants to provide surrogate informed consent for the actual participants. This strategy involves dividing a homogeneous group into two subgroups; individuals from one subgroup are given the full details of the project and research procedures, including any possible deception, and asked, singly, if they would have been willing to participate. Individuals from the second subgroup are provided with the illusions and partial information necessary to obtain their honest reaction to a situation they define as real; they are debriefed and counseled after the research experience.

Researchers would then have confidence they had given the rights of the real participants (from the second subgroup) adequate consideration because they would know that comparable individuals approved of the project. If there was concern that the surrogate participants might inform the real participants of the nature of the deception, they could be drawn from different communities or universities. Alternatively, a committee representing the participants could review a project and make a judgment for them. An unresolved issue is the percentage of surrogates that must approve a project before it is initiated (unanimity is a remote possibility); if the average cooperation rate for surveys is used as a guide, approval by more than 80 percent may be considered as constituting consent, although 95 percent approval has been suggested as a "safe standard" (Baumrind, 1971).

An alternative to surrogate informed consent would be to obtain a general consent to participate in experiments and inform the participants they may be deceived in any particular study and that the deception will be revealed after their research experience. This procedure would not require informing a specific participant that he is going to be deceived, and it would increase confidence that he is unaware of the purpose of the research (although he may be more sensitive to the possibility of an illusion). At the same time it would ensure that he had given his consent to be deceived, although not to a specific type of deception (Soble, 1978).

Perhaps the most widely employed solution to this problem has been to minimize the deception as much as possible and, after the research experience, emphasize debriefing and follow-up to determine and correct any possible ill effects. This allows a true experimental research design, focuses efforts upon those who may experience negative effects and have their rights infringed upon (rather than a set of surrogates), and acknowledges the rights and welfare of the actual participants. It may not, however, satisfy critics who claim that research deception encourages the spread of general distrust in society and specifically of social scientists (Baumrind, 1971; Rubin, 1970; Warwick, 1975).

Debriefing involves two different activities (Holmes, 1976a, 1976b): (1) *dehoaxing,* or informing the participant of the true nature of activities or procedures to eliminate the deception, and (2) *desensitizing,* or attempting to remove or correct any negative perceptions or feelings the participants may have had about themselves or others based on accurate information received in the study. A review of the literature (ten studies) on the effectiveness of dehoaxing suggests that if it is completed in such a way that participants believe explanations regarding the illusions created for the research (there are a number of techniques to facilitate this), it may correct the false impressions conveyed to the participant (Holmes, 1976a). In most cases these involve false information about the participants' personalities or other aspects of themselves; a substantial number of participants are told they were misled into improving their self-image.

Studies of the effects of desensitizing procedures have involved a replication of the obedience to authority study. Here the major issue was the effect of variation in debriefing upon the reaction of the participants (Ring, Wallston, & Corey, 1970); only 3 percent of the debriefed participants (1 out of 28) regretted participating in the project or felt that such research should be prohibited, compared to 43 percent (6 out of 14) of those not debriefed. Further, 96 percent of those fully debriefed did not resent the deception and did not consider the research unethical; they could be considered desensitized. When potential participants were given descriptions of various research procedures, some involving stress and various amounts of debriefing (Berscheid et al., 1973; Schulman & Berman, 1974), small differences were found in reactions to stressful and stress-free research, and participants reacted more positively to the research (they were more willing to participate) when they were given a full debriefing.

Current evidence suggests that a complete, thoughtful debriefing and post-research follow-up of participants not only provides evidence of the investigator's concern for the rights and welfare of the participants, but also ameliorates the effects of the research experience upon the participants. There is a slight tendency for dehoaxed participants to tell others about the study and its deceptive aspects, thereby affecting the responses of some involved later in the project; however, fewer "secrets" are divulged following a written promise of confidentiality (Lichtenstein, 1970; Walsh & Stillman, 1974). But this tendency is not significant enough to substantially affect confidence in experimental research. It seems likely that the advantages of controlled research settings for the study of complex, easily influenced phenomena will continue to encourage the use of deception—in combination with careful dehoaxing and desensitization—when it is required to achieve scientific objectives.

NATURAL (FIELD) SETTINGS

Example of Analysis: Income Maintenance Study

Typical of government experiments dealing with individual behavior is the study of the effects of the negative income tax (Kershaw, 1972; Kershaw & Small, 1972; Rivlin, 1971). The research involved the examination of the effects of different negative income tax plans (direct cash payments) to "guarantee" a predetermined minimum household income: partial reductions in payments occurred if household earnings increased. The basic question was the extent of labor-force participation of individuals in households with a guaranteed income—i.e., would they work less? The study also estimated the costs of a guaranteed income program if adopted as the major welfare strategy for the nation. The initial study involved 1,400 families in five cities in the New Jersey-Pennsylvania area randomly assigned to one of the eight plans (negative income tax schedules) or to a control group (families receiving no guaranteed income).

Effects on Rights.   There are several different categories of individuals whose rights may be affected by this research. Those paying the costs and most likely to benefit are the public at large; the project can be seen as serving the right of all citizens to an effective, efficient, and humane government. The basic purpose of the research was to determine if improved welfare programs would promote the welfare client's contributions to society. Two rights of the participants (heads of households and their families) were of major concern: (1) protecting the confidential information they provided to the investigators (every three months they were interviewed about their activities, purchasing behavior, sources of income, attitudes, and the like) and (2) ensuring they were treated with dignity and provided with a humane welfare program. Since all members of the experimental groups received more cash benefits than they might otherwise receive, it was to their economic benefit to become involved. Members of the control group were paid a fee for participating in comparable interviews, but this was substantially below the total payments to those receiving guaranteed incomes.

It is possible that other members of communities where the research was conducted may have been indirectly affected. Employers may have paid higher wages to attract workers with a guaranteed income, thereby benefiting other workers; but the program would also reduce employers' profits in comparison with competing firms located in other communities. Such indirect effects on "secondary participants" have not been systematically explored.

Research Program/Project Effects.   Prior to the first study there was no systematic empirical evidence to indicate whether the advantages of a guaranteed income plan—simplicity of administration, equity, dignity for the recipient, and work incentives (guaranteed income was only partially reduced by increased earnings)—were outweighed by the major presumed disadvantage, a tendency to reduce gainful employment. Considering the extreme dissatisfaction with the current welfare program and the cost and impact of changing it, which would involve millions of recipients, thousands of welfare staff members, and billions of dollars, the resolution of this issue is very important. The guaranteed income experiment would also help determine if a dominant assumption in economic theory—that individuals will work less if they are guaranteed an income—is accurate in all cases; thus the experiment would resolve both scientific and practical issues.

The chief reason for developing such a social experiment was the desire to minimize ambiguity over the causal relationship between variables. The sponsor of the research, the federal government, had the ability to actually modify the major independent variable—the nature of the payment procedure. Since no such guaranteed income scheme had been used previously, it was not possible to observe the effects on the basis of past experience. There appeared to be no better way to resolve the issues than to use a social experiment.

The major negative effects of the project were the rather massive costs (a full-time staff of three dozen; annual costs of several million dollars for the five-year period; complicated and elaborate computer files) and the long time required to resolve the intellectual issues. The initial study lasted five years, but this is now considered too brief. For example, many participants may have been reluctant to quit work knowing that the guaranteed income would soon terminate.) Some current studies provide guaranteed income for up to twenty years.

Participant Effects.   Positive and negative effects were experienced by individuals as members of families, for the household was the unit of analysis (if the household dissolved, the payments were continued but divided among the individual members). Participants agreed to be interviewed every three months and report all outside income (for all household members) to the project personnel. The major negative effect, therefore, was the time required to provide the information and the possible invasions of privacy that contributing such information entailed. The families in the control group received few positive benefits (other than a token fee). Families in the experimental conditions received more benefits (depending upon which of the eight plans they were in); the payments, in fact, could range up to several thousands of dollars per year per family (this was in the late 1960s).

Distribution of Effects.   If the guaranteed income plan turns out to have substantial advantages, such as lower costs or increased dignity for the recipients, both the general public and welfare recipients would benefit. The major contributors were representative of those on welfare, but the general public contributed through financial support of the project. In this case, it would be difficult to argue that disadvantaged individuals were being "used" for the benefit of the advantaged, since those in the disadvantaged situations stood to gain.

Respect for Rights, Welfare.   The research pocedure considered the participants' rights and welfare in two ways. First, all families involved signed a contract that specified the nature of the research activity and the procedures to be followed; it included a guarantee of anonymity with respect to the written description of the research. Second, rather elaborate attempts were made to insure the confidentiality of the data; a pledge of confidentiality was signed by all staff members, and confidentiality was emphasized in the operating procedures of the research organization. Local district attorneys, federal agencies, and legislatures made some unanticipated attempts to obtain information on specific families. They were told that it would not be in the best interest of society to divulge such information and thus jeopardize a major research effort. In addition, the program made payments to a state welfare agency to compensate it for any "overpayments" to families that were both on state welfare and involved in the experiment (and may have received more than the state-mandated maximum for support). Unfortunately, the need for repeated interviews with the families precluded destruction of identifying information (one of the best procedures for guaranteeing anonymity).

Personal Treatment.   Participants in any experiment are more likely to cooperate willingly if they are treated with respect, dignity, and honesty. There is no evidence to suggest that this did not occur in the guaranteed-income experiment. It would have been difficult to develop a long-term relationship (up to five years) with participants if they had not been "treated right." Individuals who have participated in later income-maintenance studies have reported being treated with dignity; the degradation of the typical welfare program was avoided (Reinhold, 1979).

Acceptability to Social Scientists.   All social science orientations seem to be compatible with this research. Those that emphasize important issues, intellectual or applied, may find this a worthwhile endeavor. Those that emphasize good relationships with participants and a wholesome reputation in society would have few reasons to complain. Those that are concerned with improving society or the situation of the disadvantaged may see this as a contribution, even if only because of the cash payments made to those with low incomes. Perhaps the absence of social scientists with strong aversions to these studies is one reason that a number of other negative-income experiments were conducted to explore additional issues not covered in this initial study.

Effects and Informed Consent
in Field Experiments

Some phenomena are too complicated to create in a controlled setting; some take a long time to reflect experimental influences; and some must be studied in a true-to-life context. All these are reasons for using a natural setting for an experimental design. The typical procedure is to select several comparable entities (individuals, families, communities, and so on) to receive special treatment and leave others unaffected (the controls) as a basis for comparison. This procedure allows researchers to study the effects of variables such as supervisory techniques upon work group productivity, variation in counseling upon family cohesiveness, advertising techniques upon sales of consumer products, or various forms of government housing subsidies upon the supply of new dwellings in a community. Experimental studies in natural settings differ from those in controlled settings in that the investigator has no control over most physical, social, and economic features of the environment; however, the phenomena being affected may be of substantial importance to the daily lives of individuals.

Analysis of the major rights associated with such research is complicated by two issues. First, uncertainty regarding the acquisition of informed consent varies with the unit of analysis. It is relatively easy to determine who and under what conditions informed consent is provided when the unit of analysis is the individual participant; it is less clear when it is a social system, such as a family, business organization, or community. When a social system is involved, it is possible to expect all members to provide informed consent (although this is more practicable with a family than with an organization or community) or just those in positions of leadership (heads of households, executives, elected officials). Second, the nature of the mechanisms that demonstrate respect for the rights and welfare of the participants, related to the nature of the investigator and the research project itself, may vary. If the investigators are individuals (natural or legally defined persons), the major procedure for demonstrating respect for the rights and welfare of the participants is informed consent—which implies a choice regarding involvement in the project. However, in government investigations, the scientifc objectives may be furthered by mandatory participation, and the participants may have no choice; in such cases other mechanisms are used to demonstrate respect for the rights and welfare of those affected.

When the government conducts a field experiment with participants without their informed consent, the endeavor falls into the same category as other government actions taken for the general benefit of all citizens (such as building a road or enacting a new program). The mechanisms designed to prevent government officials from unjustified infringement upon the rights of citizens—*due process* and *equal treatment*—become relevant. Due process was included in the Constitution to ensure that the major individual rights (life, liberty, property, and movement) would not be restricted without the "regular course of administration through courts of justice" (Fifth Amendment); due process has since been expanded to mean that the "law (government actions) shall not be unreasonable, arbitrary, or capricious, and that the means selected shall have real and substantial relation to the object (or goals)" (Black, 1968, p. 590). Equal treatment is formalization of the idea that all citizens are equal with regard to their rights and that there shall be a "strict scrutiny" if differentiation is made on the basis of sex, race, or religion, or if, fundamental rights such as privacy, association, voting, and travel are involved (Breger, 1976, p. 28). Since any experiment involves an unequal treatment of individuals (to determine if the treatment has an effect) and may involve government benefits considered as rights (such as welfare support or medical care), then some complications arise when the participants are not free to choose whether they want to be involved in a project.

Major controversies, in the form of legal action, have involved some government social experiments—for example, those designed to increase the efficiency of programs by helping welfare participants obtain training and employment or requiring those receiving medical assistance to share in the cost of the program.[3] These cases are unique in several ways. They represent a small number of special projects (though the effects on participants may be important); the experimenter (the government) may require participants to be involved; they have the character of both a research design and an experiment in administrative innovation; and at least some participants have felt their rights or welfare have not been given appropriate consideration (otherwise there would not have been the court challenges). A government-sponsored project that required participation and involved substantial negative effects (such as a study of longer prison sentences on future criminal activity) might well be prohibited by the courts (Norris, 1966). The research chosen as an example of moral analysis is different in several ways; not only are the participants allowed to provide their informed consent, they may receive a substantial positive benefit for doing so (in this case, extra income).

CONCLUSION

The same experimental research techniques that provide the greatest confidence in a causal relationship between variables also maximize the investigator's responsibility for their impact on participants. The investigator's deliberate control of the variables is the basis for both inferences. The potential moral dilemma is minimized when the benefits of the new knowledge are substantial, the negative effects are minimal, and there is clear evidence of consideration for the rights and welfare of the participants (through the use of informed consent and postrearch surveillance to determine and correct any negative effects). In laboratory settings, the investiga-

---

[3] A court action to prevent implementation of a program that would require welfare recipients to present themselves for job training and placement in 25 percent of the state welfare districts because it provided unequal treatment of welfare recipients was denied (*Aguayo* v. *Richardson*, 1973); the court held that it was not necessary to implement trial programs on a statewide basis to provide equal treatment. In California, unsuccessful attempts were made to block an experimental medical program. The program was designed to reduce medical costs without affecting the level of care by requiring recipients to pay a modest fee (one dollar for each visit to a health provider and fifty cents for each prescription, not to exceed three dollars a month). Objections were raised on the ground that the Secretary of HEW had no authority to modify programs (*California Welfare Rights Organization* v. *Richardson*, 1972). A similar medical co-payment experiment was halted by a federal judge who agreed that the participants were to be considered "human subjects at risk" (as defined by the federal guidelines) and had not been given an opportunity to provide their informed consent (*Crane* v. *Mathews*, 1976).

tor may have maximum control over the participants' environment for short periods of time; this may allow the creation of illusions, to further the study of processes or phenomena that, if made explicit, would change or disappear. Respect for participants' rights may be demonstrated by reducing the amount of deception and by careful dehoaxing and desensitization following the study. In field experiments, the minimal control over the environment when the research is conducted by an individual (natural or legal person) may inhibit deception, particularly when informed consent is involved. Government-operated experiments may require individuals to participate; in such cases, respect for their rights and welfare is demonstrated by following the standards of due process and equality of treatment.

CHAPTER THREE
OVERT DESCRIPTIONS

The development of descriptions and the attempt to increase their reliability and precision may be the most common objectives in scientific research. This includes such diverse projects as: field observation (of work groups, atypical subcultures, families, and the like), systematic analysis of paper-and-pencil personality tests (to diagnose mental disorders), use of survey interviews (to estimate political preferences, uses of leisure activity, judgments of consumer products), studying personal contact and influence relationships in a community (to portray the social structure), and so on. The list of completed projects is endless and possibilities infinite. Such endeavors have one dominant feature that separates them from experimental research: none attempts to manipulate or change the unit of analysis (individual, social system, or whatever). Their purpose is to describe things "as they are"—not to estimate the effects of a change initiated by an invesigator. Moral analysis is primarily concerned with the control of information (acquisition of confidential data and the release of sensitive information) and the possible negative effects resulting from such disclosure.

Concerns about the effects on participants and the handling of private or confidential information may be considered in two major categories: the direct effects of the actual data gathering and possible effects from disclosure of information under the investigator's control. Two common types of data gathering will be reviewed in some detail: personality measures and survey research; both have been the focus of controversy. A second set of issues involves the disclosure of information after it has been obtained, particularly information on sensitive issues such as drug use, abortion, and sexual behavior. The desire to make good on the promise of guaranteed confidentiality has led to a number of techniques for maintaining participant anonymity, reviewed below. It is often desirable to describe a specific case or situation in some detail, and some of the concerns regarding this practice are described in the third section.

AGGREGATE, ANONYMOUS DATA: PERSONALITY TESTS

Example of Analysis: Test Score Stability

Whether the focus is on the factors that affect the personality or using the personality to predict an individual's behavior or reactions, a number of features of any measurement procedure are of some interest; one is the stability of personality traits. Unfortunately, this phenomenon, variation in personality trait stability, may be confounded with measurement unreliability—variation created by an unstable technique for measuring the personality. This leads to attempts to determine the stability of measures of personality and those factors that contribute to consistency. One study involved asking 201 men and 289 women to complete a set of personality tests, including the MMPI (Minnesota Multiphasic Personality Inventory), at the beginning and toward the end of their freshman year in a religious college; there were 33 weeks between the two administrations of the materials (Mauger, 1972). All analysis and interpretation were related to the individuals as members of an aggregate (those who took the tests); there was no specific attention given to any unique individual.

Effects on Rights. The participants were asked to review and complete a series of questions about themselves, some of which asked for sensitive, private information, and take the risk of being embarrassed; in this research, participants gave up their rights to privacy and to control their own time (i.e., the time required to complete the tests). The investigators assumed the right to explore any issue; but as long as they treated the participants with respect and dignity, this did not conflict with the rights of others. The right of the society at large to expect investigators to investigate issues with both scientific and practical significance was honored by this project.

Program/Project Effects. The use of omnibus personality tests to interpret and predict personality traits has been a major activity among psychologists; there are, in addition to the ten basic MMPI scales, literally hundreds of special scales for distinctive predictions based upon this one test (for example, low back pain, delinquency, and social desirability scales). In most cases, this systematic research had led to better than chance predictions regarding features of an individual's future life; it has increased both the understanding of the effects of personality and the ability to help those with current or potential problems. Such research represents a considerable investment in financial and professional resources, to say nothing of the thousands of participants involved in the research; the scientific and practical results are major advances in the knowledge of personality and improved therapeutic techniques.

The project in question is only one of hundreds that measure personality characteristics by standard means. While it requires some costs in terms of participant, investigator, and computer time, it has improved confidence in the estimates of personality trait stability (or test-retest reliability) and identification of stable and unstable personalities.

Participant Effects. The major positive effects (benefits) on participants is the knowledge they are participating in a worthwhile scientific endeavor; and they may have found the experience of taking the tests interesting. While the positive effects are small, the negative effects are also likely to be minimal. As long as answers remain confidential, it is unlikely that participants will experience anything more than embarrassment by reading and completing the items on the schedule; this reaction is likely to be far less in the second administration of the questionnaire. If there is no detailed postresearch consultation with the participants, they will not be embarrassed by an explicit intrusion into their private feelings and thoughts.

Distribution of Effects. The major benefactors of the research will be society as a whole (from the increased knowledge) and those individuals who, in later practical applications of the information obtained in this research, will benefit personally from the increased knowledge about personality stability. Both groups of benefactors are representative of a wide, geographically diverse cross-section of society: in contrast, those participating in the research were drawn from the upper middle class in the upper Midwest. While the distribution of participant effects is quite heterogeneous, few would argue that it is unjust. Those with advantaged situations are contributing to a project that will benefit all members of society, including the disadvantaged.

Respect for Rights, Welfare. As with most descriptive research, the welfare of the participants is unlikely to be affected by the research. The major issue is the extent to which the investigator demonstrates respect for their rights. This is found in several features of the project: obtaining informed consent gives some the option of not becoming involved (only those who consent are participants), allowing participants not to answer specific items they considered too sensitive, and maintaining strict anoymity. It is not clear what additional steps could have increased the respect shown for the participants.

Personal Treatment. There is no reason to suspect that the participants were not treated with dignity and consideration, particularly since the investigator desired honest responses on two separate administrations, the second eight months after the first.

Acceptability to Social Scientists. Such a project is most likely to be approved by those social scientists whose primary role is developing empirical knowledge for predicting human phenomena (in this case, personality). Those who expect social scientists to be model citizens may consider their attempts to reduce the human personality to quantifiable elements to be a threat to the humane treatment of individuals and their problems. Those concerned with reforming and improving society may be tolerant of the project due to its relation to applied uses of personality tests, but they may also find such a slow and detailed process personally frustrating.

In summary, then, this study involving the use of personality measures and aggregate analysis of the data appears to create very little moral controversy as long as the participants give their voluntary consent to participate, are willingly responding to each item in the inventory, and have their anonymity protected by the investigator. In this regard it is typical of hundreds or thousands of such studies. The major controversy may continue to focus on the applications of the research (such as in employment screening) rather than on its conduct.

The Inner Self
and the "Private Personality"

Whether concerned with individual personality factors or the effect of distinctive personalities upon mental processes, perspectives, attitudes, or behaviors, a central problem in psychological research is the development of reliable, useful measures. Because they are inexpensive and may improve upon clinical judgments (Meehl, 1954; Sawyer, 1966), substantial effort has gone into the development of paper-and-pencil tests for measuring personality and associated techniques for analysis. Salient features of mental processes may involve sensitive, intimate aspects of life (related to sex, relationships with parents and other family members, religion, bodily functions, and so forth); many such items are found in omnibus personality tests.

Participants in such research are generally asked to spend an hour or so (sometimes more) responding to a number of simple questions, or items, regarding their thoughts, feelings, and judgments about themselves. There are few direct positive effects: perhaps a sense of contributing to a scientific endeavor, gaining increased self-knowledge, or undergoing an interesting experience; and there may be a small direct benefit such as a cash payment or course credit. The test results of those receiving therapy or counseling may help the professionals providing assistance. Individuals in normal, comparison, or control groups may not receive immediate therapeutic benefits.

Potential negative effects include the time required to participate in the research; the risk (or concern) that sensitive personal data may become public knowledge; embarrassment at being asked to read, comprehend, and respond to questions about sensitive or objectionable topics; and the possible infringement of an individual's right to a "private personality." The first of these—time to participate—does not receive much attention; and the second—the potential release of sensitive data—is more of an issue with survey research projects (discussed below). The concerns about sensitive items and private personality are of special relevance to this type of investigation.

One of the better-known omnibus personality tests, the MMPI has frequently been criticized for containing sensitive, personal items. Several studies have examined the responses of participants to MMPI items. In one study, undergraduates identified those items considered "offensive" (Walker, 1967) and in another undergraduates rated those they "generally opposed" (in contrast to those they would specifically oppose if the test were part of an employment screening) (Butcher & Tellegen, 1966). Further, the frequency with which normal adults respond "cannot say" (which means neither true nor false) may be interpreted as an indicator of item sensitivity (Dahlstrom, Welsh, & Dahlstrom, 1975).

A summary of these findings is given in Exhibit 3-1. All twenty items (one is asked twice) were considered "offensive" or "generally opposed"; four other items had high "cannot say" frequencies from normal adults. While a "cannot say" response may be due to either a reluctance or an inability to provide a true-false answer, most of the items indicated as sensitive by college students are not associated with a high adult "cannot say" frequency. Those six items rated as sensitive and with high "cannot say" frequencies may well be avoided by a cautious, truthful person not embarrassed by the content. (One would have to know the Bible very well to judge the current accuracy of the prophets' predictions.) Further, of the 550 unique items on the MMPI (16 are asked twice), only 20, or 3.6 percent, are seen as sensitive by these undergraduates; this is hardly an overwhelming rejection of the test as offensive and embarrassing. Interpretations of MMPI profiles are assumed to be unaffected unless more than 20 percent of all items are unanswered (Dahlstrom, Welsh, & Dahlstrom, 1972, p. 102).

When intrusions into the private personality are discussed, the personality is conceptualized as more than a "thing" with multiple characteristics (or traits or dimensions); it is also considered to have a set of concentric domains (Westin, 1967); those closest to the "core" are considered as most private (Pius XII, 1958):

> . . . a large portion of his inner world . . . the person discloses to a few confidential friends and shields against the intrusion of others. Certain (other) matters are kept secret at any price and in regard to anyone. Finally, there are other matters which the person is unable to consider.

The study of the personality, then, involves more complex matters than simple inquiries about things normally "kept secret at any price and in regard to anyone"; it may also involve inferences regarding aspects of the personality the individual

EXHIBIT 3-1 Offensive Items on a Personality Test (MMPI)

RATED[1] OFFENSIVE (PERCENT)	GENERALLY[2] OPPOSED (PERCENT)	"CANNOT SAY"[3] MALE (PERCENT)	FEMALE (PERCENT)	ITEM[4] NUMBER	ITEM
33	Over 20	1	0	63	I have no difficulty in starting or holding my bowel movement.
31	Over 20	8	9	542	I have never had any black, tarry-looking bowel movements.
28		1	1	462	I have no difficulty starting or holding my urine.
26		7	6	474	I have to urinate no more often than others.
26		0	2	486	I have never noticed any blood in my urine.
24	Over 20	6	1	14	I have diarrhea once a month or more.
7	Over 20	4	1	133	I have never indulged in any unusual sex practices.
5	Over 20	1	6	20	My sex life is satisfactory.
5	Over 20	29	31	58	Everything is turning out just like the prophets of the Bible said it would.
2	Over 20	19	18	237	My relatives are nearly all in sympathy with me.
	Over 20	7	8	297	I wish I were not bothered by thoughts about sex.
	Over 20	16	15	483	Christ performed miracles such as changing water into wine.
	Over 20	12	8	61	I have not lived the right kind of life.
	Over 20	24	19	287	I have very few fears compared to my friends.
		—	—	513	I think Lincoln was greater than Washington.
17		1	1	18	I am very seldom troubled by constipation.
11		2	1	519	There is someting wrong with my sex organs.
10		1	0	533	I am not bothered by a great deal of belching of gas from my stomach.
7		12	20	476	I am a special agent of god.
7		0	1	302	I have never been in trouble because of my sex behavior.
5		0	1	37	I have never been in trouble because of my sex behavior. (Asked twice.)
		28	17	415	If given the chance I would make a good leader of people.
		18	23	46	My judgment is better than it ever was.
		20	21	400	If given the chance I could do some things that would be of great benefit to the world.
		12	21	558	A large number of people are guilty of bad sexual conduct.

[1] From Walker (1967), average of responses to two administrations of the test to 21 college undergraduates.
[2] From Butcher and Tellegen (1966), items *generally* opposed by more than 20 percent of undergraduates are indicated.
[3] From Dahlstrom, Welsh, and Dahlstrom (1975), Appendix A, reporting on adults from Hathaway study.
[4] From Dahlstrom, Welsh, and Dahlstrom (1972), Appendix L.

may not have considered, and traits and characteristics inferred from sophisticated analyses of responses to relatively simple questions—items considered neither sensitive nor embarrassing.

The dilemma could not be more complex, for participants may allow investigators access to parts of their psyche they neither comprehend nor are aware of; it is difficult to provide informed consent for the examination of unknown features of the mind. But if the investigator discloses no details of the analysis, participants will not be confronted with "matters which the person is unable to consider." (On the other hand, many would consider it morally appropriate for an investigator to counsel any participant discovered to have serious mental disorders, even if such disorders are unknown to the participant.)

While there has been a substantial concern over the use of such personality tests, the controversy has not arisen over their use for scientific objectives but for screening employees in business and government (*American Psychologist,* 1965; Westin, 1967). A dominant feature has been concerned over whether applicants should be required to reveal certain information (about their sex lives, religious preferences, bodily functions, and the like) as part of a hiring evaluation. The extreme influence of a potential employer over an applicant reduces confidence that the applicant is an informed "volunteer"; the applicant's right to a private personality may be infringed in such cases. While critics are correct in pointing out the lack of a direct relationship between the specific test items ("I think Lincoln was greater than Washington") and employment demands, they have misunderstood the nature of the analysis. All items on the personality inventories are crucial in the comparison of normal applicants with those having mental disorders or distinctive problems; it is such comparisons that give the tests utility, not the item-by-item analyses (Hathaway, 1964; Dahlstrom, 1969).

A second issue, receiving somewhat less attention, is the extent to which personality inventories predict on-the-job performance; while they are generally less successful than aptitude or achievement tests for this purpose, they may help identify those with unstable personalities who should not be in certain critical jobs, such as airline pilot, secret agent, and the like (Meehl, 1969). Some of the same issues have been raised regarding polygraph (lie-detector) examinations, where the issue of accuracy is a major concern; even a small error (one in twenty) will result in a significant number of job applicants being labeled as dishonest or untrustworthy—even if none are (Lykken, 1974; Westin, 1967).

AGGREGATE, ANONYMOUS DATA: SURVEY RESEARCH

Example of Analysis: Adolescent Sexual Behavior

One study of adolescent transitions (including first experiences with alcohol, drugs, sex, and work) was completed with high school students over a four-year period; a total of four interviews, one per year, were conducted with each participant. The objective was to determine those aspects of personality, social environment, and behavior that might predict these youthful transitions. By analyzing the patterns expressed by comparable students who had and had not experienced the "transition to nonvirginity," researchers could identify factors reasonably accurate in predicting which students would experience the transition in the next year. Transition-prone students tended to value independence, greater social criticism, tolerance of deviance, and friends' models of deviance, and place less emphasis upon achievement—which subsequently led to a first sexual experience (multiple regression of 0.57). Transition proneness was also related to the initiation of drinking and marijuana use (Jessor & Jessor, 1975).

Effects on Rights.   A right to scientific freedom would certainly allow investigators to select the adolescent transition to nonvirginity as a phenomenon for study. Further, if youthful transitions (such as sexual experiences that may lead to unplanned pregnancies) are considered a significant societal issue, then research on the topic may be consistent with the general public's right to the development of systematic knowledge about it. On the other hand, the participants had a right to withhold information regarding private actions and beliefs, which may include sexual behavior as well as the use of alcohol and marijuana. Further, because the participants were minors when they were first contacted about the research, their parents may have had some right to control or supervise the type of information they divulged. Finally, as the project was conducted within and through a school system, those responsible for the school had a right to become aware of and approve any research in a school context.

Program/Project Effects.   The sexual behavior of teen-agers and their contraceptive practices are considered to be major social issues in the United States, particularly in light of the increasing number of abortions and unwed teenage mothers. The negative effects on the moral climate of society due to illegitimacy and abortions, the massive medical and welfare costs borne by society, and, perhaps most important, the disruptions to the lives of young people who find they have parental responsibilities before reaching maturity, attest to the importance of increased, systematic knowledge about youthful sexual activity. A number of research activites may investigate contraceptive practices, pregnancies, abortions, live births among teen-agers, of the consequences such live births, and the life experiences of the unplanned children. However, the present research under consideration focuses only upon the events that precede the first sexual experience. One major negative effect would be the costs of the project. A second is more controversial; some may feel that such research would encourage an open public discussion of sexual behavior, encouraging young people to seek sexual experiences and change the moral climate of society. Others may consider this a major benefit. Either way, the scope of this effect is likely to be small.

This specific project clearly provides only one contribution to the knowledge of the overall phenomenon—those factors that lead to the transition from virgin to nonvirgin, a transition that occurs to almost everyone, with some variation in timing. The major costs of the specific project are the professional and financial resources involved. The major benefits would be a more precise description—precise enough to lead to predictions—of the psychological and social context, and behavioral changes that may precede a first sexual experience. This could help parents and school personnel identify those adolescents who could benefit from counseling or contraceptive information before entering a period of sexual activity.

Participant Effects. The direct effects on the participants in this study are very modest; it is designed only to describe their lives, not to directly influence them. Those who remained in the full study completed a 50-page questionnaire (taking about one and a half hours) four times, with a year between administrations. Included was the following question: "Have you ever engaged in sexual intercourse with someone of the opposite sex?" This question may have been embarrassing to some participants, but this would have been minimized if answered privately and the responses remained confidential. After the first year of the project, each participant received a token cash payment of two dollars every time he or she completed the questionnaire. Participants could not remain completely anonymous, since each of four questionnaires was consolidated for analysis, and the investigators retained all identities until data collection was complete.

Distribution of Effects. The major benefactor of the research would be society at large, as the results would be disseminated through the scientific community. The participants would receive few direct benefits (other than the chance to talk about themselves and the money); as they were generally high school students from upper-middle-class backgrounds, the small effort on their part was confined to the more advantaged members of society. It is difficult to argue that the unfortunate or deprived have been used to provide benefits to the majority in this case.

Respect for Rights, Welfare. Respect for participants' rights was demonstrated in several ways, the most important being the acquisition of informed consent. With the cooperation of the school authorities, 1,126 students in the eighth, ninth, and tenth grades and their parents were contacted regarding the study; consent from both parents and students was obtained for 59 percent. However, only 38 percent (but 82 percent of those completing the first questionnaire) of the original group of 1,126 completed all four questionnaires and could be included in the analysis. (This led to an emphasis upon the process of youthful transitions, rather than overall sexual activity among youth.) Although each questionnaire was signed by the respondents, the data were ultimately organized according to code numbers and were separated from the names, which were stored in a secret safe deposit box in a bank vault.

Personal Treatment. It can be assumed that the student participants were treated with some degree of respect and consideration by the investigators, if only because they wished to retain their cooperation over a four-year period. It is likely that the personal treatment was equal to or more gracious than that they received from most teachers; there is little reason to expect they would be deceived or debased.

Acceptability to Social Scientists. This project would be acceptable to social scientists with different perspectives; it provides some new basic information on youthful transition of scientific interest. Further, it provides information that may help ameliorate a societal problem. The fact that the participants were treated with considerable dignity and respect may satisfy social scientists who are concerned about interpersonal treatment, although some may argue that asking sensitive questions is inappropriate under any conditions. Those who are concerned with direct action to ameliorate societal problems may prefer that the social scientists do more to counsel and educate youth about pregnancy, and may consider the information gathered to be superfluous.

Embarrassing Issues
and the Right to Privacy

Most citizen contacts with social science research are likely to involve surveys. Not only are surveys frequently used to explore scientific issues, perhaps regarding personal and sensitive behaviors and activities, but they are widely used for applied objectives such as guiding political campaigns, measuring consumer preferences for products, determining citizen needs for government services, providing background information for mass media articles, and the like. The single best-known social science project in the United States is a survey of all citizens mandated by the Constitution, the decennial census; such participation is considered an obligation of citizenship.

When individuals respond to a series of questions about themselves, the major positive effects are similar to those mentioned before: experiencing the pleasure of talking about one's self, the satisfaction of contributing to science, having an interesting experience, and—more frequent in survey research toward the end of the 1970s—receiving a cash payment. Following stressful events, an interview may actually improve the mental condition of the respondent, as after a natural disaster or family tragedy; questions may require them to collect their thoughts and develop rational responses, rather than succumb to emotion. Any interview may be a positive experience, as the respondents review their lives, self-concept, or other personal aspects and develop new perspectives or orientations towards themselves.

Direct negative effects are not a major issue for such descriptive research. If the procedure is properly designed, boredom may be kept to a minimum. The amount of time required to complete some interviews may vary quite a bit, from a few brief questions on the phone to a full day of conversation; most are designed to take about an hour. The major negative effects are related to possible disclosures of personal information and the actual embarrassment associated with some issues that may be raised (even if the respondent does not answer the question); both concerns are often related to a right to privacy.

The concept of privacy, as a right, has been developed in a number of different, though not inconsistent, ways. For example, one of the earliest legal definitions was the right "to be let alone" (Cooley, 1888; Warren & Brandeis, 1890); today this right is associated with connotations of a freedom from aggressive salespersons, junk mail, or nuisance phone calls, although it originally developed in the context of concerns over sexual assaults upon boarders, aggressive reporters writing stories about the private lives of famous persons, and the unauthorized use of photos or testimonials in advertisements. The more recent concepts of privacy center on the control of information about one's self (Westin, 1967); such control may be related to aspects of the research process such as the collection of data from individuals and the maintenance of their anonymity to ensure that private information does not become public.

Evidence of citizen concepts of privacy are available from a survey of typical adults in the United Kingdom (England, Scotland, and Wales). Spontaneously mentioned as conceptions of privacy were (Younger, 1972):

Being left alone (e.g., not receiving junk mail)	47%
Maintaining the confidentiality of one's own affairs	35
Freedom of action (behavior) in one's own home	30
General freedom of activity, without surveillance or external control	16
Unable to give any definition of privacy	5

(Total exceeds 100% due to multiple definitions from some respondents.) This broadly defined "right" was considered to be of intermediate importance with regard to a variety of societal issues; it was less important than economic problems (such as inflation and unemployment) but more important than improving the educational system. It was considered to be more significant than several other social issues; for example, it was rated above "improving race relations" and "protecting freedom of speech."

The acceptability of making selected aspects of their lives public (the question implies that a central file, such as a public directory, would retain the information) is summarized on the left side of Exhibit 3-2. While it is no surprise to discover that the vast majority would prefer that "details of sex life" be kept confidential, almost as many prefer their income to remain private; further, one-third would object to their address and phone number "being available to anyone who wanted to know" (it is not clear how they respond to the telephone directory) (Younger, 1972, pp. 242-43). (The unusual sensitivity regarding income is reflected in the British census interviews, which have never included an item on personal or household income) (Bulmer, 1979.)

The results of a U.S. study on the factors affecting responses to sensitive issues are presented on the right side of Exhibit 3-2. The sample of 1,172 adults was asked about various behaviors (the percentage responding is indicated in the far right column) and then was asked whether or not the same questions would make "most people" uneasy (indicated in the adjacent column). While the rank order is approximately the same as that in the British sample (sexual behavior at the top

EXHIBIT 3-2   Sensitivity of Survey Research Questionnaire Items

BRITISH ADULTS[1]		U.S. ADULTS[2]		
Would you object to the following being available to anyone who wanted to know?	Yes (percent)	Would a question on this topic make you very uneasy?	Percent rating very uneasy	Percent actually answering
Details of sex life	87	Masturbation	56	93.3
Income	78	Sexual intercourse	42	94.0
Medical history	51	Using marijuana	42	99.6
Political views	42	Using stimulants or	31	99.9
Telephone number	34	depressants		
Address	33	Getting drunk	29	97.7
Religious views	28	Petting or kissing	20	99.7
Leisure activities	22	Income	12	95.2
Wife's (or your)	18	Gambling with friends	10	99.8
maiden name		Drinking beer, wine, or	10	99.9
Education	17	liquor		
Occupation	12	Happiness or well-being	4	99.7
Race	10	Education	3	99.7
Nationality	8	Occupation	3	99.9
		Social activities	2	99.2
		Leisure time, leisure	2	99.8
		activities		
		Sports activities	1	99.9

[1] Younger, 1972, p. 239.
[2] Bradburn, Sudman, et al., 1979, p. 68.

and education and occupation at the bottom), there is some discrepancy between perceived sensitivity and the actual response rate. Only sexual activity (masturbation and intercourse) and income are associated with the highest rates of nonresponse (approximately 5 percent, although the cooperation rate is quite high). Questions about all other behaviors are answered by 98 percent or more of the respondents (Bradburn, Sudman, et al., 1979, pp. 66-69). Perceived uneasiness regarding questions about different types of behavior is not highly related to actual willingness to answer the questions.

One source of evidence regarding the acceptability of general population surveys is the refusal rate—the percentage of respondents who have been contacted and refused to contribute to a survey. In the United States several government surveys have been conducted continuously for a number of years (each with a new sample): both the Current Population Survey and the Health Interview Survey have been able to maintain cooperation rates of 95 to 96 percent into the early 1970s, although costs have risen as repeated call-backs are needed. This reflects a major complication in interpreting data on cooperation rates: as the number of two-worker households and time spent away from the dwelling increases, it has become more difficult to contact many respondents—which reduces the cooperation rate. Cooperation rates of 60 to 65 percent reported by commercial firms (after 3 or 4 callbacks) in the 1970 are somewhat lower than the 80 to 95 percent reported in the 1960s, but it is estimated to be equaly divided between refusals and not-at-homes (American Statistical Association, 1974). A survey of typical adults completed in the later 1970s found them positive about interviews: although half had been interviewed within the past four or five years (40 percent more than once), 68 percent said they would be "somewhat" or "very" interested in participating in another interview; 80 percent of those who had participated in four or more interviews said they would like to do so again (Scott, 1978). In short, while cooperation with surveys may have decreased slightly, a substantial majority of typical adults appear to approve and participate in them.

Informed consent in survey research leads to new complications. The problem is that an adequate informed consent agreement must be signed by the participant, but at the same time, the participant's anonymity must be assured. It has been found that a request for signatures produces a statistically significant reduction in the cooperation rate (from 71 percent to 64 percent), while variations in the completeness of descriptions of the research and the extent to which sensitive data would remain confidential did not (Singer, 1978; Boruch & Cecil, 1979b, p. 18a). The refusals, however, related to providing the signature, not to completing the interview. Further, most refusals to participate appear regardless of the explanation provided (Singer, 1978; Epstein & Lasagna, 1969); systematic variation on the introductory statements for telephone interviews has absolutely no effect on the refusal rate (Dillman, 1978, p. 242). Apparently many potential participants are not interested in providing an "informed refusal"; they have already decided they want nothing to do with any research, regardless of its nature.

The survey project selected as an example of moral analysis was atypical in several ways. First, it was not designed for a one-time interview; a crucial feature was the longitudinal design and the repeated interviews with the same individuals. This meant that the names of the respondents had to be stored and filed until the last wave of interviews was completed and assembled with the previous interviews from the same individuals. Second, it was completed with minors, in which case respect for the respondents' rights and welfare required that both participants and their parents provide informed consent.

While such a procedure may be appropriate for research on sensitive topics that involve minors, it is not without negative consequences for research. A 1975 replication of a 1965 survey of high school students (involving the occupational and educational dimensions of sex roles) utilized formal informed consent, and signed statements were obtained from all students and parents of minors. While participation in the 1965 study was required, resulting in a 100 percent response rate, the 1975 replication achieved a 70 percent response rate from adult students and 42 percent from minor students (parental consent required). This was in spite of the absence of *any* compliants from the 4,400 respondents or their parents about the study. The major basis for the lack of participation appeared to be a lack of interest or motivation to return the informed consent form, rather than concerns about privacy or confidentiality (Lueptow, et al., 1977). If parents had been asked to respond if they did *not* approve their child's involvement (called passive or negative informed consent) rather than if they did approve (active or positive informed consent), a higher cooperation rate would have been obtained in the 1975 survey.

While most investigations that involve aggregate survey data provide respondents with the opportunity to give their informed consent, one investigation is considered to be so important to the interests of all citizens that informed consent is not an option; this is the decennial Census in which responses are compulsory (not only in the United States, but in most countries). Basically, the efficient, effective, and constitutionally correct administration of society is assumed to require an accurate count of all citizens; this consideration outweighs the rights of individuals to refuse to provide information they may consider private. On the other hand, the rights of the individual respondents are recognized in both the substantial legal protection and administrative mechanisms developed to ensure that identities of individual respondents are not revealed. Even in a wartime emergency as in World War II, when the identity of Japanese-Americans was sought, the confidentiality of Census data has not been violated (Josephson, 1975).

Procedures for Maintaining Confidentiality

Except for the possible embarrassment from certain questions, there are few direct negative effects of significance for those responding to surveys. However, the disclosure of confidential information may provide substantial indirect negative effects. Both respondents and investigators are aware of these potential problems, and this has led to the development of a number of procedures for minimizing the risk that confidentiality will be breached and for increasing participant's confidence that this is the case. These include attention to the nature and form of the actual questions presented to respondents, the procedures to be followed by the research staff, the organization and format of the stored data, and public presentation of the results. (Special status for social science data that would legally prevent disclosure is generally not available; it will be discussed in Chapter 6.) Cross-sectional or one-time surveys are the most general case and will be discussed first; the additional advantages and complications associated with longitudinal studies (as in the previous example) will be reviewed later, as will the combination of research data and administrative records (usually government files).

Two major techniques for presenting questions to increase the response rate are increasing the generality of questions and the "random response method." When sensitive issues are involved, it has been found that questions in a general form ("Have you ever engaged in masturbation?") tend to be answered more often than those involving precise details ("Have you engaged in masturbation within the past 24 hours?"). For illegal behavior (underage drinking, use of drugs, self-reported crimes, and the like), only precise information could be used for legal action, were the data to be reviewed by officials. In contrast, the response to nonthreatening issues is unaffected by the design of the questions (Bradburn, Sudman, et al. 1979, p. 19). As with other techniques, there are tradeoffs; increased response rates from more general questions are associated with a reduced potential for analysis; knowing that a person engaged in a certain behavior sometime in his or her life is less useful than precise details on the context and frequency of occurrence.

The random response technique involves providing a respondent with two questions: one innocuous ("I voted in the last presidential election"), and one related to a sensitive topic ("I fudged on my last income tax return"). Only innocuous questions where the distribution of responses is already known can be used; the percentage that will answer Yes is predictable. The respondent is asked to choose one question at random (perhaps by flipping a coin) and answer that question without telling the interviewer which question was answered. If the procedure is followed correctly, only the respondent knows which question he or she answered, but the interviewer will know the proportion of respondents answering both questions. Knowing the proportion who will answer Yes to the innocuous item, the percentage who answered Yes to the sensitive item can be estimated (Warner, 1965; Bradburn, Sudman, et al. 1979, p. 4). Again, there is a tradeoff between the higher response rate and the lack of precision possible for analysis; unless there is a very large sample that is clearly separated into distinct subsamples (classified by income or residence area), the only possible analysis is an estimate of the frequency (of, for example, tax cheaters) for the entire group of respondents; cross-tabulations are not feasible (to compare tax cheating among those with different sources of income).

Another potential breach of confidentiality may come from the research staff itself, particularly if face-to-face interviews are conducted by individuals who live in the same community as the respondents. This can be partially avoided if the interviewers are assigned areas outside their own neighborhoods (in the 1970 British census, interviewers were bused to different districts to achieve this). Interviewers can be taught the importance of respecting the privacy of the data, which is likely to be more significant to those who interview for a living. Other steps can be taken to ensure anonymity for some responses, such as the use of telephone interviews, random digit dialing ensures anonymity (in fact, some responses increase under these conditions) (Bradburn, Sudburn, et al., 1979, p. 7), or placing responses in sealed envelopes and returning them without interviewer surveillance.

Once the interview has been checked and is ready for processing (coding, entering into computer files, checking files for accuracy and completeness), the single most important features for maintaining confidentiality is using a code number for each respondent in order to keep the identity of the respondents separate from their answers. This is usually not a burden for most research and is routinely done for most computer processes of any type; it is best if it is done at the earliest possible stage of the processing—immediately after the responses are reviewed for completeness and accuracy. The actual identifying information should be stored separately from the data under the investigator's care; destruction is the surest way to guarantee that identities and data will be impossible to match.

Longitudinal studies, such as the example reviewed above, provide a special case: and in some instances the names and addresses of individuals who will receive follow-up interviews are stored in safety deposit boxes or outside the country. In extreme cases the foreign custodian of the names and addresses has actually been responsible for drawing samples for follow-up research and providing the investigators with code numbers for matching the follow-up questionnaires (when they are returned from a mailed administration) with the data initially acquired. In this way, the original investigators and research staff never have access to the identities of the participants after the initial data collection; this is a useful procedure if they are concerned about potential subpoenas.

The major factor that protects the anonymity of individual respondents in the presentation of the results of survey research is the large number of individuals who contribute to the data set; proportions, correlations, regression analysis, and the like reveal little about specific respondents. The problem of disclosure becomes more serious when the data represent a complete survey of a well-defined population, such as all the district attorneys in a state, all seniors in a high school, or all the citizens in the country (as with the U.S. Census). Disclosure of identities in the analysis can be controlled by using aggregate data in tables; if the number of respondents is so small that identities might be revealed, extreme values may be omitted from tables (as the Census Bureau does when the number of individuals represented is less than 5). Further problems develop when the data are given to other investigators for analysis (conforming to the scientific norms of open access and cooperation).

If the research data have ordinary details on the respondents (such as age, sex, occupation, and residence area) that are not linked to an individual but may be publicly available in directories or official data, a successful match may be achieved between the public information and the research data for a specific person. This leads to considerable concern over the integrity of the individuals receiving the data for analysis (which cannot be guaranteed if the data are added to an omnibus research data bank) and how the information might be changed to avoid such possibilities. Security of individual anonymity can be improved by such techniques as eliminating the most salient information that might be used for identifying respondents (race, age, occupation), "microaggregation" of data (such as summary descriptions of ten-person groups), or "inoculation" (such as randomly modifying the ages by one or two years) that would have a small effect on the analysis but would prevent positive identification of the respondents.

The problems become even more substantial when large numbers of respondents are involved and the data are assembled from different government agencies (comparing welfare data and tax returns, for example). Maintaining anonymity is becoming a specialized technical area, and a recent review of the issues is available in Boruch and Cecil (1979a). In all cases there is an interrelated set of issues that investigators must resolve: the desire to protect the anonymity of the participants, the economic costs of the different mechanisms required for such protection, and the effects of the different "confidentiality protection techniques" on the analysis.

Few investigators can argue that they cannot protect their respondents' anonymity, but the procedures do involve financial costs (which may limit the objectives of a research project) and may reduce the precision or detail of the analysis.

DISTINCTIVE, PERSONALIZED DATA: FIELD OBSERVATION

Example of Analysis:
Street Corner Society

In this research the investigator selected an Italian slum area of a city in the northeastern United States and hoped to describe the structural features, social differentiation, and norms of an urban area considered a homogeneous mass by most outsiders. He moved into the district, lived with an Italian family, and made contacts among the unemployed young men (approximately the same age as the investigator). Once he had gained the confidence of the leader of one gang (the infamous "Doc"); he was accepted by other members of the group and incorporated into many of their activities, often as an equal, in spite of the fact that he deliberately informed all present that he was studying the community. (The common interpretation was, "He is writing a book about us.") At the conclusion of the study, the key informant was asked to read draft versions of the manuscript to check it for accuracy and completeness; in this case the informant resisted making changes that would lead to inaccurate but more sympathetic portrayals. The major features of the description were the systematic nature and predictable effects of the structures, processes, and norms within the community, which had a relatively complex and differentiated social structure. This was another instance where generally held stereotypes of a collection of individuals (be they physicians, criminals, executives, or urban minorities) proved to be simplistic and inaccurate (Whythe, 1955).

Effects on Rights. The right of the investigator to explore a topic of interest prevailed in this study, as did the right of the general public to expect attention to significant phenomena. The community (the particular streetcorner or block) had little choice regarding the location of the study; no community has a right to restrict the movement of others within its boundaries. However, the individual members within the community had a right not to talk with or become involved with the observer; while the nature of the observer's intentions were somewhat vague (most appeared to accept that he was "studying Cornersville"), no one was misled into thinking he was just another itinerant boarder.

Program/Project Effects. This particular project may be considered as part of an informal research program designed to describe and understand the social structure and processes of all segments or parts of society—a general objective of sociologists. Clearly, though, no coherent, focused scientific objectives were formulated in this specific study. The study itself was relatively low cost; it required the efforts of only one individual who acted pretty much on his own for several years. The potential benefits were substantially greater than the costs, primarily because the costs were so low and almost all of them were borne voluntarily by a graduate student. Other field observation projects may be substantially more expensive and complicated, particularly when they involve travel to distant (often foreign) locations and require considerable logistical support merely to sustain the investigator and a staff.

Participant Effects.   The direct effects of this study on participants were relatively modest: they were simply the normal effects of social intercourse or becoming more involved with another person. For some participants this person became more than an acquaintance and was, for a time, a close friend. An additional risk, one not normally found in friendships was that some personal activities that were usually known only by close friends within the neighborhood were eventually made known to others when the study was published. However, these activities may or may not have come to the attention of those in the neighborhood; much depended on how well individual identities were disguised by the investigator in the case descriptions.

Distribution of Effects.   In this case there is no question that the costs of the research, however small, were borne by disadvantaged members of society; the purpose of the study, after all, was to examine the social structure of a slum. To the extent that the results provided a general contribution to knowledge that benefited all members of society, this may be considered unfair. To the extent that the result was an increase understanding of and sympathy with those in urban slums, they may have received some benefits. There is little evidence that the participants of the "Cornersville" community experienced substantial negative effects from participating in the research. In the absence of any significant effects of any kind—positive or negative—it is difficult to argue that the distribution was unjust.

Respect for Rights, Welfare.   Numerous activities of the investigator demonstrated a general respect for the rights and welfare of the participants. First, no member of the community was deceived about the investigator's intentions; they were all aware he was "writing a book" or "doing a study." Second, he took no actions that would incriminate or risk criminal prosecution of the participants as they engaged in illegal activities (such as multiple voting). Third, before publishing the study, he had sections of the manuscript read by an informant to check for accuracy and completeness. Fourth, in the published study, not only are the individuals disguised as much as possible, but they are described with some sympathy and dignity. Finally, after the work had been published and copies made available to key informants, the investigator returned to ask them about their responses and the responses of their friends. In sum, aside from not conducting any field research, it is difficult to determine what else the investigator could have done to demonstrate respect for the participant's rights and welfare.

Personal Treatment. In the conduct of the research, it would appear that the investigator was gracious and polite in his personal treatment of all participants; indeed, it would have been almost impossible to develop rapport and gain their confidence with any other approach.

Acceptability to Social Scientists. The conduct of this research is likely to be approved by most social scientists. The objectivity and usefulness of the descriptions are considerable and had a significant impact on the study of social processes. Those concerned with social reform would probably not condemn such a study, as it not only provided evidence that "slum dwellers are people too," but the investigator also helped organize political demonstrations to benefit "Cornersville." (For example, one demonstration led to more hot water for the local public baths.) Finally, those who believe social scientists should be model citizens would probably approve of this investigator's activity, even though he did engage in a few quasi-illegal activities common among his respondents.

Public Privacy:
Informed Consent Between "Friends"

Field observation (or ethnography or participant observation) is one of three major types of social science research (the others being experiments and surveys). The typical field project has several distinguishing characteristics: it has no clear objective (in the sense that it tests precise hypotheses); instead, it focuses on describing, often very concretely, the norms, structural features, major processes, and the world view of a particular group. The group may be a relatively primitive culture, a sophisticated but insulated society (such as the Mennonites or Hutterites), or even a distinct subculture within the greater social system (such as drug users, athletes, or insurance salesmen). A second major feature is the tendency of field observers to consider they have understood the phenomena when they are able to interpret events or personal behavior from the perspective of the individuals involved—i.e., to present the individual's personal analyses or rationalizations. As such, there is a strong tendency to demonstrate the intellectual success of the endeavor by presenting specific events and interpretations associated with them. (See Cassell & Wax, 1980, for a thorough review of issues in ethics and field work.)

Focusing upon overt participant observation (covert studies are reviewed in the next chapter), several features complicate the application of the seven-issue moral analysis to specific projects. First, the absence of explicit objectives or purposes makes any form of utilitarian or cost-benefit analysis difficult (although such an analysis can be developed in relationship to the participants or informants) (Cassell, 1978). Second, since there is no clearly defined investigator-participant relationship, the notion of informed consent (where specific individuals agree in advance to engage in a defined series of activities) is difficult to apply. It may be more appropriate to consider informed consent as a process, rather than a discrete decision (Wax, 1980). As the investigator develops better rapport with the informants and a sense of what aspects of the society are worthy of study, the expectations for the participants (those personal thoughts and private activities that would contribute to the study) and the boundaries of the relationship (the information and behaviors considered sensitive and private within the culture) become more obvious; this helps an investigator comply with the spirit of informed consent for a specific society.

Third, as with other types of descriptive research, there are no major direct effects—positive or negative—on the participants. While participants may give up time for discussions with the investigator and divulge personal information, these are often in the context of quasi-friendship relationships. They may receive, in turn, the satisfactions normally associated with social intercourse and the attention of a knowledgeable (often very knowledgeable after careful study of a community) person of relatively high status. On the other hand, once the study is completed, the respondents may feel "used"; they may feel they have been incorporated into a friendship (with the connotations of unselfish equality) to further the instrumental purposes of the investigator. On some occasions, particularly when participants are members of disadvantaged groups (ethnic minorities, societal deviants, and the like), the investigator may provide expertise or personal representation in dealing with authorities and bureaucracies. While this may be of great assistance, the participants may feel uncomfortable if they are not able to reciprocate and fall into a subordinate relationship with the investigator. This acknowledgement of the investigator's superior influence and ability prevents a truly egalitarian relationship from forming; some consider this a negative effect on the participants. There are, in field investigations of illegal or deviant activities, risks for participants in just talking to the investigator; if others know of the research objectives, the respondent's reputation may be in jeopardy by association.

One of the major results of the lack of clear effects of field observations, either for the participants or for scientific knowledge, is a change in the basis for defending such investigations. Some emphasize the rights of the investigators, as ordinary citizens, to engage in free speech and make the analogy to the freedom of the press; they say that it is impossible to prevent any person from experiencing some risks in ordinary social intercourse (Mosteller, 1980).While the lack of additional risks (over and above those of daily life) makes it easier to defend field observation as realizing the rights of scientists, such a shift in emphasis deemphasizes the contributions to knowledge that may result from this technique.

CASE DESCRIPTIONS: ANONYMITY AND DETAIL

One of the major negative effects on participants is the public disclosure of events and activities assembled during field observations. However, case descriptions may be developed and presented on the basis of other research techniques such as interviews. These are widely used to "give life" to abstract or empirical presentations and justify attention.

Several categories of audiences may have an "unscientific" interest in case descriptions, and each may be affected by a different degree of precision and detail. For example, at one extreme are public officials (the police or the Internal Revenue Service) who could cause considerable difficulties for individuals, but only if the information regarding an "infraction"–times, dates, identity of individuals involved–is very specific. There is also the general public, as represented by the mass media, who may have less of an official effect upon the participants and fail to take an interest unless something unusual or distinctive is involved; even violent physical confrontations between friends or spouses are unlikely to cause much comment. Third, there are individuals familiar with the participants who come into contact with them on a regular basis, such as coworkers, neighbors, friends, and relatives; when the study involves an entire social system, these individuals may modify their reactions or relationships on the basis of new information obtained from the case description. Finally, an individual participant, may recognize himself and be embarrassed by interpretations of a private, sensitive nature (perhaps related to subconscious motives or the inner workings of the psyche), even though he could not be identified by others from the case description.

From the investigator's perspective, the issue becomes one of comparing the advantages of a more complete and precise case description for the scientific objectives with the potential disadvantages for the participants of being identified. Several factors may reduce the risk of identification: the use of esoteric, technical language; the limited distribution in professional journals; the incomplete and ambiguous descriptions of the case and specific individuals; and the extent to which the events are ordinary and unremarkable. Conversely, the less technical the language, the wider the distribution of the analysis, the more specific the descriptions, the greater the discussion of unique and distinctive events, the greater the probability that the participants will be recognized by themselves and others. These features will be illustrated by a number of case descriptions illustrating investigators' solutions to these dilemmas.

Clinical cases reflect attempts to assist individuals with problems, as in the case of an older man whose social and work life was disrupted by chronic abdominal pain that was partially controlled by injections received six times a day (Levendusky & Pankratz, 1975). The patient was taught how to control the pain through a program of relaxation, covert imagery, and cognitive relabeling; simultaneously, the medication was progressively diluted–without the patient's knowledge–until all pain control was due to the patient's mental processes. At this time the medication was discontinued and the patient was able to resume an active social life. The report of this treatment program reviews the patient's background in some detail; he is described as a "sixty-five-year-old retired army officer with a history that included significant military achievement, a productive teaching and research career, and numerous social accomplishments." It was noted that before the self-control treatment the patient's "mood was somewhat depressed, and he was unkempt and had poor personal hygiene: . . . to control pain in social situations with friends, he would often assume awkward or embarrassing postures" (pp. 165-66). Since the report gave the location of the treatment hospital, it may have been possible for the patient's associates to identify him (it is certain that he would have been able to identify himself). On the other hand, the limited distribution of the discussion and its technical nature would minimize the possibility that the patient's problem, treatment, and the researchers' deception of him during therapy would become public knowledge: The researchers clearly felt that this small risk to the participant was justified by the benefits of describing the successful application of this technique in a rather dramatic situation.

Investigators (generally anthropologists) dealing with less developed societies frequently do not disguise the identity of the culture or the participants. This can lead to embarrassing situations. In one case, a leader of a New Guinea political group (which had been transformed from a primitive religious cult) with a history of humanitarian activities during the Second World War was discussed by name in publications during the early 1950s. In the late 1960s, these earlier writings received considerable publicity during democratic elections in which the same individual was the key participant (Mead, 1969). The individual won reelection; and while it is not clear that the publicized reports—his political abilities were compared to those of Churchill and Roosevelt—influenced the outcome, it is a possibility. (The investigator expressed concern that the informant could have lost the election, not that a political process may have been affected.)

In studies of families, responses to crises are considered to illuminate structural features and relationships that develop among family members. For example, when a person suffers kidney failure, the probability of a successful transplant is somewhat higher if a kidney is received from a genetically similar relative rather than a nonrelative. But this raises a crucial issue within the family: who will provide the replacement kidney? (The donor experiences the risk of surgery and has a reduced chance of personal survival with one kidney.) In general, the decision to provide a new kidney does not cause stress and conflict within the family; both the donor and recipient are usually satisfied with the decision and experience an improved self-concept (Simmons, Klein & Simmons, 1977).

There are, however, some situations where the decision to donate does not go smoothly (Simmons, Klein, & Simmons, 1977, p. 289):

> The case of the most extreme guilt involved a married daughter (Brenda) who had agreed to donate to her mother, but who became extremely anxious and angry the night before the transplant after she was admitted to the hospital and some minor errors were made by the surgery resident. She alternated between indicating at some points that she was too fearful to donate and at other times that she wanted to continue with the donation. The donor doctor decided that she could not donate in her psychological state and gave her a false medical excuse so that the recipient would be unaware of her unwillingness. Her guilt at having backed out was considerable, as documented by relatives who were aware of the true circumstances.

While the investigators felt that this description provided considerable information, it is clear that the details are specific enough that it may have been possible for the family members to recognize the incident; perhaps even the recipient would have recognized the nervous donor. Such possibilities are increased by the attention of the local media to the research; newspaper accounts of several transplants have been published. To minimize possible embarrassment to family members, genders, family relationships, and minor technical or procedural details were changed. Since over 100 cases have been involved in the research, this has been effective in minimizing the disclosure of confidential information in distinctive cases; even the patients have not recognized themselves.

Perhaps the antithesis of unusual medical crises is the portrayal of individuals as they conduct their daily lives. Concerned with the details of the daily life of the urban working poor in a developing country, one observer spent considerable time producing a biographical description of the lives of four siblings and their father in an urban slum. The account portrays many of the challenges that must be faced in such situations, including family conflicts, official corruption, and sexual and emotional development; the participants often describe their problems in earthy, explicit language. While there was little complaint that the published work, *The Children of Sanchez* (Lewis, 1961), was inaccurate, considerable controversy developed in the host country (Mexico) over the portrayal of the society; most concerns were directed toward the language and sexual emphasis. One newspaper assigned two reporters the task of discovering the true identity of the family; after twenty-seven days they claim to have succeeded, although the identity of the family was not made public (Beals, 1969, p. 35). However, because the investigator had chosen a "typical" family to portray "ordinary urban slum life," it is questionable that the family was unambiguously identified; locating them was clearly not very easy (it took the reporters 54 working days). Hence, despite the wide distribution of the book in both English and Spanish and the nontechnical nature of the discussion, the general, ordinary descriptions made identification of the family difficult and protected them from repercussions for living a life that was, from their perspective, conventional.

In summary, then, there are some good reasons why descriptions of specific individuals, families, groups, organizations, or communities might be presented in some detail. Not only may they illustrate specific examples of phenomena or processes, they lend confidence that the investigator did indeed observe and record explicit phenomena ("manufactured" cases always seem too simple and the phenomena of interest are too salient); and they are instructive to those attempting to determine the correspondence between general statements and concrete phenomena. On the other hand, there is the possibility that the investigator will divulge information that may embarrass, insult, or substantially harm the participants (if the legal authorities were to take action). While investigators must decide what is to be divulged in a case description—and there is no way of predicting who will expend considerable effort to "unmask" a disguised participant—the benefits of *not* portraying participants with sympathetic respect would seem small.

CONCLUSION

One of the major activities in social science is developing descriptions through the use of personality tests, survey research, and field observation. If there is no deliberate attempt to change or manipulate the participants or their environment, or to disguise the nature of the research or its existence, concerns over the moral appropriateness will be minimized and will focus primarily upon indirect effects. Negative outcomes can result from publicizing private or confidential information or interpretations. The process of asking certain questions may be embarrassing to some respondents, but this is clearly not a major issue as long as scientific objectives are involved and respondents are not "forced" to answer questions. Hence, the major issues are demonstrating respect for the participants during their involvement with the research and maintaining their anonymity during both data analysis and in written presentations.

When large numbers of individuals are involved in research, as with studies of personality traits and survey research, their anonymity is substantially protected by the aggregation of the data. If it is possible to destroy records of their identity, anonymity is further enhanced. On the other hand, if several interviews are planned for each participant, or if distinctive data in the research files allow participants to be identified, respect for their rights and welfare may be demonstrated through careful controls or slight modifications in the data. Elaborate techniques are now available for protecting anonymity; they all increase the cost of research and tend to reduce the flexibility and precision available for analysis. This changes the problem for investigators. While they can no longer claim that techniques for protecting research records are not available, they can claim that the financial costs may be prohibitive or that scientific objectives may be compromised.

Case descriptions, as a special type of description, involve two concerns: presenting the material in such a way that participant anonymity is maintained—and different measures are required depending upon the audience to be convinced; and providing a commentary that minimizes the tendency to demean or belittle the participants. The latter is especially important when a social system or category of individuals is the unit of analysis, for it is extremely difficult to obscure the identity of either. A number of investigators have been able to resolve this problem and portray the participants and their actions in detail, sympathetically and with anonymity.

CHAPTER FOUR
COVERT RESEARCH

A variety of research procedures—participant observation, field experiments, unobtrusive measures, secondary data analysis, and archival research—share a common feature. The original source of the data, the participants, are unaware that research is being conducted; they are unable to provide their informed consent. Investigators may engage in such covert research for a variety of reasons: telling the participants may affect the phenomena under study; contacting them (as in photographs used for studying crowd behavior) may be impossible; the participants may be deceased (such as authors of ancient diaries); or the research involves secondary analysis of anonymous data.

The wide range of activities and purposes associated with different types of covert research suggests a distinctive analysis for each. All, however, tend to share one feature: they have little or no direct effect on the participants. This is in contrast to overt experimental research, where there is a deliberate attempt to change the participants' actions, attitudes, or characteristics, and overt descriptive research, where the participants may willingly contribute sensitive information. In covert research the participants either have no direct contact with the investigator or the contact is such that it appears to be part of the normal course of daily life. A recurrent concern with covert research is the morality of the systematic deception of participants; individuals who consider themselves to be just "living" are also unwittingly contributing to research. Even though they are not directly affected by the research, they may be wronged without knowing it (as, for example, when their privacy is secretly invaded).

Four types of covert investigation will be reviewed, with examples of moral analysis presented for three. The first example, participant observation (an investigator allows himself to be accepted into groups of male homosexuals), is one of those responsible for increased attention to the ethical issues associated with research; a general discussion follows the analysis. A dramatic study of altruism provides an occasion for morally analyzing surreptitious field experiments. A moral analysis of the study of household refuse (garbage) is an example of an unobtrusive measure; there is no impact upon the sources and they are unaware the data is being collected. The chapter concludes with some comments on issues in archival research—the analysis of material already collected.

PARTICIPANT OBSERVATION

Example of Analysis:
Male Homosexuals and Public Deviance

Interested in the characteristics of the participants and the patterns of behavior in clandestine homosexual activity, an investigator devised a two-stage research project to gather relevant information (Humphreys, 1970). The first stage was to engage in covert participant observation in a location (public restrooms in a city park) known for attracting individuals with a desire to participate in male homosexual acts (which were largely restricted to oral sex). In addition to frequenting these "tearooms" during the most popular times of the day (noon and immediately after 5 P.M.), the investigator also participated to the extent of acting as a lookout (a "watchqueen" in the argot of the subculture) to ensure that the participants were not interrupted by teen-age boys, the police, or those who might have been violently hostile to such behavior. (Such a contribution to the sex life of the participants was technically illegal when the study was conducted.) This procedure for gathering information was apparently successful, for behavior in public restrooms preceding, during, and following 50 completed sexual acts involving over 100 men were observed.

Once a description of the atypical sexual behavior was obtained, the next stage was to develop descriptions of the participants that could be compared with a random sample of residents of the area. In order to gather such information without alerting these men that they had been observed in illegal sexual activity, the investigator obtained their automobile license-plate numbers; most men had to drive to these public restrooms because they were in remote locations of a large city park and largely inaccessible by foot. The names and addresses of the individual car owners were obtained from the police. The participants, however, were protected because the investigator misrepresented the study; he disguised it as a project in market research. Utilizing a questionnaire designed for a health-status survey of men in the area, the investigator (with his appearance modified) and a research assistant interviewed the men eighteen months after they had been observed engaging in homosexual behavior.

The study portrayed homosexual behavior in these remote public restrooms as predictable and routinized; it was conducted in almost total silence (less than ten interpretable utterances were heard during the completion of fifty sexual acts). The few interruptions were due to the arrival of the police or hostile teen-agers. When the characteristics of the participants were compared with those of typical males from the same urban area, no striking differences in terms of occupations, marital status, socioeconomic characteristics, and the like were found. Aside from their participation in clandestine homosexual activity, there was little to distinguish these men from typical adult males.

Effects on Rights.   Attempts to analyze the rights of those associated with this project are complicated by the illegal nature of the sexual activity at the time of the study (the late 1960s) in the jurisdiction where it was conducted. While there is now widespread agreement that consenting adults have the right to engage in sexual behavior in private settings, whether or not this right extends to public settings is another matter. It can be argued that when such homosexuals have accepted all participants (including the participant observer) into the subculture, they have created a private setting, even though the physical location is public property. Otherwise the role of lookout (normally filled by a voyeur) would not have emerged; it takes "three to tango," so to speak. On the other hand, the process of evaluating and accepting new participants into the distinctive, silent world is so casual that anyone (journalist, law officer, sociologist) is easily accepted as a member. It is difficult to argue that the right to privacy has been seriously infringed when the individuals concerned are so cavalier about their own privacy, as reflected in the casual screening of participants and utilization of public settngs.[1]

The rights of the participants in the interviews in the second part of the study are also mixed. On one hand, they were selected and interviewed because of their known involvement in homosexual behavior; a truthful presentation regarding research objectives and procedures (the right to informed consent) was not fully honored. Presumably they gave their informed consent to participate in a health survey. To have provided them with the reason for their selection for an interview would have made it clear that their behavior in the public restrooms, which they considered anonymous, was not only observed and recorded, but that their identities had been determined. Any right to a minimization of anxiety over public disclosure and embarrassment would be threatened by such revelations.

Whether or not the rights of the police were given appropriate respect (they were deceived on two occasions) is another issue. The first deception occurred

---

[1] As for example, when prostitutes service their clients in cars, doorways, and parking lots in full public view; such behavior was covertly filmed and presented on national television (NBC's *Weekend,* September 4, 1976) in the United States. Apparently, it is now common for male homosexuals in privately owned but "public" bathhouses to engage in sexual acts not only in the common areas of the establishment (rather than in the seclusion of dressing rooms), but in front of spectators (Webb, 1980).

when the observer was arrested for "loitering" outside a public restroom; the investigator was able to conceal his true identity and the purpose of his "loitering" from the police, thus preventing them from having a reason to seek access to his field notes to identify the homosexuals. Second, the police were misled regarding the true purpose for wanting the names and addresses of those registering automobiles. It may be argued that the authorities have no right to a truthful presentation if they are so careless as to accept fabrications without independent attempts at verification. Further, if the illegal status of homosexual behavior is controversial, it could be argued that such a minor deception of the authorities in an attempt to study the "true" nature of the activity and its participants is justifiable as a political act, one that may lead to a change in the political (legal) status of homosexual behavior.

It would appear that the right of society at large to expect systematic research on important topics has been respected. In exercising his right to an unrestricted choice of research topics, the investigator potentially infringed upon the rights of the police and the participants. That the investigator conducted the research in such a way that no specific participant was negatively affected and that no specific police officer was embarrassed would suggest that their individual rights and welfare actually received considerable respect. The extent to which the "group rights" of the police department and the homosexual subculture received respect is another issue; "group rights" are not widely accepted and have tenuous legal standing.

Program/Project Effects.   While this study is clearly not part of a well-defined, large-scale research program, it is a contribution to the knowledge developed about atypical but potentially harmless subcultures in the society. Additional descriptive knowledge may help to determine the nature of the participants and their activities, whether or not they constitute a threat to the well-being of society, and the consequences of such involvement on the participants themselves. While no project can investigate all major issues, the study of "tearooms" and the participants provided new, and presumably accurate, information on some of these issues. (There has been a recent flurry of similar works on free and open heterosexual activity such as swinging, mate swapping, and the like.) It is quite possible, considering the widespread knowledge of this research, that it had a major effect upon the shift in the legal status of male homosexuality in the United States during the decade after it was published.

The major advantage of this particular study was that it was one of the original attempts to describe how typical adults with homosexual preferences were able to meet and engage in sexual activity. The direct costs were relatively small, requiring only the time of the investigator and some help from a research assistant. Given the absence of descriptions prior to this study, it would seem to have been a useful contribution.

Participant Effects.   As the investigator went to great lengths to make sure the participants were not aware of the research, they clearly were not in a position to gain any major benefits (the presence of the investigator, however, did assist some participants in achieving an orgasm). The major negative effects for the individual participants were the time required to participate in the interview; no direct negative effects were reported by the investigator (or the critics). There may have been indirect negative effects associated with the police response to the publication of the study; they may have temporarily increased their surveillance and arrests of male homosexuals, but there is no way of determining if this included any of the participants.

Distribution of Effects.   Although all members of society may gain from the results of this research, a small number of individuals were the source of the research data and bore any risks associated with the project. It would appear that these men were representative of the men in the city where the study was conducted (this was one major purpose of the study), hence any unjust distribution of risks and benefits was not related to socioeconomic distinctions. If there was any unjust distribution, it was related to the small group of homosexuals bearing the risks for the greater society or the larger group of homosexuals; all of these would bear the results of changes in social norms and laws regarding homosexuality—whether repressive or liberal. In this particular study, it is difficult to make a strong argument that the distribution of effects was dramatically unjust.

Respect for Rights, Welfare.   The rights and welfare of the participants were respected in several ways. Measures were taken to protect the anonymity of the participants and the purpose of the study. A safety deposit box in another state was used to maintain all records of individual identity; cover stories were used in all dealings with the police. Care was taken to prevent the participants themselves from knowing that their activities were being recorded and their identities located. This was done by the investigator's participation in the "illegal" sexual society and his use of a disguise during the interviews (although all interviews could have been completed by the research assistant).

Personal Treatment.   The exchanges between the participants and the investigator and the police and investigator were not open and honest; the investigator misrepresented himself and his objectives. Such deliberate deception is not considered an ideal personal relationship. On the other hand, aside from this deception the investigator's relationships with the participants were within the normal standards of casual social intercourse. In the case of the participants, it was important to the investigator to appear as a knowledgeable member of the subculture in order to obtain an accurate description of their behavior.

Acceptability to Social Scientists.   Social scientists who believe that their major purpose is to contribute to objective knowledge about important and sensitive phenomena would approve of this research, despite its limited intellectual aims. Social scientists who see their major purpose to be the reform of society and who personally favor increased freedom of sexual choice are likely to approve of this research, although the social reform emphasis was a separate activity that complemented this study (Humphreys, 1972). Those who feel that social scientists should be model citizens and avoid the controversial and sensitive might not wholly approve of this research, especially since both participants and the police were deceived and there was some risk that the participants' identity would be disclosed or they would discover they were more vulnerable to disclosure than they realized (Warwick, 1973).

Overt Friendship, Covert Purposes and the Limits of Effect

In participant observation research an investigator describes activities and behaviors (perhaps including conversations) of individuals who consider the investigator to be a typical member of the group; the participants are unaware of the researcher's identity or full purpose. This technique is used to prevent the participants from knowing their actions are being observed and recorded. In some cases, certain activities may be considered illegal (such as drug use) or embarrassing (such as atypical sexual behavior). However, there are instances where investigators have adopted the role and status of participants in an attempt to increase their understanding of the participants' lives—to experience the perspectives and interpretations of the participants' world. In one case, a Caucasian changed his skin color, along with his dress and demeanor, to experience discrimination as a Negro (Griffin, 1961).

Participant observation may become covert "after the fact." An individual may be involved in a distinctive setting for its own value (such as a work situation, religious organization, or recreational group) and decide afterward to use the experiences and observations as research data. The result may be a discussion of the social structure of a military unit (Homans, 1946), the socialization processes in a total institution (Dornbusch, 1955), or the norms and values of a particular occupational group; this latter is a popular topic for graduate student papers and theses (Roth, 1959). Although covert from the perspective of the participants, since they were never aware they would serve as sources of research data, such research was clearly not the result of deliberate planning by the investigator; its objectives and plan for analysis were developed after the information was "gathered."

There are numerous examples of elaborate, preconceived participant observation projects, including: the simulation of alcoholism to explore the reception of newcomers to therapy groups (Lofland & Lejeune, 1960); months of involvement with a doomsday cult to study the nature of the members' belief system and how it changed in response to disconfirmation when the world did not end (Festinger, Riecken, & Schachter, 1956); the disguise and reorientation of a military officer as a teen-ager to study the problems and reactions of basic trainees (Sullivan, Queen, & Patrick, 1958); and normal adults feigning schizophrenia to gain admission to mental institutions to determine how long it would take before their normality would be discovered and they would be discharged (Rosenhan, 1973).

The very nature of participant observation, where the investigator attempts to blend into a group of individuals, virtually guarantees that the participants will experience little or no change in their daily life. Because observers are attempting to describe reality, they usually make every effort not to have any influence upon social processes or individual participants. Occasionally the differences between observers and participants will be so great that they cannot successfully pass as participants (for example, a male attempting to study a group of women, or a large Caucasian studying a group of Pygmies); in such settings investigators must either settle for overt field observation or utilize informants among the existing members of the group.

SURREPTITIOUS FIELD EXPERIMENTS

Helping behavior is difficult to study. The opportunities to observe altruism in natural settings are very rare; inferring generalizations is difficult. Attempts to create emergencies in research settings are unsatisfactory; participants feel they and others are safe and expect the research staff to take care of emergencies. One solution has been to systematically create emergencies in public settings and then observe how ordinary people (the unsuspecting participants) respond. By varying the character of the emergency the effect of different factors on the helping behavior can be explored. Such created events accompanied by systematic observation are called field experiments.

Example of Analysis:
Subway Altruism

One example of such research involved the systematic creation of feigned collapse on a subway. The crucial data were the number and types of passengers that responded to a "fallen" passenger. The entire incident and all data recording—count of the number and types of passengers, staged emergency, and recording of the reactions—was completed in less than five minutes. This was less than the time required for a subway train to travel between two stations. The research team traveled back and forth between the same two subway stops, adding another case with every trip.

On each trip the "emergency" was a standing male passenger who started to lose his balance and fall to the floor shortly after the car left the station. Both the characteristics of the stricken person (whites versus black), the nature of his problem (alcoholism versus illness), and the severity of the problem (simple collapse versus collapse with blood trickling from the mouth) were explored (Piliavin, Rodin, & Piliavin, 1969; Piliavin & Piliavin, 1972).

A substantial percentage (up to 100 percent) of the "stricken" received assistance; the percentage was greatest when they appeared to faint, less when they were apparently drunk (82 percent assisted), and still less (65 percent) when blood trickled from their mouths. There was a slight tendency for the helper to be of the same race as the one stricken with "illness," a tendency that increased when the stricken appeared drunk. Ninety percent of the cases were helped by males, although males constituted only 60 percent of the passengers. The presence of a nonresponding "social helper" (priest or intern) had no clear effect; in those cases where no assistance was provided, the "social helper" helped the "stricken" passenger leave the car at the next station.

Effects on Rights.   Most research on altruism has been done in response to the murder of Catherine Genovese in 1964; this young woman was attacked and finally killed over a thirty-minute period in a high-density central city residential area. Her cries for help were heard and struggles observed by thirty-eight residents of the area, but none came to her assistance or called the police (Milgram & Hollander, 1964; Latané & Darley, 1970). This incident led to considerable speculation as to why bystanders would not provide assistance and resulted in a search for the conditions under which such assistance would and would not occur; research was conducted in both controlled and natural settings. Few areas of study in social psychology have been so directly related to phenomena of such considerable popular interest; investigators have clearly exercised their right to study phenomena of personal concern.

While the participants in the subway experiment were not able to provide their informed consent to engage in the research, the demands made upon them were minimal. They were exposed to a simulated emergency that could occur to any subway passenger. Assisting the "stricken" passenger involved nothing more than helping him to his feet; if participants did not come to his aid, any guilt was minimized by the assistance provided by the "social helper." Through it all, passengers who did and did not help remained anonymous; no identification was sought or collected on individual participants.

Program/Project Effects: As a research program, the study of altruism consists of a rather loosely structured, informally organized set of activities. Most studies, including the one discussed here, have involved modest costs (mostly the time of the investigator and research assistants); the major benefits have been more knowledge about the conditions under which altruism may be expected to occur. The major contributions have been an improved understanding of the cognitive processes that are activated in passers-by when an opportunity for altruism occurs. Because most major factors that favor altruism (the density of a crowd, number of observers, familiarity with the physical setting, the percentage of males among the observers) are outside the capacity of anyone to control, the practical implications for increasing the incidence of altruism are difficult to determine. (Reducing the need for altruistic behavior may be a more practical long-run approach.)

Participant Effects.   The direct effects on the participants are clearly quite small. For a few minutes on a routine subway ride they witness a stricken passenger. The passenger eventually receives help from either a participant or another person on the subway; a specific passenger providing assistance may perhaps feel satisfied with his actions. If he does not, someone else does and he had no reason to experience guilt. Throughout the participants remain anonymous and are never identified; direct effects on the unknowing participants are clearly insignificant.

Distribution of Effects.   The major benefactor of the research would be society at large, as knowledge about altruism increases. The major source of the data were ordinary passengers on a mass transit system; it seems reasonable to assume they are representative of society. Although the participants came from two cities (New York and Philadelphia) and not the country at large, there seems little reason to consider the distribution of effects unjust.

Respect for Rights, Welfare.   The major evidence that the investigators were concerned for the rights and welfare of the participants was the development of a research design that minimized participants' contributions, ensured they would remain anonymous, and prevented them from experiencing substantial guilt if they failed to provide assistance. Additional evidence comes from the second study, when some passengers responded to the fallen person with blood trickling from his mouth by pulling the emergency stop on the train—an act that could injure or delay a substantial number of passengers. When this happened, the passenger was restrained by one of the observers. This unexpected response, in combination with harassment by the subway police (who treated the research as a nuisance), led to the early termination of the study—a clear indicator of concern for the welfare of the participants (Piliavian & Piliavian, 1972).

Personal Treatment.   There was no extended or involved personal treatment of the participants by the investigators, only a brief opportunity to help a fallen passenger followed by a "thank you." While it may be argued that it is wrong to deceive and manipulate others, even in a minor way, there is no reason to suspect that any participant was mistreated.

Acceptability to Social Scientists.   Those who consider their major objective to be contributing to the store of knowledge may not be entirely satisfied by this research activity; however, they will attribute their dissatisfaction to the looseness of the intellectual structure of social psychology, rather than the nature of these particular projects. Those who emphasize acting as a model citizen may be concerned about this particular study, as knowledge of such research may increase suspicion that emergencies are created and not real, thereby reducing assistance in real emergencies in the future. Finally, those who wish to reform society and directly promote a particular program of action may find this research somewhat irrelevant and thereby unacceptable.

Limits of Influence on Daily Life

Two research problems have led to the development of surreptitious field experiments. The first stems from the major disadvantage of experiments conducted in highly controlled settings; it is not always clear that the same activities will occur when the participants are in natural settings. The second is the low frequency with which some interesting phenomena occur in natural settings; it is very inefficient to collect data on reactions to rare events. For example, it would require a great deal of unproductive observation time to determine how people react to emergencies; this can be substantially reduced if an emergency is created when it is convenient to observe the reactions of bystanders.

One solution to these problems has been to design studies to produce events that could occur as a result of natural processes, thereby providing an opportunity to systematically observe the reactions of ordinary individuals as they confront everyday occurrences. Further, some of the features of such occurrences and the setting can be varied systematically to provide estimates of the influences of different variables.

In this way, studies of social influence have examined the effect of escalating requests by asking those who agree to a small request (such as a short telephone interview) to endure an even greater burden (e.g., the systematic inventory of all consumer goods in the kitchen) (Freeman & Fraser, 1966); the effects of insults upon attitude change through the verbal abuse of individuals sitting on park benches (Abelson & Miller, 1967); or how the invasion of "personal space" (the area around a urinal in a public men's room) will affect psychophysiological measures or arousal (length of time in urination) (Middlemist, Knowles, & Matter, 1976). Variation in the nature of community norms has been studied by leaving stamped, unopened, and uncancelled letters in obvious locations to determine the percentage mailed in different communities (Milgram, 1969); by observing difference in rates at which abandoned automobiles are stripped or vandalized (Zimbardo, 1969); and by noting the extent of assistance provided to strangers asking for permission to use the phone (Milgram, 1970). Perhaps the greater number of studies have involved altruism or helping behavior. Altruism has been studied by asking students for handouts and testing variations in approaches (Latané, 1970); noting what factors affect the amount of assistance provided a female shoe store "customer" (Schaps, 1972); or observing the extent to which a bystander will correct misleading directions provided by one confederate to another (Allen, 1972).

The rights and welfare of the participants are respected by several features of the research design. First, the influence upon the participants must seem natural and ordinary to qualify as part of daily life; this prevents the use of extreme events. Second, the participants remain anonymous in many studies by virtue of the research design; it may not even be possible to inform them they have made a contribution to science. There has been no evidence that such research—bordering on the normal events of daily life—is resented by participants.

UNOBTRUSIVE (NONREACTIVE) MEASURES

Example of Analysis:
Garbageology

The systematic study of household consumption is generally complicated and expensive. The "official" procedure, used to estimate the mixture of products purchased by the typical household in computing the Consumer Price Index (the government standard for estimates of inflation) is a complex survey; each administration requires five interviews with every household and the completion of a two-week daily expenditure diary of every item (dog food, bread, toilet paper, and so on) (Carlson, 1974). Two features of this procedure reduce confidence that it reflects typical consumption patterns. First, people may change their consumption to appear "normal" if they know a record is being maintained; and second, they may forget purchases or recall them inaccurately.

An alternative is to avoid any direct contact with the individuals themselves and collect and analyze their household refuse (Rathje, 1978, 1979a, 1979b). Garbage is collected by sanitation crews using a procedure that ensures a household will be sampled at random from neighborhoods identified by socio-economic characteristics. Household members cannot distort or temporarily change their consumption patterns to "look good," and inaccurate recall does not affect the data. On the other hand, there are some disadvantages. The data are less precise measures of household consumption; only the remains can be analyzed, consumption away from the home (restaurants, travel) is not reflected in household refuse, and some types of technology (garbage disposals) can affect the mixture of material thrown away. Further, the data are related to neighborhoods, not specific households. Confidence in inferences about households is highest when the community is homogeneous.

Effects on Rights. The right of investigators to study any topic is satisfied by research on household garbage as an indicator of household consumption or nonconsumption (that is, waste). While it may be argued that the participants, the source of the waste, may have a claim to the refuse, in the city where the project was initiated (Tuscon, Arizona) the refuse is legally defined as city property once it has been placed for pickup. (Although this may be challenged if it were not disposed of anonymously.) The right of the public to expect investigators to pursue important, relevant topics is related to inerpretations, rather than the inherent economic value of the "raw data."

Program/Project Effects. While not initiated as part of an explicit research program (the initial focus was the association between socioeconomic status and consumption), garbageology has now developed into the systematic study of variation across social classes in the United States and other industrialized countries. As the technique has become more refined, with substantial support from large numbers of students sorting garbage for course credit, it has allowed more systematic attention to the nutritional character of consumption and discards as well as to the potential pollution-causing properties of matter to be buried in landfills. The initial project, developing a procedure for selecting refuse and a coding scheme and technique for describing it, provides a useful procedure for systematic analysis.

Participant Effects.   The direct effects for the participants are, for all intents, nil. The garbage is collected by sanitation crews using a procedure that ensures a randomly selected household will be sampled from neighborhoods identified by socioeconomic characteristics. Once delivered to the investigators ·(or garbage sorters), neither they nor the participants have any way of knowing whose garbage is included. A possible indirect effect on participants may occur if knowledge from the project affects private or public policies, such as a change in standards for throwaway containers—a remote link, indeed.

Distribution of Effects.   Households from all socioeconomic categories and all ethnic communities in the city were deliberately included. As the participants were representative of all segments of society and the major benefactor is society itself, there appears to be little reason to expect an unjust distribution of costs and benefits.

Respect for Rights, Welfare.   The major evidence of respect for the rights of the participants is the use of an intermediary (the sanitation workers) to gather the data (the refuse) from the households; the gathering was completed in such a way to insure their anonymity. Apparently it is almost impossible to identify specific households, despite the discarded mail that might be found in the refuse. On occasion when valuables such as rings are found, it is necessary to use newspaper advertisements to attempt to locate the owners.

Personal Treatment.   As there is no face-to-face contact with the participants creating the refuse, this issue is largely irrelevant. Investigators have tried to return valuables to their anonymous owners, which indicates some personal concern.

Acceptability to Social Scientists.   The usefulness of these data for providing a check on interview-based descriptions of household consumption and food waste ensures that this procedure is acceptable to those who emphasize the development of reliable scientific knowledge. The absence of any contact with the respondents or direct effects of any kind precludes criticism from those who emphasize a model citizen role for social scientists. Social reformers may prefer more direct attacks on the problems of society and thus be critical of such an endeavor.

And the Participants Never Know . . .

Numerous procedures, techniques, or devices have been developed to reflect human or social variables without affecting the phenomena of interest; they are referred to as nonreactive or unobtrusive measures (Webb et al., 1981; Brandt,

1972), and can be considered in three categories (Bouchard, 1976). The first, physical traces, utilizes indirect measures of psychological and social processes. For example, the nose prints on the glass in front of a museum can be used to estimate the number and height (and age) of visitors; the percentage of locked cars in an area can be used as a measure of neighborhood concern with theft; broken windows can be used as a measure of pride in public property (such as schools) or the rate of vandalism in a neighborhood.

A second category is simple observation, the careful recording of specific details of events. For example, the distance between conversational partners may be used as a measure of their psychological closeness; the extent to which different ethnic categories are interrelated in social settings (lunch breaks, playground activities, and so on) may be used as a measure of integration. Personal behavior such as eye-blink rate may be used to infer emotionality, pupil size to indicate interest, or voice frequency to indicate emotion.

Third, electromechanical devices are used to accurately record behavior, usually without the knowledge of the participants. Photoelectric cells may be used to measure the movement of crowds; sensors may be placed on chairs to measure duration of sitting (as in a theatre) or movement in the chair; or a transmitter may be placed in a book to identify its physical location.

Regardless of their exact nature, unobrusive measures have several features in common. One major advantage is that they make data collection efficient; some require only the simple measurement of physical changes (such as floor-tile wear), and others allow an automatic system to gather the data. In addition the investigator usually has high confidence that the measurement procedure has not affected the phenomenon itself—an assumption not always tenable in experiments or surveys. The major disadvantage is that investigators can never be sure that unobtrusive measures are valid indicators of the variables of interest. For example, there will always be some ambiguity over the source of emotion reflected in certain voice frequencies; it could be the stress of telling a lie, the stress of the situation, or stress from some other source. Variables must be measured in other, more direct ways to ensure that the unobtrusive measure reflects the phenomena of interest.

ARCHIVAL RESEARCH

The analysis of information developed and assembled for reasons other than those of primary interest represents a further type of covert research. Examples would be: the secondary analysis of research data that perhaps was originally collected with the knowledge, consent, and cooperation of the participants; the analysis of public documents such as birth, marriage, or death certificates, or even property tax records; the use of anonymous public data, such as that provided by the Bureau of the Census; the analysis of administrative records containing data intially assembled for organizational purposes; and the analysis of personal or family material such as letters, diaries, Bibles, or even the artifacts found in burial grounds (originally included for religious purposes). All these can be considered examples of covert research because neither the individuals originally providing the data, nor anybody else, was aware that the data would be used in the investigator's specific research project.

A number of issues are of marginal significance to the moral analysis of research involving archival material. For example, the research project has almost no direct effects, particularly from the data collection, since the information was provided before the research was initiated. The distribution of positive and negative effects among participants and possible benefactors (present generations or society in general) is rather moot if no effects are experienced by the participants. In the absence of any contact between the investigator and the participants, the nature of their personal treatment is largely irrelevant. Finally, the acceptability of a project to social scientists with different orientations will depend on the objectives and implications of the findings, rather than the contact with the participants, although those preferring social scientists to have a minimal effect may favor archival research, as long as it is not seen as "snooping." Three issues are worthy of discussion: effects on rights, program/project effects, and demonstration of respect for participant rights and welfare.

Effects on Rights.   From the perspective of the participants, the major issue centers on their expectations regarding use of the information at the time they provided it. For example, some archival information is considered to be a public record and is developed with that understanding. Birth, marriage, and death certificates, property tax records, and judicial trial records are available to anyone (journalists, lawyers, relatives, investigators, and so forth) regardless of their purpose. In the same sense, data collected as part of official government activities, such as the U.S. Census or the National Health Survey, are assumed to be used for future research. Such data are generally organized and presented anonymously; substantial attempts are made to ensure the participants' anonymity. The federal government encourages the use of such surveys by making the data available at modest cost; this helps to satisfy a public right to maximize the value of a federally sponsored research.

Such is not the case when the information has been assembled for administrative purposes, such as the detailed information in federal and state tax returns or applications for public assistance. The situation that has received most attention has been the use of administrative records from both secondary schools and colleges for research; a recent federal law has made mandatory the consent of students or their parents for the release of data for nonacademic purposes (Title 20 USC 123g; Russell Sage Foundation, 1970); this clearly includes any scientific research. As for family or culture archives, the major rights associated with research may be those of the current generations. For example, if an archaeological project necessitates excavating Native American religious artifacts or perhaps a burial ground, the rights of present generations of Native Americans may be affected if the excavation is not done with a demonstration of respect; some Native American tribes still practice the religions of their ancestors, who have become unknowing contributors to current research.

Program/Project Effects.   Some general effects on specific projects deserve comment. Three types of archival research—the use of public records, administrative data, and family or personal artifacts—have considerable merit; they reflect events, often of substantial importance for the participants, occurring in the natural course of life and are not exclusively responses to research situations or issues. When individuals complete a marriage certificate, file an application for welfare payments, or bury household items with a deceased relative to ease their afterlife, they are acting in good faith (so to speak) as members of their family, religious group, or society. Hence, investigators need have no doubt about the applicability of the findings to "real life"; in such cases, the data may be the best evidence possible for establishing an event (such as a birth or death). Further, the conduct of the research has not affected the phenomena; the participants have provided the data as part of their regular routine.

Not only do archival data represent natural behavior in daily life, they are often an economical way to gather information. This is particularly true when the data have been gathered to facilitate research, as with government surveys. This cost-advantage is not, however, always as great as might be imagined. For example, it may be expensive to separate the desired information from the total record. Costs may involve programming and computer processing expenses for data stored on magnetic tapes; much human effort may go into searching and selecting items from written data (biographies, eyewitness accounts, diaries, legal cases, administrative files, and so forth) or into the physical shifting of artifacts and earth in archaeological sites.

Finally, a major cost to the investigator may be completing the administrative procedures required to gain access to some data. While government surveys, in which the data are prepared for analysis and the participants are anonymous, can often be obtained for the cost of the computer tape and codebooks, official administrative records may require confrontation with complicated requirements. While the availability of some government records has been facilitated by the Freedom of Information Act of 1966 (Public Law 90-23), access to data on individuals has been complicated by the Privacy Act of 1974 (Public Law 95-38), and utilization of data within the jurisdiction of both acts may be quite complicated.[2] The requirements for informed consent of students and parents prior to release of educational information may not only involve considerable time and money but also reduce the number of individuals on whom information is available for analysis, due to participant indifference toward the research.

Respect for Rights and Welfare.   The major techniques for demonstrating respect for the rights and welfare of the participants (or their descendants) are: maintaining anonymity for the participants, providing descriptions and analyses that treat them with respect and dignity, and minimizing the possible misinterpretations and misapplications of the major results of the research.

[2] A continuously up-to-date reference on this issue is cited in Chapter 6, footnote 2.

In most cases maintaining the anonymity of individual participants is not difficult, although there are some cases where the use of administrative records from several sources has caused some unexpected complications. For example, it may be desirable to assemble information from several agencies, normally kept quite separate, for analysis—such as combining data from annual tax returns with welfare applications. A concern may arise regarding the access of the Internal Revenue Service to the welfare applications and vice versa. In order to protect the participants from such a comingling of data, investigations may have to specially process the data gathered from one agency in order that only major identifiers (such as names, addresses, Social Security numbers) will be interpretable, all other data having been eliminated or transformed with a special code. Crucial data from the second agency can be added to the computer tape (on a case-by-case basis), and the final version can be prepared for analysis by decoding the sensitive information once it is under the safe control of the investigator. (A number of such techniques are described in Boruch and Cecil, 1979a.)

It is very important to demonstrate respect for the participants by describing the results in such a way that will reflect sympathy and understanding for them as individuals. In addition, the possibility of indirect negative effects on groups represented by the participant is also present. This is particularly true when a unique combination of data from several sources may be assembled for the research. If the research involves social categories (minorities, unwed mothers, police officers, and the like), the new information may embarrass the individuals concerned. A more subtle indirect effect involves the impact of the research findings upon social or organizational policies, which may be changed without the knowledge or consent of individuals affected. This may be seen as an infringement upon the right of self-determination, although the extent of the infringement would depend upon the opportunity for open, public debate before the new policies were adopted, not the existence of a research project.

CONCLUSION

A number of important, valuable research procedures may be used without the knowledge of the participants. In such cases, it is impossible to demonstrate respect for the participants' rights and welfare through informed consent. However, in most of these instances there is very little risk to their immediate welfare; their rights are only threatened when issues of privacy are involved. Such are ambiguous only when "private" behavior is enacted in public settings; private settings should not be intruded upon without consent and "public" behavior in public settings causes no problems. Other ways of demonstrating respect for participants makes up for the inability to utilize informed consent.

The potential for direct effects, either positive or negative, is minimal in covert research; this is primarily due to the participants' lack of awareness that research is being conducted, an illusion that is carefully developed for many studies.

It may be argued that this is "deception" and violates the right to self-determination with regard to involvement in research; however, the concept of informed consent (reflecting the right to self-determination) was developed to ensure that participants would not experience substantial negative effects without their knowledge and willing agreement. A low possibility for negative effects substantially diminishes the justification for informed consent.

The major negative effect on participants is the potential disclosure of information of a private, confidential nature. Respect for the participants may be demonstrated through the careful protection of their anonymity or ensuring that identities are not actually collected as part of the research data. Both procedures are common; the general practice of investigators is not to collect individual identities unless absolutely necessary and then to destroy such information when it is no longer needed.

In conclusion, then, because participants are unaware of covert research there is a limited opportunity for dramatic negative effects; only in special circumstances is it possible to obtain confidential, personal information. There is ample opportunity for investigators to demonstrate respect for the participant's rights and welfare; covert research allows participants to make an effortless contribution to social science.

CHAPTER FIVE
FURTHER COMPLICATIONS: CROSS-CULTURAL RESEARCH, AND STUDIES OF SOCIAL SYSTEMS

The moral analysis of research becomes substantially more complicated when an investigator no longer conducts research with individuals from the same society (or moral community) or focuses upon supraindividual entities (groups, organizations, social systems, and the like). Research with another society or culture usually involves a different legal system or political philosophy. This may lead to different conceptions of individual rights, informed consent, costs and benefits for participants, and methods of showing respect and concern for the rights and welfare of participants. When an aggregate, cultural group, organization, or societal institution is the object of study, determining the rights and welfare of supraindividuals and relating them to those of the natural persons involved, obtaining informed consent, and demonstrating respect for the "participants'" rights and welfare becomes more complex.

The following section will review issues associated with these two complicated situations. As before, the major objective is not to provide an ultimate solution, but to review the considerations that may help an investigator to gain confidence about the conduct of his or her research.

CROSS-CULTURAL RESEARCH

Example of Analysis:
Field Observation, Starvation,
and Competition[1]

Field observation of the Ik tribes, the subject of this analysis, was the *fifth* choice for study by an anthropologist who had arranged for release time from his university and funds to pay for field work (his preferred choices were ruled out because he could not get the necessary permission from supervisory societies, tribal warfare, and the like). His final selection, the Ik, was a tribe that had been nomadic hunters-gatherers up until World War II; for twenty-five years they had been encouraged by the local government to remain in one place as farmers–and apparently survived quite well until a drought which began about the time the observer arrived. The resulting monograph is a travelogue with intermingled administrative details, personal experiences, and observations about the society and its cultural patterns (Turnbull, 1972).

After gaining an initial acquaintance with the language from two young Ik boys attending a boarding school and making contact with members of the tribe, the observer found famine created by a drought in the arid, mountainous region in which they lived (East Africa where Kenya, Uganda, and Sudan adjoin). The major result of this shortage of food was extreme interpersonal competition; this appeared to generalize into indifference and outright cruelty between family members, sexes, generations, and the healthy and the ill. The supervising government was distributing food, but it was generally eaten by tribal representatives, who were strong enough for the long trip required, and who vomited it up intermittently so as not to have to share the food when they returned; the young, the old, and the sick continued to starve. After a year of observation the investigator left to organize his field notes and returned during the second growing season. Although sufficient rain had fallen to produce abundant crops, the Ik were not actively cultivating their fields; instead, they lived off government supplies (which continued to be provided). The more violent aspects of their intermember competition had subsided (as they all had enough to eat), but the norm of callous indifference appeared to have continued.

Effects on Rights. Clearly, the investigator's right to explore any topic, phenomenon, or people of interest was respected; the financial support allowed realization of the right to investigate. The rights of the administrators in the supervisory societies were respected by the investigator; he pursued tribes and traveled

---

[1] This anthropological case study was chosen for review for several reasons: it is well known, it involves three moral communities (the investigator's home society, the supervisory society, and the participant's society), it has been the center of a controversy over the investigator's conduct and recommendations (Barth, 1974; Turnbull, 1974), and it is a rather fascinating description of a very unusual culture. It is not considered representative of all field work or all anthropology, but as an example of distinctive problems and how they are solved.

in areas only after official approval and offered to provide reports and recommendations on the groups he studied. It would appear that the immediate rights of the participants, the Ik, were shown respect, for they were not required to respond to the investigator's requests and in most cases received gifts of food and tobacco in exchange for their cooperation. (It could be argued that to offer food to the starving for participation in research is such an attractive inducement that they cannot be considered true volunteers.) There would seem to have been little intrusion upon the Ik's rights of privacy, as they were clearly quite capable of preventing the disclosure of material to an outsider. Whether or not their rights were respected in the utilization of the information is another matter, discussed below. The rights of the greater society—humankind as a whole, in this case—to expect distinctive and thought-provoking information from social scientists was clearly satisfied.

Program/Project Effects.   From the perspective of the investigator, it would appear that the study of the Ik resulted from an opportunity to "get into the field." The research is not systematically related to any specific intellectual or scientific issues. The closest the research comes to a general program is a stated desire to compare two groups of hunters living in different environments (Pygmies in a rainforest, studied earlier, and the Ik in an arid mountain region; Turnbull, 1972 p. 17) and to discover some general principles of social organization—a basic objective in anthropology. Neither, however, is a basis for the description and analysis of the Ik society; the presentation emphasizes the investigator's personal experiences and reactions to the events he encountered. While it is clear that the project resulted in a description of a distinctive culture under severe constraints—starvation conditions—it does not provide a systematic, objective analysis of the cultural features and social processes in the tribe. On the other hand, the costs of the project were relatively modest and involved only the time and support needed for one person to spend several years in a remote area of Africa.

Participant Effects.   The direct effects on participants appear to have been modest and mostly positive. As they were very careful to conceal information from the observer, his primary impact was to provide food and tobacco and some employment to a group of people who were starving and without work. While positive effects might have been greater (more food could have been given), it is clear that the Ik were not worse off for his presence. The participants did not support him in any way; they did not have the resources and were too clever to have been forced to do so. If nothing else, the observer appeared to have served as a gullible mark and a butt for their jokes.

The indirect effects, however, could have been considerable. The investigator eventually submitted a report to the supervising government that suggested that all Ik be rounded up into ten-person groups (mixed in age, sex, family identity, and village of residence) and dispersed throughout the rest of the country; this could be considered a deliberate strategy to destroy their existing society and culture (Turnbull, 1972, pp. 283-84). While this suggestion was not adopted, it could have resulted in the total obliteration of the Ik culture; the investigator felt that this would be better than to allow such a society to persist. He concluded that destruction of the Ik society was of no concern to the individual Ik and would be best for humanity—a rather weighty judgment for any individual.

Distribution of Effects.   It is clear that the Ik people would receive little benefits, and perhaps substantial harm, from the completion of the research. The supervising society's administrators might have accepted the investigator's recommendations that the surviving Ik be broken up into small groups and distributed across the entire country. The major benefactors of the research would be society as a whole, perhaps the discipline of anthropology, and the administrators in the supervising society. The potential balance of effects was not equitable, but could have been if the direct benefits (food, tobacco, employment) to the participants were not outweighted by the negative impact of any administrative action. As no such action was taken, the balance was slightly positive.

Respect for Rights, Welfare.   While the observer showed considerable respect for the rights and welfare of the Ik, particularly as individuals, during the conduct of the research, there is some question that the resulting description shows concern and understanding for a situation in which an entire society is starving to death. For example, the following comments reflect the tone of the monograph (Turnbull, 1972):

> It is difficult to know how to thank the Ik; perhaps it should be for having treated me as one of themselves which is about as badly as anyone can be treated (p. 13).
>   They were the only people who seemed to share my opinion of their incredible younger brother, Lokwam. . . . It was one of the few real pleasures I had, listening to his shrieking and yelling when they caught him and did whatever they did (for it was always out of sight behind their stockade) and then watching for him to come flying out of the *odok* holding his head and streaming with tears while Kinimei and Loruköi laughed with happiness (p. 123).

In general, the reports reflect a distrust and contempt for almost every Ik the investigator met; his sympathy is even limited for the death of Kauar, who died from exhaustion while carrying the observer's mail up from the nearest post office, and in so doing perhaps attempted to set another time record on the multiday run (p. 89).
    The monograph also identified specific members of the group by name and through photographs as they engaged in illegal activities—spear making and abetting cattle stealing—that could lead to retaliation by the government authorities (Barth, 1974). At the same time, the remoteness of the Ik villages, the periodic movement of the people, their high mortality rates, and the low probability that the authorities responsible for the Ik (the closest police referred to them incorrectly as "Teuso") would have access to the monograph in time to take action—all minimize the likelihood of official retaliation.

But the observer's contempt for individual Ik is overshadowed by his contempt for their culture, as he found it. Apparently disillusioned by the failure of the Ik culture to return to a system of mutual cooperation and personal consideration within six months after the end of a drought, he felt that a society emphasizing extreme interpersonal competitiveness and physical cruelty should be eliminated.

> Luckily the Ik are not numerous—about two thousand—and those two years [of drought] reduced their numbers greatly. So I am hopeful that their isolation will remain as complete as in the past, until they die out completely. I am only sorry that so many individuals will have to die, slowly and painfully, until the end comes to them all. For the individuals one can feel only infinite sorrow for what they have lost; hatred must be reserved for the so-called society they live in, the machines they have constructed to enable them to survive. . . . The only hope now is for the unborn or the unweaned; and had they been rounded up and carted off like cattle, they might have grown up as human beings (p. 285).

This latter is a reference to the investigator's recommendations to the responsible national government (Uganda) that the Ik culture be destroyed by dispersing the members in ten-person aggregates throughout the country.

There is ample reason to believe that the Ik society had a rather unusual set of social customs; babies were ejected from their families at age three, the young pried food from the mouths of the enfeebled, the blind and crippled were trampled while attempting to get their share of available food, neighbors defecated in one another's doorways, and all stole food from each other. However, the observer made little attempt to separate his evaluations from his observations. His attempts to encourage the destruction of the culture may represent an extreme negative effect for research participants. It is not clear, for example, why he did not recommend that the government increase the food ration or supervise its distribution to individual Ik more closely: either step might have reduced the fierce interpersonal competition for physical survival and the consequences the observer deplored. While the council of the American Anthropological Association (1971) has adopted the following statement as reflecting the ethical responsibility of anthropologists to the public,

> . . . they [anthropologists] bear a professional responsibility to contribute to an "adequate definition of reality" upon which . . . public policy may be based.

it is not clear that this is what they intended.

Personal Treatment.   The description suggests that the observer's direct personal treatment of participants was relatively benign. Not only was he dependent upon them for information necessary to the research, but there were numerous occasions where his life might have been in danger had the Ik not found him useful. By most accounts presented in the monograph, the observer's treatment of the participants was better and more rewarding (if only in terms of physical goods) than the treatment they received from each other, other Africans, or the government authorities.

Acceptability to Social Scientists.   This analysis is complicated by the multiple characteristic of this endeavor. Not only is there the observation and description of a rather unusual culture, there are policy recommendations regarding its future disposition. Social scientists who believe investigators should provide knowledge for general benefit may applaud the hazardous and unpleasant field experiences that produced a description of this distinctive tribe—whose behavior is similar to that found in concentration camps. On the other hand, they may consider recommending the destruction of a culture as inappropriate. Those who believe the investigator should be a model citizen in his or her interpersonal relationships may have little to say, as there is no reason to suspect that individual Ik were not well treated. These social scientists may also have some reservations about the policy recommendations. Finally, those who feel that social scientists should act to improve the lot of the disadvantaged may be quite critical of this effort; they would cite the investigator's obvious callousness toward the numerous Ik who starved to death daily before his eyes (while he continued to be well fed) and his recommendation to destroy the society instead of correcting its "disorders."

As a final note, most field studies by ethnographers and anthropologists are much less dramatic—this is clearly an atypical society and an atypical report. The investigator and participants usually develop substantial rapport and genuine friendship over a long period of time; the resulting descriptions generally reflect respect, dignity, and concern for the participants and their culture.

Who Is Responsible for Whom?
What Are the Norms?

Shift in moral and political philosophies can occur in cross-cultural research. For example, if an investigator from one advanced, industrialized democratic society engaged in research on another advanced, industrialized democratic society (perhaps a psychologist from the United States studying the development of personality in Norway), he or she would encounter few differences in concepts of individual rights and welfare and how to show respect for them. Another investigator from an advanced, industrialized democratic society might engage in research in a less-developed society, one that is creating an industrialized economy (perhaps a sociologist from the United States studying status attainment in Mexico). In such a case there may be some variation in the nature of, and degree of respect shown for, individual rights but these are not likely to be radically different.

The popular image of cross-cultural research is that of a lonely anthropologist camping out with the natives; the reality, however, is somewhat more complex. There are generally three different societies, moral orientations, and legal philosophies involved. In addition to the moral values of the investigator from the advanced, industrialized society and those within the native culture, there is also the moral and legal system of the supervisory society, the one responsible for the native tribes (or that claims jurisdiction over the land they occupy). This is further complicated when a social science community exists within the supervisory society; there is a tendency to feel that the investigators from the advanced society should assist and collaborate with these social scientists, particularly when they feel proprietory toward indigenous native cultures and may resent the "rich" outsiders taking data that is, or should be "theirs." (See Tapp et al., 1974, and Warwick, 1980, for a discussion of some issues related to cross-cultural research.)

Consider the most extreme case—an investigator from advanced society studying a native culture within the responsibility of a supervising country. A number of observations can be made about this type of cross-cultural research. Perhaps most important is that the research is usually descriptive in nature and is done largely through field observation and an occasional survey; seldom is an experimental design employed. Further, field observation is almost always overt, as it is impossible for the investigators to disguise themselves successfully as natives.

Given a native society with an oral culture, it is difficult to argue that they will be major benefactors of scientific knowledge or that the contribution they make to research will eventually improve their situation. This is particularly true when the scientific knowledge is shared in a scholarly community in a distant society, one with little impact upon the immediate context. For this reason, cross-cultural investigators are often encouraged to make contributions to the literature within the supervisory society, where the benefits to the native culture may be more direct, depending upon how the information is utilized. There may be some benefits to the native culture from having a record of their culture and traditions preserved, but this would contribute more to a sense of pride and the cultural continuity of future generations than it would to the welfare of the present member-participants.

Direct effects on participants may depend a great deal upon their situation and how they respond to the field observers. Field observers who are treated as guests and place a strain upon native resources (for food and housing) obviously exert an immediate, direct negative effect. For this reason field investigators attempt to be self-sufficient, providing their own food and shelter or purchasing it from the participants. But more than this, the investigators may also provide food and medical care to the native participants, a source of immediate benefit. In addition, as with some subcultures within advanced societies, the investigator may act on behalf of the group in dealing with the supervisory government and help them obtain a more satisfactory or compatible administration of their affairs. While this often occurs as the investigator develops an understanding of and identification with the culture and its members, such familiarity does not always lead to affection; the personal diary of one famous anthropologist, Bronislaw Malinowski, indicates he had little affection or respect for his informants, although he did treat the Trobriand Islanders with dignity (Wax, 1972).

Perhaps the most important procedure that can be used to demonstrate respect for the rights and welfare of the native culture and individual participants is to show concern for their individual well-being and respect their privacy—*as they define it*. The most accepted procedure is to minimize unwanted intrusions and develop mutual rapport and respect. This may take some time, but is likely to lead to more accurate and complete information in the long run. Further, the descriptions and analysis should portray the participants objectively and with sympathy, just as one might describe a community or group within one's own society.

The use of formal, explicit informed consent procedures to show respect for the rights and welfare of native peoples is unrealistic and inappropriate. Not only may they have no concept of individual rights, but they may have no concept of scientific knowledge, or how their cooperation may contribute to it, or how it may in turn benefit them. They may have a very accurate concept of an exchange relationship, whereby they talk to the investigator in exchange for food, medical care, or the prestige of being the friend of a "wealthy" visitor. As rapport and trust develops between investigator and informers, they may be willing to divulge more information and provide access to activities and ceremonies normally closed to outsiders. It is for this reason that informed consent in field observation may be referred to as a developmental process, rather than a discrete decision made at a specific time to provide or withhold information (Wax, 1980).

THE STUDY OF SOCIAL SYSTEMS

Example of Analysis:
Description of Jury Deliberations[2]

Decisions in the legal system tend to be delegated to judges or a jury. Concern over the appropriateness of using juries to resolve legal disputes led to the study of the mechanisms by which juries—composed of lay individuals—reach decisions on legal issues, as well as ways for evaluating the product of their deliberations (Amrine & Sanford, 1956; Vaughn, 1967; Katz, 1972). The major source of information on jury decision making was to be data on the discussions of several hundred "mock juries," groups of individuals similar to those of real juries, who reached a decision after hearing a tape recording of a standardized civil trial. The use of standardized trials allowed investigators to estimate the effect of factors such as age, sex, and occupation of mock jurors upon deliberations.

---

[2] This example was selected for a moral analysis for several reasons. First, it is clearly an attempt to study one feature of one institution (the legal system) in society, and no specific group of individuals experienced any negative effects from the research. Second, it represents attempts on the part of the investigators to take elaborate precautions to both protect the rights and welfare of the participants and demonstrate concern for same. Third, despite these elaborate precautions and the absence of any negative effects on any participants, the consequence was a considerable public controversy and, eventually, legislation to prohibit further research of this type. Such legislation was passed despite ignorance of the topic, the importance of the phenomenon, and the subsequent policy changes related to jury decisions (e.g., variation in size, total consensus not required for guilty verdicts, and the like).

Concerned that the major source of data was based on mock decisions without real consequences, the investigators sought evidence that might increase their confidence that the deliberations of the mock juries were similar to those of real juries. Hence, they planned to collect data on a small sample of real juries making decisions about similar cases. To this end, arrangements were completed to tape-record the deliberations of five juries in civil disputes, with the informed consent of the attorneys representing both parties and the judges supervising the cases, but without the knowledge of the jurors or the plaintiffs and defendants. It was agreed that the tape recordings would not be heard by anyone until all appeals were exhausted within the legal system and the cases were closed. Further, the transcripts of the deliberations were to be edited to insure the anonymity of the parties to the legal dispute, the jury members, and the judge. These restrictions were agreed to, and eventually tape recordings of jury deliberations for five civil trials were obtained.

Effects on Rights.   There is some ambiguity in determining just whose rights are affected by such a project. Clearly the rights of those directly involved—the plaintiff, defendant, representing attorneys, judge, and jury—need to be considered. While the legal scholars and social scientists conducting the research felt they had considered all those whose rights were directly affected, they also felt that the study demonstrated respect for the public right to research on significant issues. However, the controversy following this study suggested that a substantial number of individuals felt that the public's right to expect a confidential jury decision—regardless of the purpose for the disclosure—was not given sufficient attention; furthermore, it was not universally agreed that the jury system was in need of review and possible improvement.

Program/Project Effects.   The research program was designed to determine if the current utilization of the jury to resolve legal disputes was producing optimal results. The major effects of a successful completion of the research program would either be confidence that the current use of juries was the best way to arrive at decisions in the legal system or recommendations for changes in the decision making mechanism to better achieve the major goal of that system—justice. The negative effects would be primarily the cost and professional time required to complete the research. Considering the historical basis for jury decisions and the existing knowledge of influence processes in small groups—those with higher status in the external social system tend to have considerable influence on group decisions—it was not unreasonable to reconsider the use of juries for complex decisions.

The major advantage of this research project was that it allowed a comparison of the deliberations of five actual juries with the discussions of several hundred mock juries. But because all the juries were selected from one judicial district and because all the cases were civil disputes, it would be difficult to have total confidence that these patterns extended to juries deliberating criminal cases or to juries in other parts of the country.

An indirect negative effect of the project, which became a critical issue after the data were collected, was concern that general knowledge that the project existed—including the recording of deliberations of selected live juries—might reduce the candor and openness of discussions in other juries. While such knowledge could influence the decisions of other juries, the nature of the effect upon their decisions would be hard to predict; it could shift the emphasis toward a discussion of the merits of the case presented by each side of the dispute and away from rumors, gossip, stereotypes, and interpersonal conflict among the jurors.

Participant Effects.   There were several types of direct participants; the procedures adopted appear to have minimized any effect on them. The jury members were not aware of the covert recordings until long after they had rendered their decisions; the project staff made every attempt to maintain their anonymity. Since the recordings were not even played until after all appeals had been completed, it seems unlikely that there was any effect on the parties to the civil cases being considered. There was a slight inconvenience for the presiding judges, for the tape recorders were placed in their cloak closets (a research assistant unlocked the closets, turned on the machines, and locked the closets for the duration of the jury deliberations). In sum, there seemed to have been almost no direct or indirect effects on the participants, either positive or negative. Such minimal effects were due more to the care and attention of the research staff than to the inherent nature of the technique; abuses were clearly possible.

Distribution of Effects.   The major sources of data were the members of juries; presumably they were selected to be representative of society at large. Since the major benefactor of the research would be society at large—inasmuch as the result would be an increased confidence in the decisions made within the legal system—the social category from which participants were selected appears to be identical to that which might benefit from the research. Hence, there seems to be little evidence that an inequitable distribution of effects among different social categories occurred, although some geographic maldistribution might have existed from participants from one region providing data that might benefit all regions of the country.

Respect for Rights, Welfare.   The major indication that the rights of parties involved were given consideration was the care taken to obtain the consent of the presiding judge and attorneys to both sides of the dispute. In fact, the investigators may have felt they had obtained the consent of the legal system, since numerous legal scholars considered the project of major importance; subsequent events would indicate that the investigators had not obtained such consent. The elaborate precautions taken to ensure that the anonymity of the jurors, attorneys, parties to the dispute, and the trial judges would be maintained and that the research would not affect the normal functioning of the legal system suggest considerable concern for the rights and welfare of all participants, however broadly defined.

Personal Treatment.   As there was little direct contact with the participants themselves (the jurors), this is not a relevant issue. The problems that developed from publicizing the research are related to the personal treatment of one of the presiding judges, who was allowed to borrow one of the tapes and who subsequently played it to a conference of judges. Presumably the attorneys were also treated with some dignity, as they provided their informed consent to participate (for themselves and their clients).

Acceptability to Social Scientists.   Considering the conduct of the overall program and the significance of the issues under consideration, it is likely that most research-oriented social scientists would approve of the project. Those concerned with the image of social scientists as model citizens may have had reservations regarding the covert tape recordings of juries; they may not have defended the project when the public controversy developed. Social scientists interested in social reform may have supported the research, and would have increased their support if an active attempt had been made to improve the legal system and its delivery of justice.

While those responsible for the project were able to prevent negative effects on any of the participants, they were not able to protect the research program itself. When a tape of one jury discussion was played to a convention of judges, the nature and procedures of the project became public and considerable controversy arose. A two-day hearing was held by the Internal Security Subcommittee of the U.S. Senate Judiciary Committee; and subsequent legislation defined "jury eavesdropping" on federal juries as a felony offense (similar laws were passed by numerous states). These actions suggest that the consent of society to study jury deliberations, for whatever purpose, was not obtained. This strong reaction appears to have several bases; for some who objected to such studies the existing jury system seemed to be closely identified with the "American way of life." A second basis for the strong reaction was often related to the right to privacy, even though juries—as decision making mechanisms—have no specific rights; the conditions of deliberation are expected to provide a "fair and just" result. In sum, ambiguity over the need to "improve" the jury system and concern that the conduct of such research may affect the deliberations of all juries led to the creation of laws that prevent the covert recording of jury deliberations in the United States. Thus, any future modification of the conditions that surround jury deliberations will *not* be based on empirical evidence of the decision making processes of "real juries."

Rights, Welfare, and "Consent" of Social Systems

Much research focuses upon characteristics of social systems (such as influence or status structures, rumor transmission, norms, roles, institutions, and the like). Moral analysis of such research is complicated because the objects of study are not individuals but characteristics and processes of aggregates or systems of individuals. Hence, in addition to concerns over the rights and welfare of individual persons, there are issues related to the social system itself that must be taken into account. Major issues include: the extent to which research may affect social systems, obtaining informed consent from social systems, and demonstrating respect for the rights and welfare of a social system.

While some characteristics of social systems or their roles may be considered sensitive or private, a very large amount of public data clearly reflects system characteristics (rather than individual characteristics). For example, any natural language openly presented in verbal exchange reflects the social system; many of the norms and regularities of daily lives are easily observed, and in advanced societies many formal organizations (such as businesses and government agencies) are required to make reports and descriptive information public (whether it is accurate and complete is another issue). Even though attention to such information may be for research purposes, there is little concern that the rights and welfare of organizations or participants may be jeopardized by the project itself when the data are public and open. Concern is usually reserved for those situations where unique, distinctive information that is not normally available is recorded for research purposes.

The effects of research on a social system are distinct from the potential effects on participants. In addition to the normal range of effects on individual participants (such as time taken from other activities, stress, possible embarrassment, providing an interesting experience, increased self-knowledge, and the like), there is also the possibility that their positions within the social system may be affected. In extreme cases, their involvement could result in expulsion (firing) or a change in their relationship to the social system. For example, their roles or positions could be redefined; the amount or types of influence may change. Further, not all desirable changes for the participants would be equally beneficial for the social system (e.g., an incompetent may be promoted). Hence, while not emphasized below, the possible effects of research on the participants in a study of the characteristics of a social system need to be considered separately.

Attention to the potential effects of a research project on a social system is complicated by their diversity. For example, at one extreme are entire societies or cultures (the United States, the Peoples' Republic of China, and the like); at the other are interpersonal groups (engaged couples, athletic teams, families, work groups, and so forth). Intermediate categories include formal or complex organizations (General Motors, U.S. Air Force, Indiana University), governments (State of Montana, County of Los Angeles, City of Pittsburgh), as well as neighborhoods and communities. In addition, social systems may be formally or informally established (e.g., legal corporations and police departments versus teen-age gangs and Tuesday bridge groups). Even illegitimate or illegal social systems (such as organized crime) may be studied. The following discussion of possible effects only introduces some general features; there may be distinctive or unusual exceptions to all statements. The discussion is organized in terms of the three types of research activity reviewed in the previous chapters: experiments, overt data collection, and covert data collection.

While experimental research provides the greatest confidence in causal relationships and clearly shows the impact of an investigator upon the object of study (individuals or a social system), the need for a high degree of control over the object of study severely restricts its use with social systems. In some cases it may be possible to conduct experiments with entire social systems, as when a family may be asked to discuss case-problems or a work group asked to adopt a new procedure. In others, it is possible to conduct experiments with processes, such as influence and decision making, that may occur in a social system. In some limited situations, the impact of changes in procedures or programs may be studied as they affect a community (as the social experiments described in Chapter 2) or perhaps a unit within a large organization (say, the Chevrolet Division of General Motors). But in general it is very difficult—because of the cost alone—to utilize experimental procedures in studying the characteristics of a social system of any size. Further, for most social systems the variables under the investigator's influence have such little effect that the overall impact is negligible; the same processes that maintain system stability in response to natural disturbances tend to resist the attempts of an investigator to create change.

Overt data collection—observations of behavior and surveys—is frequently used in the study of social systems. Aside from considerations associated with individuals, the scope and momentum of processes in most social systems suggest that such research procedures will have little influence. However, some smaller, less cohesive social systems—such as an engaged couple or a counselor and a client—may be seriously affected by the nature and form of such data collection. For example, the questions raised may introduce factors into the relationship that were absent prior to the initiation of the research (for example, questioning an engaged couple about the "ideal family size" or a counselor and client about a "just fee.")

Passive, overt data collection can take at least two forms: assembling new information and reviewing existing public records. If data collection is restricted to the review of existing public data, whether public performances or information collected for public distribution (financial statements, licensing applications, and so on), there is little chance that major new effects on the social system will occur. In the event that new data are collected in a covert fashion (no action is required on the part of the social system or its participants, who may be unaware of the research), it is also unlikely that any direct effects will occur. However, as we have seen, a major controversy over research on a social system—the study of real juries—has involved the use of such techniques but not the question of direct effects upon the social system under investigation.

Once the possible effects of research upon a social system are identified, it is a major problem to determine the extent to which they are good or bad from the perspective of society as a whole. While there is some general agreement regarding desirable outcomes for individuals (good health, education, improved social position, pleasant job, and the like), this is somewhat less true for social systems. For example, while it may be considered good to enhance the task effectiveness of a social system, some may not consider this desirable if police effectiveness improves at the expense of individual rights or if organized crime expands its operations. While it may be considered good for a large social system to survive, not all may consider it best for a small one, such as an unsatisfying marriage, to continue. The most defensible position may be to conduct research in such a way that it has no effect upon the social system. Survival, task effectiveness, social characteristics and the like will not be affected in any way; and controversy over what was desirable effects will be minimized.

The acquisition of informed consent, as an indication of respect for the rights and welfare of individuals, is seriously complicated when a social system is involved. Two problems develop: the first is providing individual informed consent in certain social systems, and the second, determining how to obtain the informed consent of the social system itself. The first situation is well represented by those situations where not all members of a social system make decisions for themselves. For example, when studying the processes and structures within a family it is not clear what the consent of the children, even if they are teen-agers, would mean if all family members accept the right of the parents to make decisions regarding family participation in research. In a similar fashion, confusion may result when individuals in certain societies are asked to give their informed consent; they may feel bewilderment when offered an individual choice for the first time. Members may be part of an autocratic political structure in which the "head person" makes all the decisions for the group, or of a consensus political structure in which joint decisions are made by all members of the group (and are binding upon all). In either case, the individuals are assumed to conform to the decision made for the group, and the notion that they have a right to make an independent decision may be quite disconcerting to them. Introducing them to the idea of self-determination may produce detrimental effects, effects that may outweigh the possible increase in confidence that rights and welfare are being respected.

More typical in an advanced society are those situations in which only a portion of an individual's activities are considered to be self-determined; for example, it may be acceptable for organizational work to be controlled by administrative supervisors. If the supervisors agree to engage in a project of possible benefit to the organization, they may in fact be providing informed consent for their subordinants. In this case, to ask subordinants for their informed consent may be a meaningless gesture (if a refusal could endanger their stature in the organization), rather than a show of respect for their rights and welfare.

But the use of informed consent to demonstrate respect for rights and welfare is somewhat more complicated when the focus of research is a social aggregate or social system. In such cases, the direct effects on the rights and welfare of the participants may be negligible, and the data may not even be collected from individuals (it may be based on public records, journalistic accounts, physical traces, and so forth). There is some ambiguity about who should provide consent in such research and about the nature of the issues for which consent is actually being provided. If both individuals and the social system will be affected, consent may be obtained from both. The most appropriate source of system consent may be those who have the responsibility for its continued welfare.

Concern that obtaining the informed consent to conduct research in organizations will prevent the study of sensitive, controversial topics has led to several alternative strategies. One is to pursue research without obtaining organizational consent, and instead obtain cooperation and consent from various individuals to provide the information (Dalton, 1959). Another approach is to argue that those in positions of public responsibility are a special category of individuals, individuals who would use the aspects of informed consent to protect themselves and their organizations from criticism or negative repercussions from the research. Hence, they are not to be seen as collaborators in a cooperative research endeavor but competitors in a conflict to determine and publicize the "truth" (Lundman & McFarlane, 1976; Christie, 1976). Investigators concerned with improving society are encouraged to deceive responsible public officials regarding the purposes of the research (that is, to provide misinformation on the informed consent form) and even to fail to honor promises of confidentiality and anonymity if "public wrong-doing" is discovered and publicizing it would, in the judgment of the investigator, discourage further incidents (Galliher, 1973, 1974; Warwick, 1974). This is not, as yet, a widely accepted position among social scientists.[3]

Perhaps the most fundamental procedure used to demonstrate respect for the rights and welfare of a social system and its members (as well as those with some relationship to the social system) is to withhold the identity of the social system whenever possible. Not only does this emphasize respect for the social system and its members, but it also helps to prevent identification of specific individuals who may have revealed embarrassing or private information to the investigators. It has been suggested that this practice be abandoned for larger social systems (such as communities or large organizations) and that readers should be allowed to decide for themselves if the social system is typical (Gibbons, 1975): however, this practice continues to reflect the concern of the investigators, regardless of its practical consequences. When the social system and associated phenomena are not specific to particular individuals and there is concern that the context may not be typical, it is usually identified by the investigator; this is a frequent occurrence in the study of distinctive or unusual cultures. Note that those who have adopted a "conflict methodology" perspective and consider the investigator to have an obligation to expose wrongdoing by publicly accountable officials are likely to be less concerned over maintaining the anonymity of social systems or participants.

CONCLUSION

While cross-cultural research and the study of organizations, such as families, businesses, governments, and the like, are less common than research on individual participants, there are situations where they can pose moral issues. The seven-issue

---

[3] An alternative to the conflict (treating all participants like unscrupulous foes) or consensus (treating all participants like trusted allies) "models" is an intermediate position. An investigator would attempt to develop an exchange of services between himself and both "influential elites" and "deserving clients"; this approach is particularly appropriate for the study of community service agencies and their clients (Hessler, New, & May, 1979).

moral analysis provides a framework for arriving at a conclusion regarding the conduct of the research (although it is more suitable for research with individuals). Cross-cultural research involving up to three different cultural backgrounds and philosophies can be very complex, particularly when the participants have little understanding of science, research, and the like. The analysis is somewhat less complex in the study of the structure and process of some social systems, in which the interests of the participants must be separated from those of the social system. These special cases demonstrate two important aspects of moral analysis: such an analysis reflects a particular set of legal, political, and ethical philosophies developed within a distinctive society, and its major focus has been upon individuals (natural persons) rather than groups or aggregates (or "legal persons").

Perhaps the most important feature of research with social systems and other cultures is that the research is likely to produce few if any direct effects on the social aggregate. A few direct effects may concern individual participants, but these are likely to be small. The same process that maintains consistency in system characteristics in response to naturally produced changes will tend to resist the impact of research, even that designed to induce change. The indirect effects, actions taken by responsible authorities in response to the conclusions and interpretations from the research, may be considerable. For example, there is a substantial interest in anthropological reports of tribal units in countries subject to revolution (Wolf & Jorgensen, 1970). Fortunately, the investigator has some degree of influence on how the research findings are presented and may minimize the more extreme forms of reaction; this may moderate the indirect negative effects on participants and social systems or, if the investigator so chooses, present a dramatic case for official intervention.

CHAPTER SIX
EXTERNAL CONTROL
OF RESEARCH

The dominant model of a scientist's role has emphasized autonomy in the selection of intellectual questions and development of strategies for their resolution; the independent gentleperson-scholar has been the accepted stereotype. As those in the physical sciences adopted this orientation, they encountered few moral problems with the conduct of research—human participants were not involved and physical and chemical substances had no rights. As long as research procedures were relatively benign, dealt with innocuous topics, and the resulting knowledge was considered interesting but of little practical consequence, this model could be transferred to the social sciences with few problems. But as the results of social science research began to be taken more seriously and the techniques of research were seen to have potentially serious consequences for the participants, the situation changed. Since the 1960s both the research techniques and the applications of social science have received more public attention. In a sense, the success of the social science enterprise—in producing knowledge of consequence about phenomena of significance—has resulted in increased public concern regarding its conduct. One consequence of the success of social science has been more attention to the activities of investigators and a reduction in their autonomy and independence.

This loss of autonomy has taken place with regard to two sets of issues: the treatment of research participants and the application of social science to practical problems. Public concern over the first issue has concentrated on both social science and biomedical investigators (the other major group conducting research involving human participants). Concern over the second issue is shared by physical scientists and engineers; their applications of knowledge have become a public issue in recent years, starting with the atomic bomb and continuing as pollution and the conservation of energy increase in importance. (The application of biomedical science to improve health has not been so controversial, although the costs and distribution of health care have been). Public mechanisms for the resolution of the first issue is the major focus of this chapter; Chapter 7 will emphasize the second.

While the efforts of an investigator to engage in a moral analysis of a research project may increase confidence in his or her own judgment, a quite different issue remains: *How to convince others—colleagues, participants, the public at large—to consider the research morally acceptable.* Three mechanisms have emerged to provide a solution. The first, codes of ethics and review procedures adopted by associations of social scientists, represents a formalization of the norms and guidelines that might emerge among investigators and their immediate colleagues. The second, procedures developed and imposed by the federal government upon research within the United States, represents an attempt to exert control over biomedical research with human participants; these procedures have been extended to social science research. The third is the standards of conduct for all relationships between persons (natural and legally defined) within society, as embodied in the legal system, which is the final arbitrator of how one "person" may treat another "person." Selected issues related to research have received attention within the legal system.

PROFESSIONAL ASSOCIATIONS
AND CODES OF ETHICS

Those who study complex, technical subjects (in law, engineering, medicine, social science, or whatever) find satisfaction in discussing issues with those sharing similar interests; professional associations have thus developed in response to this universal tendency. Once established for intellectual discourse, they may be used for other goals. For example, there is often competition among professionals either for prestige or clients; professional associations may act as "referees" who set guidelines for competition for prestige (through rules related to the acceptance of articles for journal publication or election of officers) or clients (by specifying standards for advertising and attempting to regulate "client stealing").

While a number of professional codes of ethics have been adopted by associations, none seem to have developed out of a concern for assisting individual members to resolve moral dilemmas. The process seems to reflect a desire of members to exercise control over their colleagues to prevent actions they consider "unethical." When enough members express the same concerns, a set of explicit principles may be adopted to ensure that all members are aware of the rule and perhaps conform to it. Codes of ethics also reflect the shift in emphasis of professional associations. Once they are well established and their members develop a public image (of any type), the associations may begin to act as intermediaries between their members and society at large; and they will attend to those actions that promote public support of their members and their activities. A code of ethics may be developed to improve public support and avoid government and legal mechanisms designed to control the members.

Most professionals (those who deal with technical matters requiring specialized judgments) are involved with clients as lawyers, physicians, counselors, therapists, engineers, accountants, and so forth. It is no surprise to find that the majority of associations representing professionals have adopted codes of ethics that stress this relationship, one that involves the application of an explicit, accepted body of knowledge to practical affairs. The emphasis on application is found in statements and procedures regarding adequacy of preparation of those assisting the public, moderation in the promises of what can be accomplished, and mechanisms to ensure that the quality of assistance will meet minimal standards. Such control reflects one important factor that professionals emphasize: the evaluation of professional decisions by other professionals, who are aware of the situations involved and the limits on practitioner's ability to control outcomes. The lay public (which perhaps has accepted stereotypes promoted by some professionals) often expects them to have more control over outcomes (such as a disease or a court decision) than is actually possible. In extreme cases, when professional assistance to clients is of great consequence, a public regulatory mechanism may be developed in cooperation with the professional association; this often happens with physicians, lawyers, and accountants. In other cases, where most of the professionals are employed by large organizations, the associations develop codes that emphasize the characteristics of a model employee and the ideal form of the employment relationship, such as with engineers, teachers, and college professors.

If biomedical investigators are excluded, the number of associations representing professionals who do research with human participants is quite small; they include national associations of anthropologists, educational researchers, political scientists, psychologists, and sociologists. (The American Economic Association has not attended to any issues regarding the conduct of its members, either as applied professionals or investigators.) Those that have developed some position on research ethics have all followed similar procedures. A temporary committee is formed to draft a preliminary statement; they may ask for examples of unethical activities from the membership, develop issues from their own experience, or conduct a review of relevant literature or published cases. There is usually considerable controversy in developing the principles, and several revisions (with comments from members on each proposed revision) are generally produced. Once the principles have been adopted (either by a vote of all the members or an elected executive committee), they are considered binding; and a permanent committee, with a rotating membership, is formed to review complaints and problems—which tend to be few in number. In extreme cases, such a committee may recommend that a member considered to have engaged in unethical conduct be expelled from the association, but for some associations even this mild punishment is not possible.

Because of the size of its membership and the large proportion involved in applied work, the American Psychological Association (APA) has been more active in dealing with ethical concerns than other social science associations. Part of this effort has involved the systematic review of a large number of cases regarding ethical matters brought before the APA Committee on Scientific and Professional Ethics and Conduct (CSPEC)–over 200 cases in the forty-two months preceeding June 1980. Most are resolved informally, and some psychologists are temporarily suspended from membership in the APA; very seldom is a psychologist permanently ejected from the association (Sanders, 1979; Sanders & Keith-Spiegel, 1980).

Of the thirty-one cases published to demonstrate the activities of the CSPEC of the APA, only one involved a complaint regarding research (Sanders & Keith-Spiegal, 1980, p. 1105):

> A student participating in a university research subject pool complained that deception had been used during the experimental trial that caused the student to suffer considerable stress. The study did incorporate deception because the participants were led to believe that the purpose was to rate a film, when the dependent variable was their reaction to a realistically staged altercation between two people just outside a partially open door. The participant was thoroughly and immediately debriefed, made no objections at that point, but shortly thereafter complained to the department, university administration, media, and CSPEC.
>
> CSPEC wrote to the experimenter requesting an account of the incident and of what precautions had been taken to minimize stress reactions. The experimenter sent back copies of the study proposal, the human subject approval, and the debriefing procedure. A graduate assistant also supplied a letter describing favorable interactions with all other participants and of how attempts were made at the time of the debriefing to reassure the complainant. CSPEC agreed that appropriate procedures had been followed. It also noted that the experiment was exceptionally well designed and that its potential impact, regardless of the direction of the findings, would be far from trivial and could have considerable beneficial application.
>
> CSPEC wrote a sympathetic letter to the complainant indicating that after a careful review of the materials, it had decided no ethical principle violations had occurred in this instance.

The remaining thirty complaints involved work as applied professionals: incompetence, suitability of advertising, sexual relations with clients, appropriateness of psychological test interpretations, and the like. Complaints of research participant abuse is not a major source of committee work.

This procedure tends to work relatively well for applied professionals–the physician who fails to diagnose a common, obvious disease; the lawyer who steals from a client's trust fund–particularly when offenders can be prevented from continuing in their professionals capacities. But there are several problems associated with the application of this strategy to scientific investigators. The first is the absence of any meaningful sanctions—investigators can investigate even if they are not members of professional associations. Further, there is the inherent uncertainty of scientific research. If it were possible to predict the results of research (usually specified in terms of effects on participants), there would be no reason to conduct the research; research represents the study of the unknown. Hence, it is not possible to specify, in advance, what types of rules or principles should be followed to protect participants.

Finally, any code of ethics represents the current societal standards regarding current research procedures applied to phenomena of current interest to investigators. All three of these are likely to change—societal norms, research procedures, and phenomena of interest—in unpredictable ways. After such changes, fixed ethical principles may no longer apply to much research. Strangely enough, this obvious fact seems lost on most professional associations, for they prefer to create new codes of ethics every decade or so rather than develop a procedure for continuously adapting and revising ethical principles in response to the inevitable changes. One alternative—to develop general principles that will apply for a longer period of time—usually results in statements so imprecise that application to unique instances is ambiguous.

Despite the lack of any real consequences for investigators who fail to adhere to association codes of ethics and a general failure to encourage consultation in advance of conducting research, codes of ethics developed by professional associations for social science investigators do provide a set of issues that investigators should take into account when they review the moral status of a research endeavor. The codes of ethics current at the time of publication for four major social science associations are presented in Appendices 2 to 5. These rules undergo continual change, and those who have a serious interest in them should locate the most recent versions.

FEDERAL GUIDELINES:
PRIOR REVIEW

The development of federal procedures for prior review of research with human participants is dramatic evidence of the failure of associations to convince the public that either their members are to be trusted as individuals or that the associations are to be trusted to control them. (This failure is shared by associations representing biomedical investigators.) Initially implemented in 1966 and eventually extended to cover all research with federal support, the mechanism embodies two important strategies for moral analysis. The federal procedure emphasizes the necessary conditions for obtaining a full, complete informed consent from the participants, which reflects a concern for individual rights, particularly self-determination. Second, it also emphasizes prior review, or evaluation before research is initiated. Such committees (called Institutional Review Boards, or IRBs) are expected to engage in a risk (cost)-benefit analysis of research, which reflects a utilitarian approach to social issues. (See Robertson, 1979, for a more complete treatment of the legal aspects of the federal procedure.)

There are three major features of the federal mechanism for prior review of research: the scope of application, the nature of the prior review (the composition of the committees and their obligations), and standards for informed consent. The scope of application covers all research conducted within federal agencies or directly contracted by them (such as the Department of the Army, National Aeronautics and Space Administration, Environmental Protection Agency, and the like), all research on drugs and other medical devices that receive approval for use by the Food and Drug Administration (FDA) after testing (standards for treatment of human participants are part of the test specifications), and all research (contracts or grants) sponsored by the federal government, the greatest number occurring in the Department of Health and Human Services (DHHS) and the Department of Education (combined as the Department of Health, Education and Welfare until 1980). The regulation of research through the FDA is a special case; not only does it focus upon the testing of drugs and other types of medical therapy (including some mechanical devices), it must also monitor research that is often paid for by private pharmaceutical companies. Research involving human participants supported by other federal agencies is covered by separate rules and procedures of each agency. However, these are not only very similar, but there is a tendency to adopt DHHS procedures, as these are the most complete and highly developed.

The federal regulations developed by DHHS set minimal standards for the review and surveillance of research; local institutions may go beyond these federal minimums and many do. This has happened in the past and is certain to be the case for several years after January 26, 1981; on this date a substantial change was made in the federal regulations (*Federal Register 46*(16): 8366-8392) reducing the scope of prior review *required* for social science research. It may be some time before institutions revise their own procedures and "relax" the surveillance of investigators, if they wish to do so. Changes affect not only the scope of projects to be reviewed, but the criteria for review and standards for informed consent. The following discussion focuses upon the minimal procedures and criteria adopted by DHHS in January 1981; investigators should check with their own institutions to determine the regulations applicable to them.

The major change in the DHHS guidelines is the dramatic reductions in the scope of projects that must be submitted to a full committee review. This reduction in scope has occurred in three ways. First, the regulations explicitly apply only to research involving human participants conducted within the DHHS or supported wholly or in part by DHHS funds. This is in dramatic contrast to previous standards which government officials interpreted, in the midst of considerable controversy, as applying to all research conducted at an institution that accepted any federal funds for research with human participants. (It is no longer possible to claim that First Amendment rights to freedom of speech are threatened by federally imposed prior review, or prior restraint, of independent research.) However, policies regarding the review of nonfederally funded research are to be submitted as part of the material provided to DHHS (45 CFR Part 46.103[b] [1]) in the "assurance agreement," which describes how the institution will comply with the federal standards. While prior review of nonfederally funded research is no longer mandatory, it is considered evidence of an institutional "willingness to afford human research subject protections" and, by implication, a worthiness that justifies the receipt of federal funds (*Federal Register 46*(16): 8369).

Second, broad categories of research activity—regardless of the objectives of the research—have been defined as exempt from the regulations; these are listed in Exhibit 6-1. Included are experimental studies of educational innovations, secondary analysis of anonymous data (existing before the proposed research), routine use of educational tests, routine surveys and interviews, and routine field observations. These last three activities are considered so innocuous that unless *all* three critical conditions are present (sensitive data *and* ability to identify participants *and* potential for damage to participants), the research need not be reviewed; if only one or two of these features is present, review is not required. Note that except for educational innovations, no experimental research (where an investigator tries to "change" a participant) is included. This federal regulation is subject to infrequent changes; very seldom will additional research activities be added to this list.

EXHIBIT 6-1   Research Activities Exempt from Prior Review: DHHS Guidelines

---

b. Research activities in which the only involvement of human subjects will be in one or more of the following categories are exempt from the regulations unless the research is covered by other subparts of his part:

1. Research conducted in established or commonly accepted educational settings, involving normal educational practices, such as (i) research on regular and special education instructional strategies, or (ii) research on the effectiveness of or the comparison among instructional techniques, curricula, or classroom management methods.

2. Research involving the use of educational tests (cognitive, diagnostic, aptitude, achievement), if information taken from these sources is recorded in such a manner that subjects cannot be identified, directly or through identifiers linked to the subjects.

3. Research involving survey or interview procedures, except where all of the following conditions exist: (i) responses are recorded in such a manner that the human subjects can be identified, directly or through identifiers linked to the subjects; (ii) the subject's responses, if they became known outside the research, could reasonably place the subject at risk of criminal or civil liability or be damaging to the subject's financial standing or employability; and (iii) the research deals with sensitive aspects of the subject's own behavior such as illegal conduct, drug use, sexual behavior, or use of alcohol. All research involving survey or interview procedures is exempt, without exception, when the respondents are elected or appointed public officials or candidates for public office.

4. Research involving the observation (including observation by participants) of public behavior, except where all of the following conditions exist:

FIGURE 6-1 (continued)

(i) observations are recorded in such a manner that the human subjects can be identified, directly or through identifiers linked to the subjects; (ii) the observations recorded about the individual, if they became known outside the research, could reasonably place the subject at risk of criminal or civil liability or be damaging to the subject's financial standing or employability; and (iii) the research deals with sensitive aspects of the subject's own behavior such as illegal conduct, drug use, sexual behavior, or use of alcohol.

5. Research involving the collection or study of existing data, documents, records, pathological specimens, or diagnostic specimens, if these sources are publicly available or if the information is recorded by the investigator in such a manner that subjects cannot be identified, directly or through identifiers linked to the subjects.

From *Federal Register,* January 26, 1981: 8, 386-8, 387.

The third device used to reduce the need for a full, formal review of research has been the creation of a list of research techniques requiring only "expedited" review. An expedited review is performed by the chair of an IRB or an experienced committee member; they alone may approve a project, and only the full committee can disapprove it. The list of procedures that entitle a project to an expedited review is presented in Exhibit 6-2; most are related to biomedical data collection (nail clippings, blood samples, moderate exercise—but not X-rays). The expedited review list may be changed by the secretary of DHHS, which means that when he or she receives a recommendation (perhaps from the Office for Protection from Research Risks) the list may be modified. This is less cumbersome than modifying the federal regulations, and changes can be expected in the future; investigators should check for the latest version of the "expedited research activities list" in the *Federal Register.*

Some projects will require a full, formal review: these include those which receive federal funding and involve research procedures that are not exempt and do not allow for expedited review. For them, the IRB is expected to consider the extent to which risks to the participants are minimized, the relationships between risks and the anticipated benefits of research, and the importance of the knowledge to be developed. The IRB will also consider the equitable selection of subjects and the acquisition and documentation of informed consent; it will monitor participants when necessary to ensure their safety and make provisions for protecting their privacy. If participants are vulnerable to coercion (such as mental patients and children), additional safeguards should be considered.

There are two distinctive features of the analysis of risks and benefits required for an IRB. First, risks are to be considered only when they add to those that normally would be expected (e.g., the risks of experimental surgery in addition to those of routine surgery); minimal risk is equivalent to the risk of daily life. Second, the "possible long-range effects of applying the knowledge gained in research"—specifically its impact upon public policies—should *not* be considered. In short, the IRB should not speculate on the future uses of *potential* knowledge as a basis for

EXHIBIT 6-2   **Research Activities Suitable for Expedited Review:**
DHHS Guidelines

Research activities involving no more than minimal risk and in which the only involvement of human subjects will be in one or more of the following categories (carried out through standard methods) may be reviewed by the Institutional Review Board through the expedited review procedure authorized in § 46.110 of 45 CFR Part 46.

1. Collection of: hair and nail clippings, in a nondisfiguring manner; deciduous teeth; and permanent teeth if patient care indicates a need for extraction.

2. Collection of excreta and external secretions including sweat, uncannulated saliva, placenta removed at delivery, and amniotic fluid at the time of rupture of the membrane prior to or during labor.

3. Recording of data from subjects 18 years of age or older using noninvasive procedures routinely employed in clinical practice. This includes the use of physical sensors that are applied either to the surface of the body or at a distance and do not involve input of matter or significant amounts of energy into the subject or an invasion of the subject's privacy. It also includes such procedures as weighing, testing sensory acuity, electrocardiography, electroencephalography, thermography, detection of naturally occurring radioactivity, diagnostic echography, and electroretinography. It does not include exposure to electromagnetic radiation outside the visible range (for example, X-rays, microwaves).

4. Collection of blood samples by venipuncture, in amounts not exceeding 450 milliliters in an eight-week period and no more often than two times per week, from subjects 18 years of age or older and who are in good health and not pregnant.

5. Collections of both supra- and subgingival dental plaque and calculus, provided the procedure is not more invasive than routine prophylactic scaling of the teeth and the process is accomplished in accordance with accepted prophylactic techniques.

6. Voice recordings made for research purposes such as investigations of speech defects.

7. Moderate exercise by healthy volunteers.

8. The study of existing data, documents, records, pathological specimens, or diagnostic specimens.

9. Research on individual or group behavior or characteristics of individuals, such as studies of perception, cognition, game theory, or test development, where the investigator does not manipulate subjects' behavior and the research will not involve stress to subjects.

10. Research on drugs or devices for which an investigational new drug exemption or an investigational device exemption is not required.

From *Federal Register,* January 26, 1981: 8,392.

approving or disapproving research. As only the immediate importance of the knowledge is to be considered, this may be a difficult distinction to make.

The standards used by IRBs to determine if informed consent has been appropriately obtained are quite explicit and have become more elaborate. Under no condition are participants to expect they have given up any legal rights or released the investigators or sponsoring institutions from liability for negligence or mistakes. The standards are now divided into four parts, as presented in Exhibit 6-3. The first (a) covers the "basic elements" that are expected of all research. The second (b) are additional elements that may be required for projects with special hazards for participants. The third (c) refers to a major exception, social experiments with existing public programs, where informed consent may reduce the number and representativeness of the participants and affect confidence in the results. (Whether or not this new standard will quell the controversy over these social experiments is not clear.) The fourth category (d) covers "deception research," research in which participants cannot be fully informed of the research objectives if the scientific purposes are to be achieved; participants are usually informed afterwards.[1]

It is normally expected that informed consent will be documented (demonstrated) by acquiring a signature from the participant on a written consent form; participants should be allowed to keep a copy of such "minicontracts." In some cases, a "short form" is allowed, referring to an oral presentation that should be witnessed; this is designed for patients or others who may be unable to read, comprehend, and sign a written statement. Under some conditions the necessity for a signed consent statement may be waived by an IRB (45 CFR Part 46.117[c]): (1) if the only link between the participant and the data would be such a signature and there may be some potential harm from such an association; or (2) the research involves (a) minimal risk and (b) no procedures for which written consent is normally required outside a research context (such as telephone interviews). There is, then, considerable flexibility in terms of the form and documentation required for informed consent; IRBs have considerable leeway in this federal requirment.

A distinctive feature of the federal mechanism for control of research is that the actual decisions involving projects are made by the local institutions—that is, the organizational homes of investigators. In order to assure the DHHS they will make responsible decisions about research projects, the institutions must file "assurance" agreements with DHHS. These agreements describe the procedures to be used and must meet certain minimal standards regarding: institutional rules that guide evaluation of projects (they cannot take precedence over DHHS policy): the size of the institutional review board (there must be at least five members); the heterogeneity of the member's background (they can not be all of one gender or from one professional group, and at least one nonscientist must be present at each meeting); the relationship of board members to projects reviewed (none is allowed); the institutional affiliations of the members (at least one must be from outside the responsible institution): provisions for acquiring outside technical

---

[1] In a number of categories of participants the implementation of informed consent becomes more complex; special regulations have been developed for research involving fetuses, pregnant women, and human *in vitro* ("in glass"; e.g., "test tubes") fertilization (45 CFR Part 46, Subpart B), and prisoners (45 CFR Part 46, Subpart C). New regulations have been proposed for research involving children (*Federal Register 43* (141): 31,786–31,794; to be 45 CFR Part 46, Subpart C) and the institutionalized mentally disabled (*Federal Register 43* (223); 53,950-53,956; to be 45 CFR Part 46, Subpart E).

EXHIBIT 6-3   Elements of Informed Consent:
DHHS Guidelines

Except as provided elsewhere in this or other subparts, no investigator may involve a human being as a subject in research covered by these regulations unless the investigator has obtained the legally effective informed consent of the subject or the subject's legally authorized representative. An investigator shall seek such consent only under circumstances that provide the prospective subject or the representative sufficient opportunity to consider whether or not to participate and that minimize the possibility of coercion or undue influence. The information that is given to the subject or the representative shall be in language understandable to the subject or the representative. No informed consent, whether oral or written, may include any exculpatory language through which the subject or the representative is made to waive or appear to waive any of the subject's legal rights, or releases or appears to release the investigator, the sponsor, the institution or its agents from liability for negligence.

a. Basic elements of informed consent. Except as provided in paragraph (c) of this section, in seeking informed consent the following information shall be provided to each subject.

1. A statement that the study involves research, an explanation of the purposes of the research and the expected duration of the subject's participation, a description of the procedures to be followed, and identification of any procedures which are experimental;

2. A description of any reasonably foreseeable risks or discomforts to the subject;

3. A description of any benefits to the subject or to others which may reasonably be expected from the research;

4. A disclosure of appropriate alternative procedures or courses of treatment, if any, that might be advantageous to the subject;

5. A statement describing the extent, if any, to which confidentiality of records identifying the subject will be maintained;

6. For research involving more than minimal risk, an explanation as to whether any compensation and an explanation as to whether any medical treatments are available if injury occurs and, if so, what they consist of, or where further information may be obtained;

7. An explanation of whom to contact for answers to pertinent questions about the research and research subjects' rights, and whom to contact in the event of a research-related injury to the subject; and

8. A statement that participaton is voluntary, refusal to participate will involve no penalty or loss of benefits to which the subject is otherwise entitled, and the subject may discontinue participation at any time without penalty or loss of benefits to which the subject is otherwise entitled.

b. Additional elements of informed consent. When appropriate, one or more of the following elements of information shall also be provided to each subject.

1. A statement that the particular treatment or procedure may involve risks to the subject (or to the embryo or fetus, if the subject is or may become pregnant) which are currently unforeseeable;

2. Anticipated circumstances under which the subject's participation may be terminated by the investigator without regard to the subject's consent;

3. Any additional costs to the subject that may result from participation in the research;

FIGURE 6-3 (continued)

4. The consequences of a subject's decision to withdraw from the research and procedures for orderly termination of participation by the subject;

5. A statement that significant new findings developed during the course of the research which may relate to the subject's willingness to continue participation will be provided to the subject; and

6. The approximate number of subjects involved in the study.

c. An IRB may approve a consent procedure which does not include, or which alters, some or all of the elements of informed consent set forth above, or waive the requirement to obtain informed consent provided the IRB finds and documents that.

1. The research is to be conducted for the purpose of demonstrating or evaluating: (i) Federal, state, or local benefit or service programs which are not themselves research programs, (ii) procedures for obtaining benefits or services under these programs, or (iii) possible changes in or alternatives to these programs or procedures; and

2. The research could not practicably be carried out without the waiver or alteration.

d. An IRB may approve a consent procedure which does not include, or which alters, some or all of the elements of informed consent set forth above, or waive the requirements to obtain informed consent provided the IRB finds and documents that:

1. The research involves no more than minimal risk to the subjects;

2. The waiver or alteration will not adversely affect the rights and welfare of the subjects;

3. The research could not practicably be carried out without the waiver or alteration; and

4. Whenever appropriate, the subjects will be provided with additional pertinent information after participation.

e. The informed consent requirements in these regulations are not intended to preempt any applicable federal, state, or local laws which require additional information to be disclosed in order for informed consent to be legally effective.

f. Nothing in these regulations is intended to limit the authority of a physican to provide emergency medical care, to the extent the physician is permitted to do so under applicable federal, state, or local law.

From *Federal Register,* January 26, 1981: 8,389-8,390.

expertise (if needed); the frequency with which ongoing projects are reviewed (at least annually); and the actions taken if a problem is found with an ongoing project (it must be reported to the institutional officials and the secretary of DHHS).

One of the more subtle ambiguities in the federally imposed procedure is the dual purpose of the IRBs. First, they are expected to be representative of the community in which the research is being conducted, acting as surrogates for the host society (much as a jury or legislative body). Hence, the boards must include non-investigators and others who are not members of the institution. But second, IRBs are expected to represent the technical expertise necessary to evaluate the research procedures for their potential impact on the participants; this is reflected in the range of investigators and professionals (lawyers) required for the committees and in the option of acquiring highly specialized advice when needed (such advice will be more frequently needed for some experimental drug treatments or other complex technical activities). The IRBs will probably resolve these problems by adopting a different stance as they confront distinctive proposals.

This ambiguity is partially resolved by the responsibilities of others for decisions involving research. While no project can be conducted and receive federal funding without IRB approval, projects may be disapproved by other institutional officials, committees, or individuals within the federal government after receiving IRB approval. For ethically sensitive research (such as that involving human fetuses or prisoners), these additional reviews may be substantial. Very expensive projects may even be reviewed by Congress itself, which may attend to ethical or moral implications.

Several issues are unresolved regarding the current procedure for prior review of research. At present, there is no advantage for the investigators, aside from possible federal funding and a clearer conscience; even if a project is approved by an IRB, there is no provision for assisting an investigator if a participant brings legal action. The scientist's major defense is their personal poverty; in order to recover substantial damages, the institution and the funding agency would need to be the focus of a legal action. Second, there is no provision for an appeal by an investigator; there are no opportunities to present a case to other impartial decision makers if the research is disapproved by the IRB. This is, however, not a major issue since very few projects are disapproved; the usual case is to advise the investigator of changes required for approval (usually involving the informed consent form or procedure for maintaining anonymous data). Third, there is evidence that the prior review procedure has been affecting the choice of research activity, in addition to the administrative costs and project delays; some investigators report selecting research topics on the basis of IRB approval, not for their scientific or practical importance (Glynn, 1978; Seiler & Murtha, 1980). There are incidents, particularly where several ethics committee reviews are required (as when both a university and an institution responsible for participants, such as a hospital, have separate committees), of endless delays and confusion; occasionally innocuous projects fail to be initiated because of such mindless bureaucratic complications (Kipnis, 1979). Perhaps the new federal regulations will reduce some of these occurrences.

Federal Contract Research and Prior Review

An important distinction between research grants (where money is provided to support the "best efforts" of an investigator to develop knowledge) and research contracts (where money is paid for completion of a specific task) is associated with federal control of research contracts. In an attempt to improve the coordination of information collected by the federal government, the Office of Management and Budget (OMB) has the responsibility to examine and approve any new form developed by any federal agency to gather new information. The intent is to minimize unnecessary burdens on the public, especially small businesses, in filling out federal forms by improving coordination among agencies. While it is estimated that almost five thousand different reporting requirements (forms) require a total of 786 million hours of public effort each year, 73 percent of this time is associated with tax collections; and most of the effort is expended by businesses, not individual citizens. Program research and evaluation is considered to take 4 percent of this total time; general statistical reporting takes about 1 percent (Office of Management and Budget; *Federal Register, 45* (8): 2596).

While clearly the major focus of OMB prior review, required when more than nine respondents are involved, is on financial and economic matters, the review may also focus upon sensitive questions, "such as sex behavior and attitudes, religious beliefs, and other matters which are commonly considered private." To obtain approval, investigators dealing in such matters must submit a justification for collecting the data, specify the uses to be made of the data, supply explanations for the respondents, formulate procedures to secure consent, and devise mechanisms to protect participant anonymity and maintain confidentiality. This procedure has been severely criticized by investigators involved in contract research (Abt, 1979). The major complaints are related to the excessive time required for clearance and approved and the lack of attention to scientific research issues (preference is given to the total time required of the participants). OMB officials can express concern over the total research design, which they may not be competent to judge. Those engaged in federal contract research often add a cost, up to 20 percent of the total contract, for the OMB review. From $6 to $40 million of the $200 million spent annually for federally contracted survey research may be absorbed by this prior review requirement (Abt, 1979, p. 162). There is, as discussed in Chapter 3, little evidence that respondents are "damaged" or resent most research questionnaires.

LEGAL CONSTRAINTS

The final resolution of issues regarding the treatment of individuals by investigators, applied professionals, and government agencies rests with the legal system. Resolutions that develop within the legal system tend to be less precise than those produced by professional associations, legislation, or administrative procedures; but legal standards are considerably more influential in defining the boundaries for the treatment of research participants, as they have universal application, and violation may lead to substantial personal sanctions, including financial loss and incarceration.

Legal standards regarding the social science research enterprise—legislation and judicial decisions—emphasize the rights (or liberties) of parties (individuals, organizations, or the state) and the relationships (cooperative, competitive, or conflicting) between parties. Most of the attention in the legal system is given to resolving disputes between different parties when their rights are in conflict in a particular situation. However, this attention is selective, and only when a problem becomes obvious (because the parties involved or observers become aware of the major issues) and attracts the attention of the political or legal system is legislation passed or a court decision made. There are four such issues associated with the social science enterprise: individual rights that may be affected by research, the criteria for legally valid informed consent, rights of investigators (both individuals and governments), and special legal privileges for investigators (to maintain the anonymity of participants).

Individual Rights

Individual citizens become involved in scientific research in two different ways: as members of the general public they benefit from the results of research, and as participants they may experience some risk to their rights and welfare. While the U.S. Constitution mentions no specific right to conduct research, a number of important public benefits or rights are recognized through legislation, including:

1. The right to a general expansion of knowledge.
2. The right to the development and maintenance of a body of knowledge useful for societal problems.
3. The right to a public accounting of the conduct of programs designed to promote public objectives.
4. The right to assurance that scientific programs are conducted within accepted moral and ethical standards.

While individual investigators, with public support, may be involved in the exercise of these rights, several—particularly the second and third—are often emphasized in government research.

Individual participants may be involved with two types of investigators: individuals (or an organization legally defined as an individual, such as a research center) or the government (as represented by a specific project conducted under contract to the government). In either case, a number of individual rights are legally established: self-determination (choice, liberty), life (personal security, freedom from physical abuse or mental stress), privacy, dignity and respect, thought, travel, and property. When the government acts as the investigator, and partcularly when participation is not voluntary, special individual rights become involved—especially those dealing with the individual's relation to the state: equality of treatment and due process.

Relinquishing Rights

The ultimate legal justification for guaranteed rights or liberties is to provide a restraint on the influence or power of the government leaders responsible for the administration of the state. As rights are "owned" by the individual, it is assumed that the individual may forego such rights if he or she wishes; they are transferable, or "noninalienable." However, this is not true for all rights, such as the right to life, freedom from mayhem, or actions that would constitute a public nuisance (violating the rights of others). Because the king in earlier times (representing the state) was thought to be entitled to healthy, productive citizens (who could engage in work and combat), it was illegal for the individual to forego the right to life (agree to self-murder or suicide) or mayhem (an action that disables, disfigures, or renders a body useless). The modern justification for a nontransferable right to life and avoidance of mayhem is the assumption that all individuals should be capable of making productive contributions to society; to consent to mayhem could lead to becoming a ward of the state (Annas, Glantz, & Katz, 1977, pp. 50-53). This is the major rationale for prohibiting or regulating activities such as dangerous sports that could maim or cripple willing participants and for encouraging individuals to take "reasonable" safety precautions, such as using seat belts in cars and wearing helmets when riding motorcycles.

Except for these special rights, individuals are allowed the privilege of relinquishing almost any other rights they may have. The legal action (which is recognized by the courts) that transfers these rights is the giving of *consent*. A concise history of the development of the legal notion of consent, and its increasing importance, is provided by Capron (1975, p. 137): "In the thirteenth century the criminal law against forcible injuries was extended to civil action for trespass. The interferences encompassed by the early law were so direct, severe, and even violent that the absence of consent could be assumed; as the scope for action for trespass increased, the absence of consent became an element of the cause of action. Some offenses might be illegal if committed without consent, but permissible with it or if consent were implied from the context. The rule that absence of consent is an element of action for assault and battery applied to medical treatment, as elsewhere." In short, if a person is modified or changed in substantial ways without his consent, that may be considered a trespass upon, or battery (unlawful touching) of, the person.

Legal developments regarding the consent of research participants have revolved around medical research, most frequently in a clinical setting where the physician is "trying out" a new therapy for the benefit of the participant. Criteria specifying legally valid consent were explicated (along with other important principles) by the Nuremberg tribunal during the trial of Nazi medical researchers accused of misusing prisoners (Jews, political dissents, prisoners of war, and so on). Emphasizing the existing practices in medical research (the tribunal was advised by a physician-investigator), the first statement of the Nuremberg Code (see Appendix 1) focuses upon informed consent, which is interpreted as having four important characteristics (Annas, Glantz, & Katz, 1977, pp. 6-7):

1. The individual must be legally competent to give consent.
2. The consent must be voluntary (free from force, fraud, duress, coercion, and the like).
3. The individual should have sufficient knowledge to make an enlightened decision.
4. The individual should understand, or comprehend, the elements of the subject matter (should know the possible outcomes and risks associated with each).

A review of judicial decisions related to medical research suggests that only the first three elements are required for therapeutic situations (where a patient is expected to receive direct benefits from the new procedure), but all four are considered necessary for any nontherapeutic research (Annas, Glantz, & Katz, 1977, p. 54).

Two important points have emerged from the recent trends in court decisions on medical research. First, the standard regarding what information is to be provided to a participant has shifted from what other physician-investigators have done to "all the facts, probabilities, and opinions which a reasonable man might be expected to consider before giving his consent." The standard is set by judicial judgments of what a "reasonable" person would want to know. Second, a review of court decisions on physicians engaged in medical practice (not research) suggests that "while many physicians complained bitterly about the informed consent doctrine, it is, in fact, almost impossible for a patient to win a suit founded on failure to obtain informed consent in the absence of independent negligence in the treatment by the physician" (Annas, Glantz, & Katz, 1977, p. 58). And if the absence of informed consent alone has not been sufficient in these medical cases, it is unlikely to be the basis for any action against social science investigators. If a participant (and his lawyer) could show that substantial harm had been created by the research experience and that legally valid informed consent had not been obtained, then a suit for damages may prevail—if there is some legal way to estimate the monetary value of social science "damages." The difficulty of the latter makes it unlikely that a lawyer (who expects a percentage of the settlement) would be interested in developing such a case.

The major problems with the informed consent criteria for social science research lie not so much in the information provided to the participants as in determining if they are legally competent to give consent and are free from coercion and duress. For example, special concerns develop about research with children, prisoners, and the mentally infirm. In most cases the guardians of children are expected to make a decision for them as long as they may receive direct therapeutic benefit; if nontherapeutic research is involved, the children must give consent as well. (But when is a child too young to give such consent?) Concerns develop about individuals in situations where minor rewards and privileges gain substantial value; there is concern that prisoners are never able to choose voluntarily, and special standards have been developed for research with them. Institutionalized mental patients involve both problems, concern about competence to make a decision, and unpleasant conditions that may make them unusually susceptible to inducements. A distinction is now made between legal competence and the basis for institutionalization; the conditions under which a legal guardian may make a decision for a mental patient are uncertain.

The legal definition of informed consent causes two problems for research. First, there is the assumption that the participant's knowledge of the research will not affect the research phenomenon itself; it is now clear that in many cases a participant's knowledge of the details of the scientific objectives does affect his experiencing and reporting of the phenomenon. The second lies in the assumption that informed consent should be required for all research, even if the data are collected in public or there are no direct effects on the participants. While alternatives have been developed in federal research regulations, there has been little specific attention to these issues within the legal system, perhaps because no cases of "damage" have been associated with social science research, whether or not informed consent was acquired.

Investigators' Rights

There is little question that investigators have a "right to research." While not specifically mentioned in the First Amendment, one analysis suggests that if a case arose such a right would be recognized by the Supreme Court (Robertson, 1978); since the publication and reading of a scientific article cannot be prohibited (a First Amendment freedom), it would be anomalous to prevent the research leading to its publication. This does not mean, however, that research procedures affecting the rights of others, such as participants, would not be restricted by the legal system. But there are at least two other rights of investigators that have received some attention from the legal system: the right of privacy with regard to unfunded research proposals and the right to maintain the confidentiality of research data and participants' identities.

Some of the most careful and thoughtful work of scientists is incorporated into research proposals, formal requests for government financial support for a research project. Obviously, investigators want to have the first opportunity to conduct research and determine if an idea has scientific or practical utility. Any premature disclosure would be considered an invasion of privacy and a threat to an investigator's right to receive credit for intellectual contributions. While there is little controversy over making a proposal public after it has been awarded government funds, there has been uncertainty over the status of proposals before funding decisions are made. Requests for the disclosure of unfunded research proposals have been made under the Freedom of Information Act and have been supported by judicial decisions (*Washington Research Project* v. DHEW et al., 1973). The most recent interpretations of the DHHS have led to maintainence of research proposal confidentiality, but the names of investigators submitting proposals that are not funded may not be confidential.[2] In fact, investigators will be informed if

---

[2] A civil action in a First Circuit District Court (Kurzon vs. DHHS; No. 76-3505; Judge Mazzone; August 21, 1980) was decided in favor of retaining confidentiality of unfunded investigators' identities. Dr. Kurzon (who requested the names to study the extent to which the peer review system was biased against innovation and creative ideas) appealed and the decision was reversed by the U.S. Court of Appeals for the First Circuit (No. 80-1695; Chief Judge Coffin, May 22, 1981). The DHHS argued that the identity of investigators who were not funded was "sensitive" and that the stigma associated with a failure to receive support could have a negative effect upon their careers. The basis for the DHHS position was Exemption 6 of the Freedom of Information Act; this protects "personnel and medical files and similar invasions of personal privacy"; the court of appeals did not consider failure to obtain support for research particularly sensitive. As this case may be appealed to the U.S. Supreme Court, the final decision has yet to be made. A useful source of summaries, explanations, and analyses of new and pending government disclosure laws (including the Freedom of Information Act, the Privacy Act of 1974, and the Government in the Sunshine Act), regulations, court decisions, guidelines, and forms is the Prentice-Hall loose-leaf service, *Government Disclosure*.

someone has requested a copy of funded research proposal and been given an opportunity to remove sensitive data (e.g., salary schedules) or critical information (a patentable idea that has not been processed).

Perhaps the greatest amount of discussion, particularly among social scientists, has been on the right to keep research data and participants' identities private and immune from legal subpoena. Rumors and actual examples of infringement upon this "right," knowledge that physicians and lawyers have such a privilege, and the well-publicized cases involving newspersons (who appear to be gaining support for a "newsperson's shield")—all have encouraged social science investigators to think that such a right is justified.[3] Given this perspective on empirical research and its potential for contributing toward society, social scientists are concerned—and are often indignant—when they discover that research data and sources are not immune from the subpoena process, even when cooperating respondents are promised confidentiality and anonymity.

The legal basis for not recognizing promises of confidentiality is based upon the assumption that all citizens have a duty to provide information to assist the legal and legislative systems in executing their responsibilities; these encompass criminal trials, grand juries, legislative bodies (e.g., Senate hearings), civil trials, and administrative agencies. It is assumed that the interest of all citizens—the public interest—is best served when such disclosures can be expected as an obligation and duty. The power to require individuals to produce relevant information—personal accounts or written records—encourages individuals to discharge this "duty." For this reason, private information exchanged between close friends is not considered to be immune from legal subpoena. Even the legal protection given to communication (verbally, in writing, by gesture, personal presence, and so forth) between spouses is carefully defined and does not extend to information exchanged before or after marriage, communications overhead by a third party, civil cases in federal courts, legal action related to the marital relationship, or criminal proceedings affecting the interests of the other spouse or family members, such as child abuse (Gard, 1972, p. 748). In brief, there is no legal recognition of guarantees of confidentiality between individuals.

Social scientists, aware of professional-client relationships receiving legal protection, may consider these as analogous to the investigator-participant relationship and support giving legal protection to confidential information. While it is true that physician-patient, lawyer-client, priest-penitent relationships have some protection, these are carefully circumscribed and have almost always been established by legislative statute, instead of emerging through a history of court descisions. The lawyer-client privilege does not extend to knowledge of future intentions to commit a crime; advice on how to minimize the illegality of future actions makes the attorney an accomplice. The physician-patient privilege generally extends to civil actions only, not to criminal cases; and physicians may be required to report cer-

---

[3] See Carroll, 1973; Carroll and Knerr, 1976, 1977; Feuillan, 1976; Hendel and Bard, 1973; Kershaw and Small, 1972; Nejelski and Lerman, 1971; Nejelski and Finsterbusch, 1973; Shaw, 1969; "Social Research and . . . ," 1970.

tain information to the authorities: wounds made by weapons, certain contagious diseases, and suspected cases of child abuse (Gard, 1972).

Psychologist-client relationships are perhaps closest to those of social science investigators; at least thirty-three states have laws that provide a privilege of confidentiality for psychologists in consulting relationships with clients (Shah, 1969). A recent incident modified the scope of this privilege. The parents of a young woman murdered by a clinical psychologist's patient sued for damages on the grounds that the psychologist had advance knowledge of the intent to harm the victim (the young woman) and failed to warn the victim or her parents; the court determined that the psychologists' "duty to warn" was more serious than the patient's right to a confidential conversation (Annas, 1976).

This latter case involves the critical feature of all professional-client legal protection: they are established for the benefit of the client, patient, penitent, or whatever. The privilege does not apply to the professional, but to the client; if a client chooses to disclose the information, it must be done, regardless of the consequences to the professional (Gard, 1972).

The special legal protection afforded newspersons is often seen as analogous to a social scientist's privilege, but the justification for the former is quite different. First, it is part of the First Amendment to the Constitution. Second, a newsperson's privilege is not widely recognized in federal laws, although by 1973 at least twenty-five states had adopted legislation related to privileges for newspersons (Cook, 1973). Newspersons are currently required to seek federal immunity on a case-by-case basis—after a supoena has been issued (Nejelski & Finsterbusch, 1973).[4] While there has been considerable controversy, it has been related to criminal cases (newspersons generally receive immunity for civil cases). The "newsperson's shield" argument was part of a general argument against providing research documents subpoenaed as part of a civil trial. A study of organizational decision making was conducted at the time major equipment was ordered by a public utility, and this purchase was the focus of a civil case. However, the decision in favor of the investigator was based on the source of "best evidence"; executive testimony was preferred over research notes. Neither issue was related to the "freedom to research" (Culliton, 1976).

While the status of newspersons' privilege is currently less than clear cut, the relationship of an investigator's status to the First Amendment privilege of freedom of the press is even more ambiguous. Although much descriptive social science is similar to the activities of newspersons (it has been referred to as "slow journalism"), a great deal of social science research is distinctly different, particularly when natural events are affected by the investigator (as in experiments), when

---

[4]However, the Privacy Protection Act of 1980 (Public Law 96-440) restricts *unannounced* searches for background material collected to produce a work product intended for sale and distribution in interstate commerce (book, newspaper or journal article, television or radio show, and so on). Applicable to newspersons, scholars, authors, or ordinary persons, the act does not prevent the legal subpoena of material, but does require an advance notice (with a few exceptions) and will allow a legal challenge to the subpoena before the material can be seized by authorities.

special data collection techniques are used (as in projective tests, measures of physiological responses, sophisticated questionnaires, and the like), or when special analysis is conducted to determine patterns and relationships not obvious on initial examination. Attempts to provide legal protection for social science investigators by the analogy to newspersons would, at best, only cover a portion of social science research activities. For this reason, and because there is no court-established legal protection, several model statutes have been proposed (Boness & Cordes, 1973; Nejelski & Peyser, 1975); all specify that the privilege is that of the investigator, not the participant providing the information, although the permission of both would be required to divulge specific information.

Despite the general lack of legal protection for social science data, there are several exceptions. Two are related to the federal collection of social science data. While it is permissible to provide summaries of the U.S. Census data, the data collection itself is required by the Constitution, and the legal status of the original data is quite clear: ". . . in no case shall information furnished . . . be used to the detriment of the persons to whom such information relates" (Title 13, USC, Statute 8 [C]). Further, only sworn officers and employers are allowed to examine individual reports, and no data may be furnished that would allow identification of any establishment or individual. Regulations covering the records of the Social Security Administration emphasize the preservation of confidentiality, although a number of administrative activities, such as settling claims for benefits, require that information be made available (Title 20, CFR Part 401); nineteen purposes are described as justifying disclosure.

There is also a mechanism that gives a measure of legal protection to individual projects, usually in response to an application by an investigator. This was first provided as part of the Drug Abuse Prevention and Control Act of 1970 and later incorporated in the Drug Abuse Office and Treatment Act of 1972. If an investigator studying drug abuse or drug treatment programs makes application to the secretary of DHEW (now DHHS), he may be authorized to protect the "privacy of patients" (research subjects). Persons so authorized "may not be compelled in any federal, state, or local civil, criminal, administrative, legislative or other proceedings" to identify research subjects. The guarantees of the 1970 act were the key issue when a witness to a murder testified that he had seen the offender run into a drug treatment clinic where she had been a patient; she thought she had seen the individual in a waiting room on a previous visit. Photographs of all research participants with characteristics similar to those of the suspect were subpoenaed; the director of the project refused to provide the information and was cited for contempt. The contempt ruling was overturned by the U.S. Court of Appeals on the grounds that the federal statute was unambiguous and that all proper procedures had been followed to acquire authorization for immunity from subpoena before the project was initiated; several federal agencies filed briefs on behalf of the investigator (*People* v. *Newman*, 1973).

A further extension of this general plan, legal protection for specific projects, was incorporated in the Omnibus Crime Control and Safe Streets Act of 1976, generally known as the act establishing the LEAA (Law Enforcement Assistance Administration). Those applying for federal support, in whole or in part, for a project under this act are *required* to submit a "privacy certificate" as a condition of approval if information that could lead to the identification of a private person is to be collected. Personal information may not be revealed without the consent of the individual involved (an investigator may be fined if he were to do so), and "shall be immune from legal process, and shall not, without the consent of the person furnishing such information, be admitted as evidence or used for any purpose in any action, site, or other judicial or administrative proceedings" (Title 42 USC Statute 3771 (1976)). Unfortunately, in at least one instance local authorities did not recognize the authority of this federal law, and investigators were not able to prevent a local subpoena (Carroll & Knerr, 1977, p. 3). It might be mentioned that the protection of the act does not extend to specific plans regarding future criminal conduct, which may be demanded by law enforcement authorities (Reatig, 1979).

The third version of this procedure (Title 42 CFR Part 2a, published in the *Federal Register* on April 4, 1979) allows investigators conducting any type of research to apply for a "confidentiality certificate," authorized by the secretary of DHHS. The secretary may authorize persons engaged in research to protect the privacy of individuals who are subjects of such research by withholding their names or other identifying characteristics from those not connected with the research; investigators may not be compelled in any federal, state, or local civil, criminal, administrative, legislative or other proceedings to identify such individuals. A distinctive feature of this procedure is that the research need not be federally funded— any investigator may apply. Investigators must observe a number of limitations in the confidentiality certificate that are specific to projects and are not provided in a general program of research, such as informing the participants of the certificate's existence and that it does not constitute approval of the research objectives by the secretary of DHHS. Nor does it prevent, as does the LEAA privacy certificate, investigators from voluntarily disclosing information; participants are not able to prevent such actions.

The State as Investigator

There are many situations in which the state (in the form of federal, state, or local government agencies) may conduct research. If the participants have the freedom not to particiapte, the relationship of the investigator (the state) to the participants is similar to a project conducted by a natural person. However, there are a number of instances where the state may actually conduct experiments without the consent of those most directly affected. Such experiments may involve simple technical devices, such as noise barriers separating a freeway from a residential area (which may also interfere with the sunlight, view, and breezes for the dwellings adjacent to the barriers) or complex plans such as those that provide work training and employment counseling for welfare recipients or that require a token payment for medical services provided to the financially disadvantaged. In these latter cases, the critical legal feature is the lack of choice on the part of the participants; the confidence in the effects of such administrative innovations would be severely reduced if substantial numbers of potential participants elected not to participate.

From a legal perspective, such research programs can be considered government activities and are thereby related to the rights of any citizen with regard to all government actions—specifically, the rights to due process and equal treatment (Breger, 1976; Capron, 1975). The basic justification for the procedural criteria of due process and equal treatment is to ensure that the judiciary and elected officials, who are responsible for administering society, do not take capricious and irresponsible actions that will infringe upon the fundamental rights of citizens or that such infringements take place only when there is ample justification. In a sense, this justification recognizes that contributions to public well-being require the infringement of individual rights. But it also calls for careful attention to all critical elements and a mechanism that will allow for the implementation of decisions based on a utilitarian analysis. As with the basic justification for rights themselves, due process and equal treatment are seen as additional protections of citizens against unjustified abuse by public officials.

Due process was included in the Constitution to ensure that major individual rights—life, liberty, property, and movement—would not be restricted without the "regular course of administration through courts of justice" (Fifth Amendment to the Constitution). Legitimate infringement upon these rights takes the form of penalties for a violation of a criminal law (that is, a serious infringement upon the rights of others). This concept has since been expanded to mean that "law shall not be unreasonable, arbitrary, or capricious, and that means selected shall have real and substantial relation to object (or goals)" (Black, 1968, p. 590). In other words, due process is now applied to a wide variety of government programs, many of which are not directly related to trials of those accused of criminal acts.

The second constraint, equal treatment, has been legally defined as: "Equal protection and security shall be given to all under like circumstances in his life, liberty, and his property, and in the pursuit of happiness, and in the exemption from any greater burdens and charges than are equally imposed upon all others under like circumstances" (Black, 1968, p. 631). In essence, there should be very strong justification for treating individuals unequally, and courts have given "strict scrutiny" if differentiation is made on the basis of sex, race, or religion or if fundamental rights are involved (Breger, 1976, p. 28).

While the requirement of equal treatment is not critical for descriptive research, where the effects on participants are usually minor, it is of greater consequence when true experiments are conducted; they necessarily involve "unequal treatment" so that the effects of such "inequality" can be systematically measured and related to the variation in the outcome. A number of court cases have arisen over social experiments, and the provision of differential treatment has been one of the major issues.

In general, government-sponsored experimental research is more likely to receive approval by the courts if several characteristics are present:

1. The objectives of the research activity have been approved (legitimated) by elected officials.
2. The purpose of the research activity is reasonably related to legitimate objectives of a public program.
3. The design of the research provides appropriate means for achieving the research objectives.
4. The design of the research minimizes the burdens and discomforts of the participants, compared to alternative designs, while achieving the research objectives.
5. No participant is expected to experience burdens greater than those that would occur in the absence of the research.
6. Any procedure that discriminates among participants does so because of the research objectives; random assignment is an appropriate procedure for some goals.

If the participants can choose not to be involved, many of these features may not be considered crucial.

The fundamental basis for government-sponsored research—in which citizens are required to participate—is the "consent of the governed," which is represented by the approval of elected officials. The elected officials provide surrogate informed consent for all the members of society. The more details of the research procedures and techniques approved by the elected officials, the greater the possibility that the courts will approve the research. Societal administrators have systematically tried to develop better, or more efficient, programs ever since there have been administrators, but only recently have the intellectual and methodological techniques of science been incorporated into such activities. It would appear that the administrators of society have a right—almost a duty—to engage in research to improve their effectiveness or efficiency; it is clear that such research is expected to provide recognition of the individual rights of liberty, self-determination, equality of treatment, and due process.

CONCLUSION

Investigators are likely to continue to confront two problems: developing confidence in their decisions on the conduct of research and convincing others that their actions are morally acceptable. There may be some assistance for the first problem from the statements in the professional codes of ethics, but professional associations themselves are generally not designed to provide assistance prior to the conduct of the research. They do provide a forum for initiating investigations into the activities of members, if members are suspected of unethical conduct. The codes of ethics provide general guidance on issues to consider; seldom can they provide unambiguous guidance regarding a specific project.

Federally required prior review of research by an Institutional Review Board may provide "quasi-official" approval of a project, but the membership is generally composed of individuals with such diverse training that it is unlikely they are able to evaluate the scientific worth of many projects. In some cases they are able to provide technical assistance in informed consent procedures or in improving the confidentiality of data. A growing number of IRBs apply criteria more stringent than those required by the federal guidelines or warranted by the evidence regarding the effects of research experiences for the participants (when virtually no evidence of permanent damage is available). Despite the administrative costs and redirection of research generated by the IRB prior review, there have been no systematic attempts to determine the "benefits" of the review procedure; research that is approved is assumed to be "more ethical." The new federal regulations allow institutions to avoid prior review of a great many social science research projects (especially those whose procedures have little effect on participants); if institutions will take advantage of this opportunity to modify their own procedures, they may avoid a substantial administrative expense and inconvenience that has provided little advantage for most participants or investigators.

Though the development of legal standards for medical experimentation has a long history, few established legal principles are directly applicable to social science investigations. The major effect upon social science research has been exerted by legal and political philosophies related to individual rights and the conditions under which they may be relinquished—the criteria for informed consent. While the threat of a legal subpoena of social science data is an ever-present danger, it has not been exercised very often (less than a dozen have been identified; Reynolds, 1979, p. 317); they are much more frequent among newspersons (as many as one in five may have received one; Blasi, 1971). The various confidentiality certificates may allow projects exploring sensitive issues to receive, in advance, federal immunity from subpoenas (but they may not prevent a financial audit or review of the quality control).[5] One alternative is to collect and organize data in such a way to make it impossible for anyone to identify individual participants from the information in the research files, an expensive and cumbersome procedure (Boruch & Cecil, 1979a).

It would appear that investigators will continue to be required to complete their own moral analysis to determine if they will be comfortable with a research project. Conforming to external control systems may provide some evidence they have not grossly transgressed professional, local, or societal standards; their own detailed analysis may provide the most convincing evidence that the research is morally acceptable.

---

[5] Federal legislation has, however, been introduced that would provide more general protection to social science research data; as of the fall of 1980, it has not yet reached the stage of committee hearings (Gray, 1980).

CHAPTER SEVEN
APPLICATIONS OF
SCIENTIFIC KNOWLEDGE

Social scientists, much like other investigators, are generally motivated by two interests: a fascination with phenomena, to be understood through study and research, and a concern for improving the human condition. A crucial feature in the organization of advanced societies is that the responsibility for the development of knowledge is generally separate from the responsibility for practical affairs in business, government, or the applied professions; different groups specialize in each. The major issue becomes how and to what extent scientific investigators may influence those responsible for practical affairs—business executives, government leaders, and applied professionals—when they utilize scientific knowledge.

Two different situations will be singled out for discussion. The first is the case where scientific knowledge has been developed and made publicly available (until it is openly shared, scientific knowledge is not generally considered to be useful), and there is concern that the public at large is not receiving maximum, or appropriate, benefits from this new information. The major issue is the extent to which the originating scientists are responsible for and can control the application of new knowledge, or minimize the negative effects or benefits foregone. The second situation is the case where social scientists become involved in applied problems, either by participating in basic research directly related to specific objectives, developing programs that implement scientific knowledge for practical purposes, or assisting in assembling information for decisions regarding action programs (the focus of evaluation research). In this latter case, they may have more personal influence on the use of knowledge.

INFLUENCING APPLICATIONS
OF EXISTING KNOWLEDGE

The application of existing knowledge may be a cause for concern to investigators in a number of ways. It may be used to achieve questionable objectives: it may result in inappropriate or misleading interpretations: it may be applied in the wrong way; or it may not be used for its maximum potential benefit. For each type of "harm," as defined by the social scientist, a systematic analysis could consider the nature of the negative effects, the source of responsibility for them and, finally, how a social scientist might control them.

The Misuse of New Knowledge

Social scientists may experience moral reservations when the application of newly developed scientific knowledge results in negative consequences—consequences inconsistent with their personal values.

Perhaps the most dramatic examples of misapplication of social (and biomedical) science involve its use in the torture or interrogation of prisoners, particularly those considered politically "dangerous." Social science techniques, including those developed in sensory deprivation research (Watson, 1978, pp. 266-76), may be used to mislead prisoners into revealing information they wish to keep secret (Vasquez & Resezcynski, 1976). Procedures may be applied to increase the discomfort of political prisoners or return them to a "preinterrogation" condition; this could facilitate the effectiveness of additional interrogation or help to disguise the techniques that had been used (Gellhorn, 1978; Sagan & Josen, 1976). It is not clear whether such therapeutic treatments serve the interests of the "patient-prisoners" or of the interrogators. Concern over the misuse of medical knowledge and the moral status of cooperating physicians led to the adoption of an explicit policy on torture by the World Medical Association ("Declaration of Tokyo . . . ," 1976).

Less heinous and more controversial examples of possible misuse would include behavior modification techniques. Behavior modification refers to a series of techniques for modifying the behavior of individuals by providing systematic, explicit rewards following desired behavior and, in some cases, the imposition of punishment following undesirable behavior (Krasner & Ullman, 1965). While most successful applications have occurred in situations where the "modifying agent" has complete control over the life of the individual undergoing modification, as in mental institutions, the army, or educational settings, some success has occurred where only partial control over the individual was possible. (There are even cases where individuals reward and punish themselves.)

Now that these techniques have had a history of success, those who help refine them are often concerned that they will be used for purposes other than the best interests of the individuals being "modified." Others have been worried that the power to affect the autonomy of an individual—who may not be able to distinguish between voluntary actions and action taken, perhaps unconsciously, to receive rewards in a behavior modification treatment—will be misused. The controversy is somewhat complicated by ambiguity over the nature of "legitimate" rewards (grades, job promotions, pay raises) and punishments (fines or jail sentences) versus those rewards (candies, prison pay, inmate privileges) or punishments (denials of privileges, mild electric shock, or noxious buzzers) considered by some to be "illicit" or "unnatural."

In ordinary usage, the concept of responsibility usually carries the connotations of an intent to achieve some objective and an ability to control the utilization of a device or procedure. While scientists may provide individuals with new alternatives for achieving objectives, they may not make the final decision regarding the objective and how it is to be achieved. Hence, desensitization techniques may be used to reduce the stress of daily life by helping individuals to overcome excessive fears of snakes, water, or heights; on the other hand, such techniques can be used to acclimate individuals to violence and brutality and increase their efficiency as assassins (Watson, 1978, p. 249). Aptitude tests may be used to select individuals who will be more effective as physicians or members of elite antiterrorist teams. Behavior modification techniques have been considered appropriate for calming hyperactive school children so they and their classmates can learn more but inappropriate for use with convicted child molesters (it is argued they should not be "involuntary" discouraged from future acts of child molestation). In all cases, the actual application of these techniques has been a conscious decision by those who have a specific objective and control over how it is to be achieved. It would be inappropriate to blame the originating scientists for specific and unforeseen—indeed, unforeseeable—applications if the ordinary sense of responsibility is retained (with its connotations of intent and control).

Four options are available to social scientists wishing to have an impact upon the utilization of new scientific or technical knowledge. If neither the scientific theories nor operational devices and techniques exist, investigators may influence the application of new knowledge in two ways: (1) they can refuse to participate in the development of new knowledge or techniques when applications are expected to be inconsistent with their own personal or political values; or (2) they can participate with the understanding that applications will be under the control of the contributing investigators or others approved by the investigators. The refusal to participate will always be effective in reducing personal responsibilty; it will be effective in blocking the ultimate development and application of scientific knowledge only if no other competent investigators are willing to contribute to the endeavor—an unlikely event in most areas of social science. The second alternative, investigator control over the final applications, seems quite unlikely, particularly after the knowledge or technique becomes widely available.

If, however, the knowledge, techniques, or devices have been fully developed and can be utilized to achieve practical effects at any time, two additional alternatives are available to investigators: (3) they can attempt to inform the decision makers or the general public of the consequences of various applications and recommend policies or procedures that may minimize negative effects; or (4) they can encourage the development of supranational organizations to control the use of new devices or techniques in such a way that the interests of the entire world, rather than a specific country, are given consideration (Auger, 1956). This last alternative does not appear to warrant serious consideration; existing international governments seem to have limited influence upon the member nations. It is unlikely that one organized by scientists would be more effective, even if it could come into existence.

The third alternative, influencing and persuading decision makers or the general public, is widely mentioned as a responsibility of scientists—the responsibility to inform others of the possible consequences of a new technique or procedure. The major problem that arises is differentiating technical judgments from personal political values. If these are not clearly seperated, it is difficult for the audience to determine whether they are being presented with objective technical advice worthy of careful consideration or just another political message with a new gimmick to gain attention. The long-term consequences for not maintaining a clear distinction between technical judgments and personal values could be substantial; the perceived value of the social science enterprise for society will be reduced if it is considered to be another avenue for political pressure and not a source of unbiased knowledge. This may already be occuring (Brandl, 1978).

Misleading Interpretations
of Research Data

The misuse of new knowledge may involve the descriptive data collected in the course of a project. While there is little potential for damage to participants during the collection of descriptive data, they may experience negative effects if the data are used by others who have some influence on their lives.

For example, a study designed to establish the relationship between XXY chromosome patterns in adolescent boys and violent delinquent behavior would have involved the examination of 6,000 youths incarcerated in juvenile jails and 7,500 from underprivileged families. Controversy developed when it was made public that the research data on the incarcerated youths would be given to the staff of the juvenile correctional agencies. This would constitute a breach of confidential information on research subjects regarding characteristics that were not (and are not) considered to be reliably related to delinquent and criminal behavior (Katz, 1972, pp. 342-46). This information could have been used by correctional facility personnel in their decisions about these individuals; the project was cancelled before any data were collected.

A second variation of the problem of data on aggregates or social categories occurs when a social scientist publishes data that are given unexpected and unintended interpretations—to the disadvantage of the research participants. One such example, reported by the social scientists involved (Rainwater & Pittman, 1967), turns on interpretations of the use of contraceptives among lower-class women before the introduction of birth control pills and intrauterine devices. The original report emphasized that such women could not sustain the habits required to practice contraception effectively. This was later interpreted, by those who opposed the establishment of family-planning services, as evidence that such women did not want to limit their families. But this conclusion was inconsistent with the true state of affairs; these women did want fewer children, but they had difficulty following the careful schedule required for effective contraception in chaotic and stressful personal situations.

Another incident was associated with a survey completed in the late 1950s that was designed to determine the health status and attitudes of the elderly (Cain, 1967). The survey directors enlisted the help of sociologists around the country, each of whom was to supervise interviews conducted in his or her area. The respondents were to be white, over 65, living in their own homes, and preferably from an upper- or upper-middle-class background. Minorities, those living in institutions, or the "senile or impossible to interview" were not to be included in the sample. During the summer of 1960, the results were released as demonstrating that "typical" older Americans were satisfied with their health care, able to pay substantial medical bills from their own resources, and were "not characteristically dependent, inadequate, ill, or senile." Heavily promoted by the American Medical Association (AMA) in its lobbying efforts to oppose the federally sponsored Medicaid program, the study quickly came to the attention of the sociologists who supervised the interviews and who were named in the report; many issued public statements calling attention to the distinctive sample they were instructed to obtain, which eliminated the elderly most likely to be in poor health, of modest means, and dependent upon the assistance of their families or the government Eventually, the report was so thoroughly discredited (in part because its conclusions were inconsistent with most research on the elderly) that it was ignored by all major policy-making bodies in government. However, if the report had not received substantial public attention, due to the efforts of the AMA, it might not have been so widely criticized and might have influenced federal decision makers.

If an investigator collects sensitive information on specific individuals and allows it to be divulged to others who are able to affect the lives of participants providing the information, the investigator is generally assumed to bear full responsibility for this breach of confidentiality, particularly when respondents are promised or expect confidentiality. A substantial range of options is available for minimizing the misuse of descriptive data on individual research participants; there are numerous ways for maintaining the anonymity of participants, and every effort should be made to ensure that confidentiality is obtained. If the various procedures (reviewed in Chapter 6) for immunizing the data from legal subpoena are not successful, it may be considered morally appropriate for the investigator to go to jail rather than disclose the participants' identities; a substantial number of news-persons and an occasional social scientist have done so.

The second type of data misuse—inappropriate interpretations of data on an aggregate or group of individuals—is a more subtle and difficult problem, perhaps because it is hard to establish who will make such misinterpretations or for what purpose. If the mistake is made by persons with professional or scientific training, they would be expected to be acquainted with the problems and techniques of data interpretation; and if the original presentation meets the normal standards for the scientific community, they would be considered responsible for gross errors, not the original investigator. If the interpretations are made by ordinary citizens or others (such as journalists) without the training required to interpret such data, the attribution of responsibility is more ambiguous. It is argued that the originating scientist is responsible for clearly formulating appropriate interpretations and warning others about inappropriate interpretations; on the other hand, it is impossible to anticipate *all* inappropriate interpretations. Some are very anxious to "see" supporting trends in scientific data, present or not.

Misinterpretation of data representing aggregates of individuals is a difficult form of misuse to control, since there is no way to anticipate which individuals will make the misinterpretations or what they might be. The major suggestions have emphasized care in the presentation of data and the descriptions of appropriate interpretations. This is combined with vigilance with regard to further uses of the data and public statements to correct any misinterpretations that may come to the attention of the investigator. But once the final report has been completed and widely distributed for a research project, it may be impossible for an investigator to keep track of all possible uses and misinterpretations.[1]

Improper Applications
of Existing Knowledge

Once scientific knowledge becomes embodied in devices and techniques that can be routinely applied, there is always the possibility that it may be misused. This is true even when the new knowledge is widely accepted by applied professionals and can have beneficial effects when properly applied. Whether it results from mis-understanding or incompetence, failure to properly utilize such techniques represents a benefit foregone, usually to the clients.

Such misuse is found with the widespread administration of polygraph tests to employees in the hopes of detecting those who have stolen property or funds from a company or who might do so in the future; such tests are often used in screening applicants for new positions. It has been observed that if a "lie-detector

---

[1]Others considering this issue are convinced that "Social scientists are responsible for how their discoveries are used" (Diener & Crandall, 1978, p. 217). Many examples of the "predictable" uses of social science knowledge do not always support this conclusion, however, (pp. 195-204); most suggestions on how this responsibility may be discharged are similar to those included in this analysis.

procedure" is 90 percent accurate and 5 percent of 1,000 employees in a firm are or may be thieves, then the procedure will identify forty-five out of fifty potential thieves as "thieves," but ninety-five honest employees will also be identified as "thieves." Thus, 68 percent of those identified as "thieves" will actually be honest (Lykken, 1974, 1975a, 1975b, 1980; Abrams, 1975). Even if polygraph procedures were 95 percent accurate—and 90 percent accuracy may be a liberal figure—50 percent of those identified as "thieves" in the example would be honest. Since there may be no other evidence on which to base a judgment, particularly if a polygraph is used in job screening, this may be an infringement on the right of individuals to be considered "innocent until proven guilty."

The widespread use of this technique in industry appears to have resulted in part from the promotional activities of professional polygraphers, whose confidence is based mainly on experience in criminal proceedings, where individual confessions and court decisions may provide validating evidence. But it also stems from the concern of executives over economic loss due to employee theft, a concern that makes them receptive to easy solutions to the problem, and to naïvely assume that individuals can be classified as honest or dishonest without reference to their situational context (Burton, 1976). It seems appropriate to consider this a misuse of a well-developed procedure although it has some potential value in criminal proceedings, where the number of innocents examined is smaller—thereby substantially reducing the probability of them being falsely identified as guilty—and the final decisions are left to the judicial procedure.

Responsibility for such misapplication would appear to rest with the applied professionals, not those who originated the procedure. This seems particularly true in the application of lie-detector tests in mass screenings, as those who apply the technique in practical settings have a financial incentive to expand its use as much as possible. Similar uses—of detecting whether or not someone is being truthful— are now claimed for voice analyzers, which are being promoted to assist business executives in lie detection during phone conversations. In part, the acceptance of this application is due to the different standards used by decision makers and scientists for evaluating techniques; the former are willing to accept much less complete and more ambiguous evidence, often anecdotal, than are scientific investigators. Hence, they may consider, adopt, and utilize a procedure or technique that a scientist would not consider effective, or at least would regard as not proven to be effective. One reason for the establishment of the Food and Drug Administration was to determine the safety and effectiveness of substances and devices that had multiple, subtle effects. It was found that executives of drug companies and physicians tended to promote treatments for general use on the basis of brief incomplete analyses and evaluations.

The ability of investigators to control such negative effects is obviously limited, as the techniques or devices are in the public domain and are widely available. An individual investigator with special expertise may make public statements outlining the issues and problems and directed toward those misapplying the device or technique or toward the public at large. This was done in the case of the misuse of lie detectors in both professional and mass-circulation journals

(*American Psychologist* and *Psychology Today;* Lykken, 1974, 1975b). In this special case, concerned social scientists also helped develop and pass state laws prohibiting misuses.

Many professional associations provide a genuine service by systematically attempting to regulate the improper application of existing knowledge by their members; competent application of accepted knowledge is a fundamental objective of most legal, medical, engineering, and accounting associations. In general, most applied professionals recognize and accept the blame for improper applications of scientific knowledge. Individuals who are not professionals, either because the professionalism of their field is not well developed or because they are outside a well-defined occupational group, are free from any control mechanism. Fortunately, much of the most potent scientific knowledge is utilized by applied professionals under some form of supervision.

Failure to Utilize New Knowledge

When new knowledge has been developed and has proven its value for providing benefits, it is often some time before it is applied in general practice. Such delays can cause the loss of many benefits. For example, the delay in introducing new procedures to help individuals stop smoking or use contraception more effectively will increase the incidence of ill health or the number of abortions or unplanned children. In psychology, one of the major successes has been the development of tests to detect those schoolchildren who have either more or less than a normal capacity to learn. Far more reliable than the intuitive judgments of teachers and administrators, the tests are very useful in identifying children who would benefit from either remedial or accelerated classes. The recent emphasis upon equality and the equal treatment of all schoolchildren—based upon the assumption that there are no significant differences in ability—has curtailed the use of aptitude tests in several school systems; the cost of this decision for both less-than-average and bright students is probably enormous. There has also been a loss to society from failure to optimize the amount of material learned by school children.

Attribution of responsibility for benefits foregone from failure to utilize new knowledge requires examining both the originating investigators and those who deal with specific problems, usually applied professionals. If the originating individuals (scientists, technicians, administrators, or societal decision makers) withhold information that may have benefits, it seems reasonable to assign them the responsibility for benefits foregone. But if the information is freely and fully available to all, then those who apply such information are responsible for adopting the new techniques as quickly as possible. Unfortunately, these individuals (for example, teachers, executives and administrators, and members of service professions) are often quite casually organized and are not able to disseminate new techniques and devices rapidly; the adoption of new biomedical and engineering knowledge for practical applications is much more efficient in this regard.

The adoption of new medical and social science knowledge is influenced by prevailing beliefs and values among scientists, applied professionals, and members of society. Perhaps because they are often inconsistent with existing ideas, many new valuable techniques are only gradually adopted. It seems unlikely that there will be any simple procedure for controlling this type of fesistence, especially since it occurs among most conscientious professionals, who are often conservative about changing accepted procedures. As long as scientists continue to publicize advances and their potential applications, they will probably have little influence over utilization of knowledge or the magnitude of the benefits that will be foregone during the delays in adoption.

DEVELOPMENT OF KNOWLEDGE
FOR PRACTICAL AFFAIRS

There are a number of ways in which social scientists may help promote practical objectives. They may contribute to a basic research program or project designed to produce "fundamental" scientific knowledge directly related to specific objectives, such as a project on the effects of stress on the combat performance of military troops. If the basic scientific knowledge is at least partially developed, investigators may help apply scientific knowledge in ways that will change individuals or social systems, presumably for the better. An example would be programs designed to increase the adoption of contraceptive techniques in grossly overpopulated developing countries. A recent and widespread social science activity is the utilization of research techniques to provide information about action programs that give estimates of their effectiveness and how they might be improved. Evaluation research on education, social welfare, health, crime, and the like is one of the fastest growing areas of social science; all major substantive specialties are involved.

Social scientists are generally motivated by intellectual interest or curiosity and a desire to benefit humanity. While an ideal project would satisfy both motives, most projects present less clear-cut choices. Much basic science, which is often intellectually challenging, may have only the most tangential practical benefits; conversely, many projects with substantial applied potential may be of limited intellectual interest. As scientists become more involved in government or business, the more they must share in decisions that affect their research; they must be prepared to give up some personal autonomy—so prized by researchers doing basic science—and accept the need for making joint decisions or for letting them be made by those who have legitimate responsibility (administrators, executives, elected officials, and the like).

Basic Research and Applied Objectives

There are numerous examples where basic research has been completed to further applied objectives. A recent review of social science research done by the military since 1960 indicates attention to: combatants' response to stressful situations, both short- and long-term (to improve effectiveness under the stress of battle and during long, hazardous missions); personality factors related to the toleration and commitment of atrocities (to select leaders who will minimize atrocities or to select potentially effective assassins); determining what smells are offensive to different cultral and ethnic groups (in order to produce substitutes for tear gas); information on the task effectiveness of groups and individuals in different situations (to improve their fighting efficiency); and situations and treatments that lead to personal disorientation and compliance (to facilitate or prevent successful interrogations) (Watson, 1978). In all cases the knowledge acquired before applications are possible can be considered to be basic science.

Investigators faced with a choice of contributing to such research may be in two types of organizational contexts. It may be relatively easy for those associated with a university to refuse to participate in a specific project; in a university organizational rewards (promotions, pay) are related to a broad variety of activities (teaching, research, and service), and some researchers may have tenured positions (their job security is assured unless gross negligence or incompetence is demonstrated). Refusals to participate will not, of course, prevent a project from being conducted (unless a researcher has a unique skill that others do not possess); a refusal simply means that a specific social scientist has made a personal choice in order to preserve a clear conscience.

In contrast, the freedom of an investigator working in an organization or agency where the sole purpose is the completion of research (perhaps under contract or as a service to an operating unit or agency) to withdraw from a project he or she considers personally unacceptable may be more limited. While most such agencies prefer to engage in a range of activities and allow each employee to choose his own projects, survival in a competitive market may not allow agencies the luxury of supporting those who are not comfortable with any current projects. There is always the possibility that no project within the organization is morally acceptable to specific individuals and they can no longer be carried by the rest of the organization.

An even greater problem develops in such organizations when a member, whether or not he has participated in a specific project, finds that the application of research may result in effects—intended or unintended—that are inconsistent with his personal values. If the individual is convinced that the project or proposed applications pose a significant hazard for individuals or society, he may try to convince the decision makers in the organization to change their plans. If he is not successful, the individual may attempt to contact those outside the organization by appealing to official agencies (or other government agencies) or the general public. Individuals who take such actions—for example, lawyers, engineers, accountants, physicians, and so forth—are now referred to as "whistle-blowers"; the phrase refers to blowing a whistle to attract attention to a "misdeed." While it is widely suggested that all scientists, including social scientists, have a social responsibility to draw attention to potential problems (Diener & Crandall, 1978; Edsall, 1975), it has not been possible so far to insulate whistle-blowers from the usual consequences: job loss and a substantial, if not fatal, career disruption.

Program Implementation

Social scientists who are asked to become involved in the implementation of a program designed to change individuals or their relationships (as when the structure of a social system is modified), may enter at least three different roles. There are the individuals who will experience the attempts at change, those who have the major responsibility for selecting the objectives to which change is directed and the programs to be implemented, and those who participate in the actual design and implementation of the programs. In most cases, social scientists are involved in the last category, assisting in the specific design and implementation of a program; but they may also select objectives and programs to achieve them, as when a client visits a therapist for individual assistance.

There are at least two major ethical issues associated with attempts to implement change. The first is whether or not the change promised by the social scientists can in fact be produced; it is considered wrong to make promises that cannot be fulfilled. The second—more significant in programs introduced for entire societies or categories of people—is the extent to which the participants themselves are willing volunteers. Have they provided their informed consent? Has the investigator contributed to an endeavor that is being imposed upon individuals and that violates their right to self-determination?

The extent to which most types of counseling or therapy, particularly psychotherapy, have beneficial effects—over and above the improvements that often occur spontaneously—has been a subject of substantial controversy (Back, 1972; Eysenck, 1961; Marshall, 1980a). Recent attempts of clinical psychologists (by far the largest group of applied social scientists) to have their assistance to patients qualify for payments under federal health care programs has resulted in renewed concern regarding a demonstrated positive effect for clients. (The available evidence suggests that harm almost never occurs.) The problem is often seen to be demonstrating the effectiveness of a particular type of therapy. Most evidence suggests, however, that the problem is to identify the conditions under which patients improve, which involve a complex interaction between a patient's characteristics, his or her problem, the therapist's skill, and the type of procedure (Marshall, 1980b; Luborsky et al., 1971). Nonetheless, it may be considered wrong for applied social scientists to promise improvements when they have little evidence they can do so, particularly when they are paid from public funds for their efforts.

While there may be some concern about therapists' intervening in the lives and psyches of clients and promising improvements, there is not much question that clients are willing volunteers, particularly when they seek out the assistance, eagerly cooperate with the recommended therapy, and offer to pay for it. In such cases the person who designs the program also selects the program objectives (patient improvement). In contrast, in many societal programs these two activities are performed by different individuals. Elected officials or government administrators may define program objectives, and social scientists may develop a program to achieve them. In such cases, social scientists share responsibility for a program's effects, whether positive and negative. Concerns develop when specific individuals are involved in a program and it is not clear they have wholeheartedly provided their "informed consent." Not all are convinced that the general "consent of the government" to programs implemented by their duly elected officials is satisfactory (Bermant, Kelman, & Warwick, 1978).

For example, a series of programs may be developed to reduce the population growth in a developing country, such as India. Services that provide family-planning information or low-cost (or perhaps free) contraceptives may demonstrate respect for individual autonomy as long as the decision to accept these services is up to the individuals involved. Other programs may be more controversial, such as those that offer a substantial incentive to participants for undergoing surgical sterilization; if a cash bonus equal to several months' wages is offered to patients, there may be concern that they are not fully able to resist the inducement and may not be, deep in their hearts, enthusiastic volunteers. Going even further, various education, work, welfare, medical, and retirement policies may be officially related to the number of live births born by a married woman—the greater the number of children, the lower the benefits (the opposite plan is used in some countries where the birth rate is below that needed to sustain the population). In such cases the suspicion that a program is being imposed upon individuals (those of childbearing years) without their full consent may be even greater; the moral dilemma for the social scientist is whether or not to participate in programs that may not fully recognize individual autonomy, even though they may provide substantial benefits for other members of society and future generations. Essentially, this is one of the fundamental conflicts that develops between solutions to societal problems and the standards for individual morality, reviewed in Chapter 1.

Research for Applied Decisions

There is a growing tendency to involve social scientists in activities to gather information directly relevant to decision making, usually to evaluate the effectiveness of operating programs designed to educate, reduce crime, improve physical health, promote mental health, and the like. In such situations, social scientists may identify a number of different constituencies they feel obligated to serve: the clients presumed to benefit from the program; those responsible for the operation of the program; decision makers who determine the existence, form, or size of the program; and the public-at-large, who may be paying for the program and the evaluation. While a number of rather obvious issues arise—the honesty of negotiations that lead to an explicit contract for research, the care and attention to detail in the collection and analysis of data, the kind of assistance during the interpretation of results, and the development of policy recommendations—special dilemmas may also develop. To the extent that investigators develop a vague feeling that "something" is wrong, such issues may be considered moral complications.

The first is that clients will often expect more from an evaluation than is possible, or they may be willing to accept a less than satisfactory (from the investigator's point of view) research design. While this may be an attempt to minimize costs, as careful research is always expensive, it probably reflects a difference of perspective on "standards of evidence." Decision makers and administrators are often quite willing to draw inferences on the basis of less complete data than are most scientifically oriented investigators. Decision makers and administrators, many with legal training, may reflect the tendency in legal analysis to stress anecdotes and dramatic cases, even if they are rare events. From the investigators' point of view, they may be making decisions on the basis of inadequate or partial evidence; from their own point of view, they may be getting far more information than they have been accustomed to or feel they need.

A second problem develops in experimental evaluation designs to determine the effectiveness of a program. This problem is relationships between the operating staff, who attempt to "do good," and the research staff, who attempt to determine if they are actually "doing good." The operating staff is usually committed to one procedure or program and is constantly attempting improvements to increase the benefits to the client. The research staff usually assumes that the program is a fixed, known activity and focuses upon the changes experienced by the clients, using before-and-after measures or comparisons with a control group. If the operating program tends to vary, then it is more difficult for the research staff to determine if it is having a positive effect on the clients or, in the more usual case, what features of the program are responsible for any improvements. Hence, the investigators are faced with a dilemma: whether to provide information that may improve the current program and benefit current clients or to keep the operating program constant until its effects are known so that future clients may be better served. Needless to say, the operating staff may resent the latter alternative; if their cooperation is vital—and it usually is—this may cause problems.

A third problem, one that also occurs in evaluation of biomedical therapies, is associated with experimental programs that measure the effectiveness of a new technique or device. The most useful procedure, in terms of providing strong inferences about relative effects, is to assign individuals with an identified problem to different conditions at random; some receive the new, unproven treatment, and others—the controls—receive either no treatment or the current standard. After a period of time, the effectiveness of the new treatment can be estimated through comparison with the controls. The moral dilemma comes from systematically denying a group of individuals the opportunity to receive a potentially effective therapy. One solution is to allow those in the control group the opportunity to receive the new treatment after all follow-up measures have been gathered. While this is a satisfactory solution when the problems are not critical and susceptible to a range of treatments (as with learning problems, mild medical problems, or some psychological distresses), it is not so satisfactory in other programs that deal with less malleable complaints. Once a study is completed it may be too late to benefit participants who have passed a critical period (for example, once a couple is divorced, it is too late to try another type of counseling). This is often a source of controversy with advocates of a new treatment who consider scientific standards of evidence a luxury, since they already "know" the new treatment is responsible for major benefits.

A final problem that concerns many investigators is the utilization of the results by decision makers. There is substantial evidence that many evaluations are not given serious consideration when the final decisions are made. This may be considered either a problem in the relationship between the investigators and the decision makers or a moral issue; it may be considered a moral issue if large sums of public money are spent on research that is disregarded. In some cases, federal legislation has required that money be spent on action-program evaluations; when the research has been completed it has then been ignored, because the legislation did not require that it be considered in any decisions. In order to avoid this dilemma, which discourages many investigators who consider their efforts wasted, there is a growing tendency to incorporate decision makers at all important stages of the project and familiarize them with its progress and the basis for the major conclusions. This helps to increase decision makers' confidence in the results and improve investigators' awareness of the issues to which the results should be directed. This procedure is considerably better than leaving reports unread or buried in the files.

CONCLUSION

Scientists are often seen as individually responsible for the impact of new knowledge upon society, for without their efforts there would be no impact. But such responsibility is often collective, because the social impact of new knowledge is due to the cumulative efforts of the casually organized scientific enterprise. While such advances could not occur without the individual efforts of specific investigators, each investigator may play only a small part in the overall scheme— a part easily played by another investigator. Individual responsibility is further reduced when others have the responsibility for applying knowledge. Politicians, administrators, executives, and applied professionals not only intend to make changes but they are able to control events to achieve such changes.

The ability of individual scientists to affect the use of knowledge is severely restricted by the fact that they are seldom in positions of responsibility with regard to applications. Some may personally refuse to become involved in specialized projects in the development or application of scientific knowledge, but this only reduces their personal responsibility; other investigators who take their places keep the responsibility within the scientific community. The most effective tactic may be to inform decision makers and the general public of the possible effects of new applications of scientific knowledge, for if others have complete knowledge, they then share the responsibility for application.

Investigators who are offered the opportunity to develop knowledge specific to a particular applied problem are often concerned with fulfilling their responsibilities to various constituencies: clients, colleagues, and the public-at-large. The most useful device for minimizing complications may be for investigators to draw up explicit, written statements regarding as much of their activities as possible. If, when their responsibilities and obligations are made clear, investigators are uncomfortable with the purpose of a project or the possible uses of the data, they may withdraw. At later stages their efforts to control the applications of the knowledge may or may not be effective. A major, and currently unresolved, issue affecting the freedom of investigators to select projects of their own choosing is the need for personal financial support. While those in tenured academic positions are assured of receiving paychecks others may have to choose between having a career and participating in a morally questionable project.

CHAPTER EIGHT
CONCLUSION

Attention has focused upon investigator's judgments regarding the moral acceptability of a project. Due to the inadequacies of explicit statements (such as codes of
ethics) as guides, a strategy for pursuing a personal, individual analysis to develop
a moral judgment was presented. This strategy considered the major moral, legal,
and political philosophies that have been developed to resolve the problems of
determining personal moral goodness, justifying the political structure of a society,
and selecting optimal social programs. The strategy proposed for moral evaluation
of research included attention to individual rights, the effects of general research
programs and specific projects, the risks and benefits for participants, the distribution of positive and negative effects, the methods for demonstrating respect for
the rights and welfare of the participants, and the personal treatment of participants by investigators. Finally, several societal roles of social scientists were
considered: the role of a societal agent developing scientific knowledge for the
common good, that of social reformer concerned with improving the human condition (or the condition of selected humans), or that of a model citizen setting an
example for others. For most social scientists, the issue is choosing which role to
emphasize, rather than selecting one and excluding the others.

As long as the dominant form of scientific understanding involves causal
mechanisms, the use of experiments to establish confidence that a causal relationship has been identified will be important. The moral dilemmas associated with the

conduct of experiments, where investigator responsibility for the effects upon participants is considerable, will not soon be resolved. The major issues will continue to be the benefits of the research in relation to negative effects on participants and the ways in which respect for the participants' rights and welfare may be demonstrated. The achievement of some scientific objectives will continue to require the use of alternatives to informed consent. These alternatives are important not only in laboratory or highly controlled settings (where illusions may be created) but in societal experiments conducted by governments without all participants' consent. Of all research activities, these investigations are most likely to create a difference of opinion between investigators committed to the development of scientific knowledge and those concerned with improving society or setting an example for others; for some experiments may deemphasize direct benefits and require an investigator-participant relationship that is less than ideal.

Moral dilemmas are substantially less dramatic in descriptive research, primarily because the direct effects on participants are usually modest or nonexistent. It is possible to ask embarrassing questions of participants, and public disclosure of sensitive information may produce negative effects, perhaps severe. However, millions of individuals complete personality tests, provide interviews, or are observed in their daily lives, and almost never suffer any serious negative effects. Descriptive research is a major activity for investigators with a commitment to scientific knowledge, but it is also a frequent pursuit of those concerned with social reform; if the topics are noncontroverial, such research may be conducted by those hoping to set an example for society.

Covert research of all types—participant observation, surreptitious field experiments, the use of unobtrusive (nonreactive) measures, or secondary data analysis—produces very few direct effects on participants; in most cases they are unaware that research is being done. Because participants are not aware they have provided data, negative effects will occur only if an investigator discloses information about sensitive or illegal behavior. Most investigators have been careful to avoid such problems and to demonstrate respect for the rights and welfare of participants by concealing their identities. Covert research is likely to create the most concern among social scientists who want to set an example to others; ideal citizens should refrain from being sneaky. Those concerned with societal reform may use such techniques to gather data on individuals they consider responsible for major problems; and in some cases, these investigators may reveal their data in order to achieve reforms.

Several types of research activity prove difficult to analyze—specifically, research on social systems and cross-cultural research. Research on social systems is complicated because the unit of analysis, a collection of people, has a quite different status in terms of "rights." Most rights are associated with natural persons, and both the effects on individual participants as well as on the social system must be considered; moral decisions tend to emphasize individual effects. Cross-cultural research involves a diversity of projects involving investigators, host countries, and research participants with widely varying conceptions of individual rights, autonomy, and "damage." In many cases, there is no way for participants to benefit from the knowledge developed from the research; one moral solution is to establish an equitable exchange relationship during the actual conduct of the investigation (for example, money, food, medical care can be traded for cooperation and information).

Two additional concerns are related to social science research and knowledge. One is demonstrating to outside observers that the conduct of research with human participants would be considered morally acceptable, regardless of the investigator's personal judgments. A lack of faith in the judgments of those conducting research with human participants (social and biomedical scientists) has led to the development of codes of ethics by professional associations. The inadequacies of control by professional associations has, in turn, led to the creation of the federally developed prior review procedures now imposed upon the social science community. Until 1981, all social science research in universities was expected to receive prior review and approval from committees (Institutional Review Boards); new federal regulations substantially reduce the need for universal prior review. Such prior review is expected to consider the extent to which participant rights and welfare are shown respect and, in cases of extreme risk, whether benefits justify risks associated with the research. Many such committees are now going well beyond requirements of new federal standards adopted in 1981; unnecessary administrative costs and procedural complications may be imposed upon investigators. In the final analysis, it is the legal system that sets standards for the treatment of one person by another; but there are few areas in social science research where effects have become so extreme that legal standards have been involved.

The second additional issue is related to the application of social science knowledge for practical purposes. Those who develop new knowledge are often considered responsible for major benefits; it is therefore reasonable that they should be considered responsible for major harms. But in both cases, investigator responsibility may be overemphasized; in the case of new devices or techniques, others usually have both the intent and the means to implement knowledge. In those few cases where scientists can affect the application of knowledge, the most morally defensible procedure is to consider the interests of both present and future generations. For the majority of situations, where scientists have little control over applications (because the knowledge is openly available), the best procedure is to inform decision makers and the public at large of possible complications and undesirable effects. The credibility of the individual scientist and the social science enterprise is likely to be promoted if technical judgments are clearly separated from personal values.

Social scientists, individually and collectively, have a choice between studying important, critical, human and social phenomena that may involve moral dilemmas, or focusing upon tangential, insignificant, safe issues. The more important the phenomenon, the greater likelihood that the research may involve a risk of negative effects, stress, or embarrassment for the participants. Investigators must then be diplomatic, imaginative, and conscientious in demonstrating respect for the participants' rights and welfare. They may take comfort from two facts: participants almost never experience lasting damage from social science research and seldom resent or take offense when they are involved. Those choosing to pursue important phenomena may find themselves confronted with a series of moral dilemmas; there will be obvious, permanent solutions, only temporary compromises.

APPENDIX 1
NUREMBERG CODE

APPENDIX 1

Nuremburg Code[1]

1. The voluntary consent of the human subject is absolutely essential.

This means that the person involved should have legal capacity to give consent; should be so situated as to be able to exercise free power of choice, without the intervention of any element of force, fraud, deceit, duress, over reaching, or other ulterior form of constraint or coercion; and should have sufficient knowledge and comprehension of the elements of the subject matter involved as to enable him to make an understanding and enlightened decision. This latter element requires that before the acceptance of an affirmative decision by the experimental subject there should be made known to him the nature, duration, and purpose of the experiment; the method and means by which it is to be conducted; all inconveniences and hazards reasonably to be expected; and the effects upon his health or person which may possibly come from his participation in the experiment.

The duty and responsibility for ascertaining the quality of the consent rests upon each individual who initiates, directs, or engages in the experiment. It is a personal duty and responsibility which may not be delegated to another with impunity.

[1] Katz, Jay, *Experimentation with Human Beings* (New York: Russell Sage Foundation, 1972), pp. 305-6.

2. The experiment should be such as to yield fruitful results for the good of society, unprocurable by other methods or means of study, and not random and unnecessary in nature.

3. The experiment should be so designed and based on the results of animal experimentation and a knowledge of the natural history of the disease or other problem under study that the anticipated results will justify the performance of the experiment.

4. The experiment should be so conducted as to avoid all unnecessary physical and mental suffering and injury.

5. No experiment should be conducted where there is an *a priori* reason to believe that death or disabling injury will occur; except, perhaps, in those experiments where the experimental physicians also serve as subjects.

6. The degree of risk to be taken should never exceed that determined by the humanitarian importance of the problem to be solved by the experiment.

7. Proper preparations should be made and adequate facilities provided to protect the experimental subject against even remote possibilities of injury, disability, or death.

8. The experiment should be conducted only by scientifically qualified persons. The highest degree of skill and care should be required through all stages of the experiment of those who conduct or engage in the experiment.

9. During the course of the experiment the human subject should be at liberty to bring the experiment to an end if he has reached the physical or mental state where continuation of the experiment seems to him to be impossible.

10. During the course of the experiment the scientist in charge must be prepared to terminate the experiment at any stage, if he has probable cause to believe, in the exercise of the good faith, superior skill, and careful judgment required of him that a continuation of the experiment is likely to result in injury, disability, or death to the experimental subject.

APPENDIX 2
PRINCIPLES
OF PROFESSIONAL
RESPONSIBILITY

APPENDIX 2

Principles of Professional Responsibility
(Adopted by the Council of the American Anthropological Associaton, May 1971)[1]

Preamble
Anthropologists work in many parts of the world in close personal association with the peoples and situations they study. Their professional situation is, therefore, uniquely varied and complex. They are involved with their discipline, their colleagues, their students, their sponsors, their subjects, their own and host governments, the particular individuals and groups with whom they do their field work, other populations and interest groups in the nations within which they work, and the study of processes and issues affecting general human welfare. In a field of such complex involvements, misunderstandings, conflicts and the necessity to make choices among conflicting values are bound to arise and to generate ethical dilemmas. It is a prime responsibility of anthropologists to anticipate these and to plan to resolve them in such a way as to do damage neither to those whom they study nor, in so far as possible, to their scholarly community. Where these con-

---

[1] This statement of principles is not intended to supersede previous statements and resolutions of the association. Its intent is to clarify professional responsibilities in the chief areas of professional concern to anthropologists. [Dates of addenda indicated in parentheses.] For further information, contact the Association at 1703 New Hampshire Ave. N.W., Washington, D.C. 20009.

ditions cannot be met, the anthropologist would be well-advised not to pursue the particular piece of research.

The following principles are deemed fundamental to the anthropologist's responsible, ethical pursuit of his profession.

1. Relations with those studied

In research, an anthropologist's paramount responsibility is to those he studies. When there is a conflict of interest, these individuals must come first. The anthropologist must do everything within his power to protect their physical, social and psychological welfare and to honor their dignity and privacy.

   a. Where research involves the acquisition of material and information transferred on the assumptions of trust between persons, it is axiomatic that the rights, interests, and sensitivities of those studied must be safeguarded.
   b. The aims of the investigation should be communicated as well as possible to the informant.
   c. Informants have a right to remain anonymous. This right should be respected both where it has been promised explicitly and where no clear understanding to the contrary has been reached. These strictures apply to the collection of data by means of cameras, tape recorders, and other data-gathering devices, as well as to data collected in face-to-face interviews or in participant observation. Those being studied should understand the capacities of such devices; they should be free to reject them if they wish; and if they accept them, the results obtained should be consonant with the informant's right to welfare, dignity and privacy.
      1. Despite every effort being made to preserve anonymity it should be made clear to informants that such anonymity may be compromised unintentionally (November 1975).
      2. When professionals or others have used pseudonyms to maintain anonymity, others should respect this decision and the reasons for it by not revealing indiscriminately the true identity of such committees, persons or other data (May 1976).
   d. There should be no exploitation of individual informants for personal gain. Fair return should be given them for all services.
   e. There is an obligation to reflect on the foreseeable repercussions of research and publication on the general population being studied.
   f. The anticipated consequences of research should be communicated as fully as possible to the individuals and groups likely to be affected.
   g. In accordance with the Association's general position on clandestine and secret research, no reports should be provided to sponsors that are not also available to the general public and, where practicable, to the population studied.
   h. Every effort should be exerted to cooperate with members of the host society in the planning and execution of research projects.
   i. All of the above points should be acted upon in full recognition of the social and cultural pluralism of host societies and the consequent plurality of values, interests and demands in those societies. This diversity complicates choice-making in research, but ignoring it leads to irresponsible decisions.

2. Responsibility to the public

The anthropologist is also responsible to the public—all presumed consumers of his professional efforts. To them he owes a commitment to candor and to truth in the dissemination of his research results and in the statement of his opinions as a student of man.

  a. He should not communicate his findings secretly to some and withhold them from others.
  b. He should not knowingly falsify or color his findings.
  c. In providing professional opinions, he is responsible not only for their content but also for integrity in explaining both these opinions and their bases.
  d. As people who devote their professional lives to understanding man, anthropologists bear a positive responsibility to speak out publicly, both individually and collectively, on what they know and what they believe as a result of their professional expertise gained in the study of human beings. That is, they bear a professional responsibility to contribute to an "adequate definition of reality" upon which public opinion and public policy may be based.
  e. In public discourse, the anthropologist should be honest about his qualifications and cognizant of the limitations of anthropological expertise.

3. Responsibility to the discipline
An anthropologist bears responsibility for the good reputation of his discipline and its practitioners.

  a. He should undertake no secret research or any research whose results cannot be freely derived and publicly reported.
  b. He should avoid even the appearance of engaging in clandestine research, by fully and freely disclosing the aims and sponsorship of all his research.
  c. He should attempt to maintain a level of integrity and rapport in the field such that by his behavior and example he will not jeopardize future research there. The responsibility is not to analyze and report so as to offend no one, but to conduct research in a way consistent with a commitment to honesty, open inquiry, clear communication of sponsorship and research aims, and concern for the welfare and privacy of informants.
  d. He should not present as his own work, either in speaking or writing, materials directly taken from other sources (October 1974).
  e. When he participates in actions related to hiring, retention and advancement, he should ensure that no exclusionary practices be perpetuated against colleagues on the basis of sex, marital status, color, social class, religion, ethnic background, national origin, or other nonacademic attributes. He should, furthermore, refrain from transmitting and resist the use of information irrelevant to professional performance in such personnel actions (November 1975).

4. Responsibility to students
In relations with students an anthropologist should be candid, fair, non-exploitative, and committed to their welfare and academic progress.

As Robert Lekachman has suggested, honesty is the essential quality of a good teacher, neutrality is not. Beyond honest teaching, the anthropologist as a teacher has ethical responsibilities in selection, instruction in ethics, career counseling, academic supervision, evaluation, compensation and placement.

  a. He should select students in such a way as to preclude discrimination on the basis of sex, race, ethnic group, social class, and other categories of people indistinguishable by their intellectual potential.
  b. He should alert students to the ethical problems of research and dis-

courage them from participating in projects employing questionable ethical standards. This should include providing them with information and discussions to protect them from unethical pressures and entice-ments emanating from possible sponsors, as well as helping them to find acceptable alternatives (see point i below).

c. He should be receptive and seriously responsive to students' interests, opinions, and desires in all aspects of their academic work and relation-ships.

d. He should realistically counsel students regarding career opportunities.

e. He should conscientiously supervise, encourage and support students in their anthropological and other academic endeavors.

f. He should inform students of what is expected of them in their course of study. He should be fair in the evaluation of their performance. He should communicate evaluations to the students concerned.

g. He should acknowledge in print the student assistance he uses in his own publications, give appropriate credit (including coauthorship) when student research is used in publication, encourage and assist in publication of worthy student papers, and compensate students justly for the use of their time, energy, and intelligence in research and teaching.

h. He should energetically assist students in securing legitimate research support and the necessary permission to pursue research.

i. He should energetically assist students in securing professional employ-ment upon completion of their studies.

j. He should strive to improve both our techniques of teaching and our techniques for evaluating the effectiveness of our methods of teaching.

5. *Responsibility to sponsors*
In his relations with sponsors of research, an anthropologist should be honest about his qualifications, capabilities and aims. He thus faces the obligation, prior to entering any commitment for research, to reflect sincerely upon the purposes of his sponsors in terms of their past behavior. He should be espec-ially careful not to promise or imply acceptance of conditions contrary to his professional ethics or competing commitments. This requires that he require of the sponsor full disclosure of the sources of funds, personnel, aims of the institution, and the research project, disposition of research results. He must retain the right to make all ethical decisions in his research. He should enter into no secret agreement with the sponsor regarding the research, results, or reports.

6. *Responsibilities to one's own government and to host government*
In his relations with his own government and with host governments, the research anthropologist should be honest and candid. He should demand assurance that he will not be required to compromise his professional re-sponsibilities and ethics as a condition of his permission to pursue the re-search. Specifically, no secret research, no secret reports, or debriefings of any kind should be agreed to or given. If these matters are clearly under-stood in advance, serious complications and misunderstandings can generally be avoided.

Epilogue
In the final analysis, anthropological research is a human undertaking, de-pendent upon choices for which the individual bears ethical as well as scien-tific responsibility. That responsibility is a human, not superhuman responsi-bility. To err is human, to forgive humane. This statement of principles of

professional responsibility is not designed to punish, but to provide guidelines which can minimize the occasions upon which there is a need to forgive. When an anthropologist, by his actions, jeopardizes peoples studied, professional colleagues, students or others, or if he otherwise betrays his professional commitments, his colleagues may legitimately inquire into the propriety of those actions, and take such measures as lie within the legitimate powers of their Association as the membership of the Association deems appropriate.

APPENDIX 3
RULES OF CONDUCT
Abridged

Rules of Conduct (Abridged)
(American Political Science Association)[1]

A. Teacher-Student Relations

Rule 1. A faculty member must not expropriate the academic work of his students. As a dissertation advisor, he is not entitled to claim joint authorship with a student of a thesis or dissertation. The teacher cannot represent himself as the author of independent student research; and research assistance, paid or unpaid, requires full acknowledgement.

Rule 2. The academic political scientist must be very careful not to impose his partisan views—conventional or otherwise—upon his students or colleagues.

B. Conduct of Officers and Employees of the Association

Rule 3. When an officer, member, or employee of the Association speaks out on an issue of public policy, endorses a political candidate, or otherwise participates in political affairs, he should make it as clear as possible that he is not speaking on behalf of the Association unless he is so authorized by the Association, and he should not encourage any inference that he acts for the Association unless he is so authorized by the Association.

---

[1] Discussions preceeding each subset of rules and the last discussion related to foreign area research have been omitted. Contact the Association (1527 New Hampshire Ave. N.W., Washington, D.C. 20036) for a complete and recent set of rules.

Rule 4.   Officers and employees of the Assocaition are free to engage in activities outside their obligations to the Association provided that such activities are consistent with their duties and responsibilities to the Association. When doubts arise about the activities of subordinate staff members, they should be resolved by the Executive Director in consultation with Executive Committee of the Association. Similarly when doubts arise about the activities of the Executive Director, they should be resolved by the Executive Committee.

Rule 5.   An officer or employee of the Association should not knowingly participate in a transaction involving the Association in the consequences of which he has a substantial economic interest. In such event he should disqualify himself from participating in a transaction involving the Association when a violation of this rule would result. Procedures for such disqualification shall be established by the Executive Committee.

C. *Political Activity of Academic Political Scientists*

Rule 6.   The college or university teacher is a citizen, and like other citizens, he should be free to engage in political activities insofar as he can do so consistently with his obligations as a teacher and scholar. Effective service as a faculty member is often compatible with certain types of political activity, for example, holding a part-time office in a political party or serving as a citizen of a governmental advisory board. Where a professor engages in full-time political activity, such as service in a state legislature, he should, as a rule, seek a leave of absence from his institution. Since political activity by academic political scientists is both legitimate and socially important, universities and colleges should have institutional arrangements to permit such activity, including reduction in the faculty member's workload or a leave of absence, subject to equitable adjustment of compensation when necessary.

Rule 7.   A faculty member who seeks a leave to engage in political activity should recognize that he has a primary obligation to his institution and to his growth as a teacher and scholar. He should consider the problems which a leave of absence may create for his administration, colleagues and students, and he should not abuse the privilege by asking for leaves too frequently, or too late, or for too extended a period of time. A leave of absence incident to political activity should not affect unfavorably the tenure status of the faculty member.

Rule 8.   Special problems arise if departments or schools endorse or sponsor political activities or public policies in the name of the entire faculty of the department or school. One of the purposes of tenure—to shelter unpopular or unorthodox teaching—is in some degree vitiated if the majority of a departmental faculty endorses or sponsors a particular political position in the name of the faculty of the department. The simple way out of this dilemma is to adhere strictly to the rule that those faculty members who wish to endorse or sponsor a political position or activity do so in their own names without trying to bind their colleagues holding different views. Departments as such should not endorse political positions.

D. *Freedom and Integrity of Research*

The Paramount Concern. In administering research funds the paramount concern of a university and its faculty and research staff should be to maintain an environment in which the freedom and integrity of research can flourish. The purpose of research is to advance knowledge. The ability of scholars to advance knowledge will depend in no small measure on two factors: first, on their freedom to seek and use all relevant evidence and to draw conclusions from it by the rigorous application of the methods of science and the disciplines of humane learning; secondly, on the integrity of their personal commitment to the spirit of free inquiry. To the extent to which the range of evidence open to them is narrowed or their ability to draw unbiased conclusions from it is impaired either by external pressures or by the infirmity of their scholarly purposes, to that extent their research will be deficient in qualities which are essential for the advancement of knowledge.

* * *

Rule 9. Financial sponsors of research have the responsibility for avoiding actions that would call into question the integrity of American academic institutions as centers of independent teaching and research. They should not sponsor research as a cover for intelligence activities.

Rule 10. Openness concerning material support of research is a basic principle of scholarship. In making grants for research, government and non-government sponsors should openly acknowledge research support and require that the grantee indicate in any published research financed by their grants the relevant sources of financial support. Where anonymity is requested by a non-government grantor and does not endanger the integrity of research, the character of the sponsorship rather than the identity of the grantor should be noted.

Rule 11. Political science research supported by government grants should be unclassified.

Rule 12. After a research grant has been made, the grantor shall not impose any restriction on or require any clearance of research methods, procedures, or content.

Rule 13. The grantor assumes no responsibility for the findings and conclusions of the researcher and imposes no restrictions on and carries no responsibility for publication.

Principles for Universities: The Committee urges academic members of the Association to work within their universities for the adoption of the following princples:

Rule 14. A university or college should not administer research funds derived from contracts or grants whose purpose and the character of whose sponsorship cannot be publicly disclosed.

Rule 15. A university or college that administers research funds provided through contracts and grants from public and/or private sources must act to assure that research funds are used prudently and honorably.

Rule 16. In administering research funds entrusted directly to its care, a university or college should do its best to ensure that no restrictions are placed on the availability of evidence to scholars or on their freedom to draw their own conclusions from the evidence and to share their findings with others.

Principles for Individual Researchers: The following rules are proposed for the guidance of academic political scientists in their relations with any governmental or private sponsor of research.

Rule 17. In applying for research funds, the individual researcher should:
a. clearly state the reasons he is applying for support and not resort to strategems of ambiguity to make his research more acceptable to a funding agency;
b. indicate clearly the actual amount of time he personally plans to spend on the research;

c. indicate other sources of support of his research, if any; and
d. refuse to accept terms and conditions that he believes will undermine his freedom and integrity as a scholar.

Rule 18.   In conducting research so supported, the individual

a. bears sole responsibility for the procedures, methods, and content of research;
b. must avoid any deception or misrepresentation concerning his personal involvement or the involvement of respondents or subjects, or use research as a cover for intelligence work;
c. refrain from using his professional status to obtain data and research materials for purposes other than scholarship; and
d. with respect to research abroad, should not concurrently accept any additional support from agencies of the government for purposes that cannot be disclosed.

Rule 19.   In managing research funds, the individual researcher should:

a. carefully comply with the time, reporting, accounting, and other requirements set forth in the project instrument, and cooperate with university administrators in meeting these requirements; and
b. avoid commingling project funds with personal funds, or funds of one project with those of another.

Rule 20.   With respect to publication of the results of his research, the individual researcher:

a. bears sole responsibility for publication;
b. should disclose relevant sources of financial support, but in cases where anonymity is justified and does not endanger the integrity of research, by noting the character of the sponsorship;
c. should indicate any material condition imposed by his financial sponsors or others on his research and publication;
d. should conscientiously acknowledge any assistance he receives in conducting research; and
e. should adhere strictly to the requirements, if any, of the funding agency.

APPENDIX 4
ETHICAL PRINCIPLES
OF PSYCHOLOGISTS

APPENDIX 4

Ethical Principles of Psychologists
(American Psychological Association)[1]

Preamble

Psychologists respect the dignity and worth of the individual and strive for the preservation and protection of fundamental human rights. They are committed to increasing knowledge of human behavior and of people's understanding of themselves and others and to the utilization of such knowledge for the promotion of human welfare. While pursuing these objectives, they make every effort to protect the welfare of those who seek their services and of the research participants that may be the object of study. They use their skills only for purposes consistent with these values and do not knowingly permit their misuse by others. While demanding for themselves freedom of inquiry and communication, psychologists accept the responsibility this freedom requires: competence, objectivity in the application of skills, and concern for the best interests of clients, colleagues, students, research partici-

---

[1] Approved by the Council of Representatives (January 1981). [For further information, contact the Association at 1200 17th St. N.W., Washington, D.C. 20036.]

These Ethical Principles apply to psychologists, to students of psychology and others who do work of a psychological nature under the supervision of a psychologist. They are also intended for the guidance of nonmembers of the Association who are engaged in psychological research or practice.

pants and society. In the pursuit of these ideals, psychologists subscribe to principles in the following areas: 1. Responsibility, 2. Competence, 3. Moral and Legal Standards, 4. Public Statements, 5. Confidentiality, 6. Welfare of the Consumer, 7. Professional Relationships, 8. Assessment Techniques, 9. Research with Human Participants, and 10. Care and Use of Animals.

Acceptance of membership in the American Psychological Association commits the member to adherence to these principles.

Psychologists cooperate with duly constituted committees of the American Psychological Association, in particular, the Committee on Scientific and Professional Ethics and Conduct, by responding to inquiries promptly and completely. Members also respond promptly and completely to inquiries from duly constituted state association ethics committees and professional standards review committees.

Principle 1: Responsibility

In providing services, psychologists maintain the higher standards of their profession. They accept responsibility for the consequences of their acts and make every effort to insure that their services are used appropriately.

   a. As scientists, psychologists accept responsibility for the selection of their research topics and the methods used in investigation, analysis, and reporting. They plan their research in ways to minimize the possibility that their findings will be misleading. They provide thorough discussion of the limitations of their data, especially where their work touches on social policy or might be construed to the detriment of persons in specific age, sex, ethnic, socioeconomic, or other social groups. In publishing reports of their work, they never suppress disconfirming data, and they acknowledge the existence of alternative hypotheses and explanations of their findings. Psychologists take credit only for work they have actually done.
   b. Psychologists clarify in advance with all appropriate persons and agencies the expectations for sharing and utilizing research data. They avoid relationships which may limit their objectivity or create a conflict of interest. Interference with the milieu in which the data are collected is kept to a minimum.
   c. Psychologists have the responsibility to attempt to prevent distortion, misuse, or suppression of psychological findings by the institution or agency of which they are employees.
   d. As members of governmental or other organizational bodies, psychologists remain accountable as individuals to the highest standards of their profession.
   e. As teachers, psychologists recognize their primary obligation to help others acquire knowledge and skill. They maintain high standards of scholarship by presenting psychological information objectively, fully, and accurately.
   f. As practitioners, psychologists know that they bear a heavy social responsibility because their recommendations and professional actions may alter the lives of others. They are alert to personal, social, organizational, financial, or political situations and pressures that might lead to misuse of their influence.

Principle 2: Competence

The maintenance of high standards of competence is a responsibility shared by all psychologists in the interest of the public and the profession as a whole.

Psychologists recognize the boundaries of their competence and the limitations of their techniques. They only provide services and only use techniques for which they are qualified by training and experience. In those areas in which recognized standards do not yet exist, psychologists take whatever precautions are necessary to protect the welfare of their clients. They maintain knowledge of current scientific and professional information related to the services they render.

    a. Psychologists accurately represent their competence, education, training, and experience. They claim as evidence of educational qualifications only those degrees obtained from institutions acceptable under the Bylaws and Rules of Council of the American Psycholgoical Association.

    b. As teachers, psychologists perform their duties on the basis of careful preparation so that their instruction is accurate, current, and scholarly.

    c. Psychologists recognize the need for continuing education and are open to new procedures and changes in expectations and values over time.

    d. Psychologists recognize differences among people, such as those that may be associated with age, sex, socioeconomic, and ethnic backgrounds. When necessary, they obtain training, experience, or counsel to assure competent service or research relating to such persons.

    e. Psychologists responsible for decisions involving individuals or policies based on test results have an understanding of psychological or educational measurement, validation problems, and test research.

    f. Psychologists recognize that personal problems and conflicts may interfere with professional effectiveness. Accordingly, they refrain from undertaking any activity in which their personal problems are likely to lead to inadequate performance or harm to a client, colleague, student, or research participant. If engaged in such activity when they become aware of their personal problems, they seek competent professional assistance to determine whether they should suspend, terminate, or limit the scope of their professional and/or scientific activities.

Principle 3: Moral and Legal Standards
Psychologists' moral and ethical standards of behavior are a personal matter to the same degree as they are for any other citizen, except as these may compromise the fulfillment of their professional responsibilities, or reduce the public trust in psychology and psychologists. Regarding their own behavior, psychologists are sensitive to prevailing community standards and to the possible impact that conformity to or deviation from these standards may have upon the quality of their performance as psychologists. Psychologists are also aware of the possible impact of their public behavior upon the ability of colleagues to perform their professional duties.

    a. As teachers, psychologists are aware of the fact that their personal values may affect the selection and presentation of instructional materials. When dealing with topics that may give offense, they recognize and respect the diverse attitudes that students may have toward such material.

    b. As employees or employers, psychologists do not engage in or condone practices that are inhumane or that result in illegal or unjustifiable actions. Such practices include but are not limited to those based on considerations of race, handicap, age, gender, sexual preference, religion, or national origin in hiring, promotion, or training.

    c. In their professional roles, psychologists avoid any action that will violate or diminish the legal and civil rights of clients or of others who may be affected by their actions.

d. As practitioners and researchers, psychologists act in accord with Association standards and guidelines related to the practice and to the conduct of research with human beings and animals. In the ordinary course of events psychologists adhere to relevant governmental laws and institutional regulations. When federal, state, provincial, organizational, or institutional laws, regulations, or practices are in conflict with Association standards and guidelines, psychologists make known their commitment to Association standards and guidelines, and wherever possible work toward a resolution of the conflict. Both practitioners and researchers are concerned with the development of such legal and quasi-legal regulations as best serve the public interest, and they work toward changing existing regulations that are not beneficial to the public interest.

Principle 4: Public Statements

Public statements, announcements of services, advertising, and promotional activities of psychologists serve the purpose of helping the public make informed judgments and choices. Psychologists represent accurately and objectively their professional qualifications, affiliations, and functions, as well as those of the institutions or organizations with which they or the statements may be associated. In public statements providing psychological information or professional opinions or providing information about the availability of psychological products, publications, and services, psychologists base their statements on scientifically acceptable psychological findings and techniques with full recognition of the limits and uncertainties of such evidence.

a. When announcing or advertising professional services, psychologists may list the following information to describe the provider and services provided: name, highest relevant academic degree earned from a regionally accredited institution, date, type and level of certification or licensure, diplomate status, APA membership status, address, telephone number, office hours, a brief listing of the type of psychological services offered, an appropriate presentation of fee information, foreign languages spoken, and policy with regard to third-party payments. Additional relevant or important consumer information may be included if not prohibited by other sections of these Ethical Principles.

b. In announcing or advertising the availability of psychological products, publications, or services, psychologists do not present their affiliation with any organization in a manner that falsely implies sponsorship or certification by that organization. In particular and for example, psychologists do not state APA membership or fellow status in a way to suggest that such status implies specialized professional competence or qualifications. Public statements include, but are not limited to, communication by means of periodical, book, list, directory, television, radio, or motion picture. They do not contain: (i) a false, fraudulent, misleading, deceptive, or unfair statement; (ii) a misinterpretation of fact, or a statement likely to mislead or deceive because in context it makes only a partial disclosure of relevant facts; (iii) a testimonial from a patient regarding the quality of a psychologist's services or products; (iv) a statement intended or likely to create false or unjustified expectations of favorable results; (v) a statement implying unusual, unique, or one-of-a-kind abilities; (vi) a statement intended or likely to appeal to a client's fears, anxieties, or emotions concerning the possible results of a failure to obtain the offered services; (vii) a statement concerning the comparative desirability of offered service; (viii) a statement of direct solicitation of individual clients.

c. Psychologists do not compensate or give anything of value to a representative of the press, radio, television, or other communication medium in anticipation of or in return for professional publicity in a news item. A paid advertisement must be identified as such, unless it is apparent from the context that it is a paid advertisement. If communicated to the public by use of radio or television, an advertisement shall be prerecorded and approved for broadcast by the psychologist, and a recording of the actual transmission shall be retained by the psychologist.

d. Announcements or advertisements of "personal growth groups," clinics, and agencies give a clear statement of purpose and a clear description of the experiences to be provided, The education, training, and experience of the staff members are appropriately specified.

e. Psychologists associated with the development or promotion of psychological devices, books, or other products offered for commercial sale make reasonable efforts to insure that announcements and advertisements are presented in a professional, scientifically acceptable, and factually informative manner.

f. Psychologists do not participate for personal gain in commercial announcements or advertisements recommending to the public the purchase or use of proprietary or single-source products or services when that participation is based solely upon their identification as psychologists.

g. Psychologists present the science of psychology and offer their services, products, and publications fairly and accurately, avoiding misrepresentation through sensationalism, exaggeration, or superficiality. Psychologists are guided by the primary obligation to aid the public in developing informed judgments, opinions, and choices.

h. As teachers, psychologists insure that statements in catalogs and course outlines are accurate and not misleading, particularly in terms of subject matter to be covered, bases for evaluating progress, and the nature of course experiences. Announcements, brochures, or advertisements describing workshops, seminars, or other educational programs accurately describe the audience for which the program is intended as well as eligibility requirements, educational objectives, and nature of the materials to be covered. These announcements also accurately represent the education, training, and experience of the psychologists presenting the program, and any fees involved.

i. Public announcements or advertisements soliciting research participants in which clinical services or other professional services are offered as an inducement, make clear the nature of the services as well as the costs and other obligations to be accepted by the participants of the research.

j. Psychologists accept the obligation to correct others who represent that psychologist's professional qualifications, or associations with products or services, in a manner incompatible with these guidelines.

k. Individual diagnostic and therapeutic services are provided only in the context of a professional psychological relationship. When personal advice is given by means of public lecture or demonstration, newspaper or magazine articles, radio or television programs, mail, or similar media, the psychologist utilizes the most current relevant data and exercises the highest level of professional judgment.

l. Products that are described or presented by means of public lectures or demonstrations, newspaper or magazine articles, radio or television programs, or similar media meet the same recognized standards as exist for use in the context of a professional relationship.

Principle 5: Confidentiality
Psychologists have a primary obligation to respect the confidentiality of information obtained from persons in the course of their work as psychologists. They reveal such information to others only with the consent of the person or the person's legal representative, except in those unusual circumstances in which not to do so would result in clear danger to the person or to others. Where appropriate, psychologists inform their clients of the legal limits of confidentiality.

a. Information obtained in clinical or consulting relationships, or evaluative data concerning children, students, employees, and others, are discussed only for professional purposes and only with persons clearly concerned with the case. Written and oral reports present only data germane to the purposes of the evaluation and every effort is made to avoid undue invasion of privacy.

b. Psychologists who present personal information obtained during the course of professional work in writings, lectures, or other public forums either obtain adequate prior consent to do so or adequately disguise all identifying information.

c. Psychologists make provisions for maintaining confidentiality in the storage and disposal of records.

d. When working with minors or other persons who are unable to give voluntary informed consent, psychologists take special care to protect these persons' best interests.

Principle 6: Welfare of the Consumer
Psychologists respect the integrity and protect the welfare of the people and groups with whom they work. When there is a conflict of interest between a client and the psychologist's employing institution, psychologists clarify the nature and direction of their loyalties and responsibilities and keep all parties informed of their commitments. Psychologists fully inform consumers as to the purpose and nature of an evaluative, treatment, educational or training procedure, and they freely acknowledge that clients, students, or participants in research have freedom of choice with regard to participation.

a. Psychologists are continually cognizant of their own needs and of their potentially influential position vis-à-vis persons such as clients, students, and subordinates. They avoid exploiting the trust and dependency of such persons. Psychologists make every effort to avoid dual relationships which could impair their professional judgment or increase the risk of exploitation. Examples of such dual relationships include but are not limited to research with and treatment of employees, students, supervisees, close friends, or relatives. Sexual intimacies with clients are unethical.

b. When a psychologist agrees to provide services to a client at the request of a third party, the psychologist assumes the responsibility of clarifying the nature of the relationships to all parties concerned.

c. Where the demands of an organization require psychologists to violate these Ethical Principles, psychologists clarify the nature of the conflict between the demand and these principles. They inform all parties of psychologists' ethical responsibilities, and take appropriate action.

d. Psychologists make advance financial arrangements that safeguard the best interests of and are clearly understood by their clients. They neither give nor receive any remuneration for referring clients for professional services. They contribute a portion of their services to work for which they receive little or no financial return.

e. Psychologists terminate a clinical or consulting relationship when it is reasonably clear that the consumer is not benefitting from it. They offer to help the consumer locate alternative sources of assistance.

Principle 7: Professional Relationships
Psychologists act with due regard for the needs, special competencies, and obligations of their colleagues in psychology and other professions. They respect the prerogatives and obligations of the institutions or organizations with which these other colleagues are associated.

a. Psychologists understand the areas of competence of related professions. They make full use of all the professional, technical, and administrative resources that serve the best interests of consumers. The absence of formal relationships with other professional workers does not relieve psychologists of the responsibility of securing for their clients the best possible professional service nor does it relieve them of the obligation to exercise foresight, diligence, and tact in obtaining the complementary or alternative assistance needed by clients.
b. Psychologists know and take into account the traditions and practices of other professional groups with whom they work and cooperate fully with such groups. If a person is receiving similar services from another professional, psychologists do not offer their own services directly to such a person. If a psychologist is contacted by a person who is already receiving similar services from another professional, the psychologist carefully considers that professional relationship and proceeds with caution and sensitivity to the therapeutic issues as well as the client's welfare. The psychologist discusses these issues with the client so as to minimize the risk of confusion and conflict.
c. Psychologists who employ or supervise other professionals or professionals in training accept the obligation to facilitate the further professional development of these individuals. They provide appropriate working conditions, timely evaluations, constructive consultation and experience opportunities.
d. Psychologists do not exploit their professional relationships with clients, supervisees, students, employees, or research participants sexually or otherwise. Psychologists do not condone nor engage in sexual harrassment. Sexual harrassment is defined as deliberate or repeated comments, gestures, or physical contacts of a sexual nature that are unwanted by the recipient.
e. In conducting research in institutions or organizations, psychologists secure appropriate authorization to conduct such research. They are aware of their obligation to future research workers and insure that host institutions receive adequate information about the research and proper acknowledgement of their contributions.
f. Publication credit is assigned to those who have contributed to a publication in proportion to their professional contribution. Major contributions of a professional character made by several persons to a common project are recognized by joint authorship, with the individual who made the principal contribution listed first. Minor contributions of a professional character and extensive clerical or similar nonprofessional assistance may be acknowledged in footnotes or in an introductory statement. Acknowledgement through specific citation is made for unpublished as well as published material that has directly in-

fluenced the research or writing. A psychologist who compiles and edits material of others for publication publishes the material in the name of the originating group, if appropriate, with his/her own name appearing as chairperson or editor. All contributors are to be acknowledged and named.

g. When psychologists know of an ethical violation by another psychologist, and it seems appropriate, they informally attempt to resolve the issue by bringing the behavior to the attention of the psychologist. If the misconduct is of a minor nature and/or appears to be due to lack of sensitivity, knowledge, or experience, such an informal solution is usually appropriate. Such informal corrective efforts are sensitive to any rights to confidentiality involved. If the violation does not seem amenable to an informal solution, or is of a more serious nature, psychologists bring it to the attention of the appropriate local, state, and/or national committee on professional ethics and conduct.

Principle 8: Assessment Techniques

In the development, publication, and utilization of psychological assessment techniques, psychologists make every effort to promote the welfare and best interests of the client. They guard against the misuse of assessment results. They respect the client's right to know the results, the interpretations made and the bases for their conclusions and recommendations. Psychologists make every effort to maintain the security of tests and other assessment techniques within limits of legal mandates. They strive to assure the appropriate use of assessment techniques by others.

a. In using assessment techniques, psychologists respect the right of clients to have a full explanation of the nature and purpose of the techniques in language that the client can understand, unless an explicit exception to this right has been agreed upon in advance. When the explanations are to be provided by others, the psychologist establishes procedures for insuring the adequacy of these explanations.

b. Psychologists responsible for the development and standardization of psychological tests and other assessment techniques utilize established scientific procedures and observe the relevant APA standards.

c. In reporting assessment results, psychologists indicate any reservations that exist regarding validity or reliability because of the circumstances of the assessment or the inappropriateness of the norms for the person tested. Psychologists strive to insure that the results of assessments and their interpretations are not misused by others.

d. Psychologists recognize that assessment results may become obsolete. They make every effort to avoid and prevent the misuse of obsolete measures.

e. Psychologists offering scoring and interpretation services are able to produce appropriate evidence for the validity of the programs and procedures used in arriving at interpretations. The public offering of an automated interpretation service is considered as a professional-to-professional consultation. The psychologist makes every effort to avoid misuse of assessment reports.

f. Psychologists do not encourage or promote the use of psychological assessment techniques by inappropriately trained or otherwise unqualified persons through teaching, sponsorship, or supervision.

Principle 9: Research with Human Participants

The decision to undertake research rests upon a considered judgment by the individual psychologist about how best to contribute to psychological science and human welfare. Having made the decision to conduct research, the psychologist considers alternative directions in which research energies and resources might be invested. On the basis of this consideration, the psychologist carries out the investigation with respect and concern for the dignity and welfare of the people who participate and with cognizance of federal and state regulations and professional standards governing the conduct of research with human participants.

a. In planning a study, the investigator has the responsibility to make a careful evaluation of its ethical acceptability. To the extent that the weighing of scientific and human values suggests a compromise of any principle, the investigator incurs a correspondingly serious obligation to seek ethical advice and to observe stringent safeguards to protect the rights of human participants.

b. Considering whether a participant in a planned study will be a "subject at risk" or a "subject at minimal risk," according to recognized standards, is of primary ethical concern to the investigator.

c. The investigator always retains the responsibility for insuring ethical practice in research. The investigator is also responsible for the ethical treatment of research participants by collaborators, assistants, students, and employees, all of whom, however, incur similar obligations.

d. Except for minimal risk research, the investigator establishes a clear and fair agreement with the research participants, prior to their participation, that clarifies the obligations and responsibilities of each. The investigator has the obligation to honor all promises and commitments included in that agreement. The investigator informs the participant of all aspects of the research that might reasonably be expected to influence willingness to participate, and explains all other aspects of the the research about which the participant inquires. Failure to make full disclosure prior to obtaining informed consent requires additional safeguards to protect the welfare and dignity of the research participant. Research with children or participants who have impairments which would limit understanding and/or communication, requires special safeguard procedures.

e. Methodological requirements of a study may make the use of concealment or deception necessary. Before conducting such a study, the investigator has a special responsibility to: (i) determine whether the use of such techniques is justified by the study's prospective scientific, educational, or applied value; (ii) determine whether alternative procedures are available that do not utilize concealment or deception; and (iii) insure that the participants are provided with sufficient explanation as soon as possible.

f. The investigator respects the individual's freedom to decline to participate in or to withdraw from the research at any time. The obligation to protect this freedom requires careful thought and consideration when the investigator is in a position of authority or influence over the participants. Such positions of authority include but are not limited to situations when research participation is required as part of employment or when the participant is a student, client, or employee of the investigator.

g. The investigator protects the participants from physical and mental discomfort, harm, and danger that may arise from research procedures. If risks of such consequences exist, the investigator informs the participant of that fact. Research procedures likely to cause serious or lasting harm to a participant are not used unless the failure to use these procedures might expose the participant to risk of greater harm, or unless the research has great potential benefit and fully informed and voluntary consent is obtained from each participant. The participant should be informed of procedures for contacting the investigator within a reasonable time period following participation should stress, potential harm, or related questions or concerns arise.

h. After the data are collected, the investigator provides the participant with information about the nature of the study and attempts to remove any misconceptions that may have arisen. Where scientific or humane values justify delaying or withholding information, the investigator incurs a special responsibility to monitor the research and to assure that there are no damaging consequences for the participant.

i. Where research procedures result in undesirable consequences for the individual participants, the investigator has the responsibility to detect and remove or correct these consequences, including long-term effects.

j. Information obtained about the research participant during the course of an investigation is confidential unless otherwise agreed upon in advance. When the possibility exists that others may obtain access to such information, this possibility, together with the plans for protecting confidentiality, is explained to the participant as part of the procedure for obtaining informed consent.

Principle 10: Care and Use of Animals
An investigator of animal behavior strives to advance our understanding of basic behavioral principles and/or to contribute to the improvement of human health and welfare. In seeking these ends, the investigator insures the welfare of the animals and treats them humanely. Laws and regulations notwithstanding, the animal's immediate protection depends upon the scientist's own conscience.

a. The acquisition, care, use, and disposal of all animals is in compliance with current federal, state or provincial, and local laws and regulations.

b. A psychologist trained in research methods and experienced in the care of laboratory animals closely supervises all procedures involving animals and is responsible for insuring appropriate consideration of their comfort, health, and humane treatment.

c. Psychologists insure that all individuals using animals under their supervision have received explicit instructions in experimental methods and in the care, maintenance, and handling of the species being used. Responsibilities and activities of individuals participating in a research project are consistent with their respective competencies.

d. Psychologists make every effort to minimize discomfort, illness, and pain to the animals. A procedure subjecting animals to pain, stress, or privation is used only when an alternative procedure is unavailable and the goal is justified by its prospective scientific, educational, or applied value. Surgical procedures are performed under appropriate anesthesia; techniques to avoid infection and minimize pain are followed during and after surgery.

e. When it is appropriate that the animal's life be terminated, it is done rapidly and painlessly.

APPENDIX 5
CODE OF ETHICS

APPENDIX 5

Code of Ethics (1981)
(American Sociological Association)[1]

Preamble

Along with other scholarly and scientific disciplines, sociology subscribes to the general tenets of science and scholarship. Teaching sociologists are also guided by ethical and professional principles that govern that activity. In addition, because of its specific subject matters, sociologists are especially sensitive to the potential for harm to individuals, groups, organizations, communities and societies that may arise out of the misuse of sociological work and knowledge.

As a discipline committed to the free and open access to knowledge and to self regulation through peer review and appraisal, sociology shares with other disciplines the commitment to the pursuit of accurate and precise knowledge and to public disclosure of findings. However, because sociology necessarily entails study of individuals, groups, organizations and societies, these principles may occasionally conflict with more general ethical concerns for the rights of subjects to privacy and for the treatment of subjects with due

---

[1] Approved by the Council (governing body of the association) on May 16, 1981; not yet submitted to the membership for approval. For further information, contact the Association at 1722 N Street, N.W., Washington, D.C. 20036.

164

regard for their integrity, dignity and autonomy. This potential conflict provides one of the justifications for a code of ethics.

The styles of sociological work are diverse and changing. So also are the contexts within which sociologists find employment. These diversities of procedures and context have led to ambiguities concerning appropriate professional behavior. These ambiguities provide another justification for this code.

Finally, this code also attempts to meet the expressed needs of sociologists who have asked for guidance in how best to proceed in a variety of situations involving subjects of investigation, relations with colleagues, and public authorities.

This code establishes feasible requirements for ethical behavior. These requirements cover many—but not all—of the potential sources of ethical conflict that may arise in scholarship, research, teaching and practice. Most represent *prima facie* obligations that may admit of exceptions but which should generally stand as principles for guiding conduct. The code states an associational consensus about ethical behavior upon which the Committee on Professional Ethics will base its judgments when it must decide whether individual members of the Association have acted unethically in specific instances. More than this, however, the code is meant to sensitize all sociologists to the ethical issues that may arise in their work, and to encourage sociologists to educate themselves and their colleagues to behave ethically. To fulfill these purposes, we, the members of the American Sociological Association, affirm and support the following Code of Ethics:

I. Sociological Research and Practice
  A. Objectivity and Integrity
  Sociologists should strive to maintain objectivity and integrity in the conduct of sociological and research practice.

1. Sociologists should adhere to the highest possible technical standards in their research. When findings may have direct implications for public policy or for the well-being of subjects, research should not be undertaken unless the requisite skills and resources are available to accomplish the research adequately.
2. Since individual sociologists vary in their research modes, skills and experience, sociologists should always set forth *ex ante* the disciplinary and personal limitations that condition whether or not a research project can be successfully completed and condition the validity of findings.
3. Regardless of work settings, sociologists are obligated to report findings fully and without omission of significant data. Sociologists should also disclose details of their theories, methods and research designs that might bear upon interpretation of research findings.
4. Sociologists must report fully all sources of financial support in their publications and must note any special relations to any sponsor.
5. Sociologists should not make any guarantees to subjects—individuals, groups or organizations—unless there is full intention and ability to honor such commitments. All such guarantees, once made, must be honored unless there is a clear, compelling and overriding reason not to do so.
6. Consistent with the spirit of full disclosure of method and analysis, sociologists should make their data available to other qualified social scientists, at reasonable cost, after they have completed their

own analyses, except in cases where confidentiality or the claims of a fieldworker to the privacy of personal notes necessarily would be violated in doing so. The timeliness of this obligation is especially critical where the research is perceived to have policy implications.

7. Sociologists must not accept grants, contracts or research assignments that appear likely to require violation of the principles above, and should dissociate themselves from research when they discover a violation and are unable to achieve its correction.

8. When financial support for a project has been accepted, sociologists must make every reasonable effort to complete the proposed work, including reports to the funding source.

9. When several sociologists, including students, are involved in joint projects, there should be mutually accepted explicit agreements, preferably written, at the outset with respect to division of work, compensation, access to data, rights of authorship, and other rights and responsibilities. Of course, such agreements may need to be modified as the project evolves.

10. When it is likely that research findings will bear on public policy or debate, sociologists should take particular care to state all significant qualifications on the findings and interpretations of their researches.

B. Sociologists must not knowingly use their disciplinary roles as covers to obtain information for other than disciplinary purposes.

C. Cross-national Research

Research conducted in foreign countries raises special ethical issues for the investigator and the professional. Disparities in wealth, power, and political systems between the researcher's country and the host country may create problems of equity in research collaboration and conflicts of interest for the visiting scholar. Also, to follow the precepts of the scientific method—such as those requiring full disclosure—may entail adverse consequences or personal risks for individuals and groups in the host country. Finally, irresponsible actions by a single researcher or research team can eliminate or reduce future access to a country by the entire profession and its allied fields.

1. Sociologists should not use their research or consulting roles as covers to gather intelligence for any government.

2. Sociologists should not act as agents for any organization or government without disclosing that role.

3. Researchers should take culturally appropriate steps to secure informed consent and to avoid invasions of privacy. Special actions may be necessary where the individuals studied are illiterate, of very low social status, and/or unfamiliar with social research.

4. While generally adhering to the norm of acknowledging the contributions of all collaborators, sociologists working in foreign areas should be sensitive to harms that may arise from disclosure, and respect a collaborator's wish and/or need for anonymity. Full disclosure may be made later if circumstances permit.

5. All research findings, except those likely to cause harm to collaborators and participants, should be made available in the host country, ideally in the language of that country. Where feasible, raw data stripped of identifiers should also be made available. With repressive governments and in situations of armed conflict, researchers should take particular care to avoid inflicting harm.

6. Because research and/or findings may have important political repercussions, sociologists must weigh carefully the political effects of conducting research or disclosure of findings on international tensions or domestic conflicts. It can be anticipated that there are some circumstances where disclosure would be desirable despite possible adverse effects; however, ordinarily research should not be undertaken or findings released when they can be expected to exacerbate international tensions or domestic conflicts.

D. Work Outside of Academic Settings

Sociologists who work in organizations providing a lesser degree of autonomy than academic settings may face special problems. In satisfying their obligations to employers, sociologists in such settings must make every effort to adhere to the professional obligations contained in this code. Those accepting employment as sociologists in business, government, and other non-academic settings should be aware of possible constraints on research and publication in those settings and should negotiate clear understandings about such conditions accompanying their research and scholarly activity.

E. Respect for the Rights of Research Populations

1. Individuals, families, households, kin and friendship groups that are subjects of research are entitled to rights of biographical anonymity. Organizations, large collectivities such as neighborhoods, ethnic groups, or religious denominations, corporations, governments, public agencies, public officials, persons in the public eye, are not entitled automatically to privacy and need not be extended routinely guarantees of privacy and confidentiality. However, if any guarantees are made, they must be honored unless there are clear and compelling reasons not to do so.

2. Information about persons obtained from records that are open to public scrutiny cannot be protected by guarantees of privacy or confidentiality.

3. The process of conducting sociological research must not expose subjects to *substantial* risk or personal harm. Where modest risk or harm is anticipated, informed consent must be obtained.

4. To the extent possible in a given study, researchers should anticipate potential threats to confidentiality. Such means as the removal of identifiers, the use of randomized responses, and other statistical solutions to problems of privacy should be used where appropriate.

5. Confidential information provided by research participants must be treated as such by sociologists, even when this information enjoys no legal protection or privilege and legal force is applied. The obligation to respect confidentiality also applies to members of research organizations (interviewers, coders, clerical staff, etc.) who have access to the information. It is the responsibility of the chief investigator to instruct staff members on this point.

II. *Publications and Review Processes*

A. Questions of Authorship and Acknowledgment

1. Sociologists must acknowledge all persons who contributed significantly to the research and publication processes.

2. Claims and ordering of authorship must accurately reflect the contributions of all major participants in the research and writing process, including students.

3. Material taken verbatim from another person's published or un-

published work must be explicitly identified and referenced to its author. Borrowed ideas or data, even if not quoted, must be explicitly acknowledged.

B. In submission for publication, authors, editors and referees share coordinate responsibilities.

1. Journal editors must provide prompt decisions to authors of submitted manuscripts. They must monitor the work of associate editors and other referees so that delays are few and reviews are conscientious.
2. An editor's commitment to publish an essay must be binding on the journal.
3. Editors receiving reviews of manuscripts from persons who have previously reviewed those manuscripts for another journal should ordinarily seek additional reviews.

C. Participation in Review Processes

Sociologists are frequently asked to provide evaluations of manuscripts, research proposals, or other work of professional colleagues. In such work, sociologists should hold themselves to high standards of performance, in several specific ways:

1. Sociologists should decline requests for reviews of the work of others where strong conflicts of interest are involved, such as may occur when a person is asked to review work by teachers, friends, or colleagues for whom he or she feels an overriding sense of personal obligation, competition, or enmity, or when such requests cannot be fulfilled on time.
2. Materials sent for review should be read in their entirety and considered carefully. Evaluations should be justified with explicit reasons.
3. Sociologists who are asked to review manuscripts and books they have previously reviewed should make this fact known to the editor requesting the review.

III. Teaching and Supervision

The routine conduct of faculty responsibilities is treated at length in the faculty codes and AAUP rules accepted as governing procedures by the various institutions of higher learning. Sociologists in teaching roles should be familiar with the content of the codes in force at their institutions and should perform their responsibilities within such guidelines.

A. Sociologists are obligated to protect the rights of students to fair treatment.

1. Sociologists should provide students with a fair and honest statement of the scope and perspective of their courses, clear expectations for student performances and fair evaluations of their work.
2. Departments of Sociology must provide graduate students with explicit policies and criteria about recruitment, admission, courses and examination requirements, financial support, and conditions of possible dismissal.
3. Sociology Departments should help to locate employment for their graduates.
4. Sociologists must refrain from disclosure of personal information concerning students where such information is not directly relevant to issues of professional competence.

B. Sociologists must refrain from exploiting students.
    1. Sociologists must not coerce or deceive students into serving as research subjects.
    2. Sociologists must not represent the work of students as their own.
C. Sociologists must not use their professional positions or rank to coerce personal or sexual favors or economic or professional advantages from students, research assistants, clerical staff or colleagues.
D. Sociologists may not permit personal animosities or intellectual differences vis-a-vis colleagues to foreclose student access to those colleagues.

The Standing Committee on Professional Ethics, appointed by the Council of the American Sociological Association, shall have primary responsibility for the interpretation of this Code, for the investigation of complaints brought under it, and for recommendations to Council pertinent to such complaints.

REFERENCES

FEDERAL LAWS CITED

Public Law 90-23. Freedom of Information Act of 1966.
Public Law 92-255. Drug Abuse Office and Treatment Act of 1972.
Public Law 95-38. Privacy Act of 1974.
Public Law 96-440. Privacy Protection Act of 1980.

UNITED STATES CODE CITATIONS

Title 13 USC Statute 8-9 (1976). Census Administration (Information as Confidential).
Title 20 USC Statute 1232g (1976). Education (Family Educational and Privacy Rights [Buckley Amendment]).
Title 42 USC Statute 3771 (1976). Law Enforcement Assistance (Information Available for Prescribed Purposes).

CODE OF FEDERAL REGULATIONS CITATIONS

Title 20 Part 401 (1976), Social Security Administration (Disclosure of Official Records and Information).
Title 42 Part 2a (1979), Public Health (Protection of Identity: Research Subjects).
Title 45 Part 46 (1979), Public Welfare (Protection of Research Subjects).

FEDERAL REGISTER CITATIONS

Department of Health and Human Services: Office of the Secretary. Public Health Service Human Research Subjects. *46*(16), January 26, 1981: 8,366-8,392.

Department of Health, Education, and Welfare: Public Health Service, Protection of Identity: Research Subjects. *44*(66), April 4, 1979: 20,382-20,387.

Department of Health, Education, and Welfare: Food and Drug Administration, Office of the Secretary. Protection of Human Research Subjects. *44*(158), August 14, 1979: 47,688-47,709.

Department of Health, Education, and Welfare: Office of the Secretary. Protection of Human Subjects: Research Involving Children. *43*(141), July 21, 1978: 31,786-31,794.

Department of Health, Education, and Welfare: Office of the Secretary. Protection of Human Subjects: Proposed Regulations on Research Involving Those Institutionalized as Mentally Disabled. *43*(223), November 17, 1978: 53,950-53,956.

Office of Management and Budget. Controlling Paperwork Burdens on the Public: Proposed Rule Making. *45*(8), January 11, 1980: 2,586-2,600.

LEGAL CASES CITED

Aguayo v. *Richardson,* 473 F. 2d 1090 (1973).

California Welfare Rights Organization v. *Richardson,* 348 F. Supp. 491 (1972).

Crane v. *Mathews,* 417 F. Supp. 532 (1976).

People v. *Newman,* 298 NE 2d 651 (N.Y. 1973).

Washington Research Project v. *Department of Health, Education, and Welfare,* 366 F. Supp. 929 (1973), 504 F. 2d 238 (1975).

AUTHORS CITED

ABELSON, R. P. and J. C. MILLER   1967   Negative Persuasion via Personal Insult. *Journal of Experimental Social Psychology, 3:* 321-33.

ABRAMS, S.   1975   A Response to Lykken on the Polygraph. *American Psychologist, 30:* 709-11.

ABT, CLARK C.   1979   Federal Regulation of Social Research; Survey Instrument. Chapter 9 in M. L. Wax and J. Cassell (Eds.), *Federal Regulations: Ethical Issues and Social Research.* Boulder, Colo.: Westview Press, Pp. 151-72.

ALLEN, H.   1972   Bystander Intervention and Helping on the Subway. In L. Bickman and T. Henchey (Eds.), *Beyond the Laboratory: Field Research in Social Psychology.* New York: McGraw-Hill.

AMERICAN ANTHROPOLOGICAL ASSOCIATION   1971   Statement on Ethics: Principles of Professional Responsibility. Adopted May 1971.

AMERICAN PSYCHOLOGIST   1965   Vol. 20, issues 2 and 11.

AMERICAN STATISTICAL ASSOCIATION   1974   Is the Public Acceptability of Social Survey Research Declining? *The American Statistician, 28:* 30-33.

AMRINE, M. and F. H. SANFORD   1956   In the Matter of Juries, Democracy, Science, Truth, Senators, and Bugs. *American Psychologist, 11:* 54-60.

172   References

ANNAS, G.   1976   Confidentiality and the Duty to Warn. *The Hastings Center Report, 6*(6): 6-8.

ANNAS, G. J., L. H. GLANTZ, and B. F. KATZ   1977   *Informed Consent to Human Experimentation: The Subject's Dilemma.* Cambridge, Mass.: Ballinger.

AUGER, P.   1956   Science as a Force for Unity Among Men. *Bulletin of the Atomic Scientists, 12*(6): 208-10.

BACK, KURT W.   1972   *Beyond Words: The Story of Sensitivity Training and the Encounter Movement.* New York: Russell Sage Foundation.

BARTH, F.   1974   On Responsibility and Humanity: Calling a Colleague to Account. *Current Anthropology, 15*(1): 99-102.

BAUMRIND, D.   1964   Some Thoughts on Ethics of Research: After Reading Milgram's "Behavioral Study of Obedience." *American Psychologist, 19:* 421-23.   1971   Principles of Ethical Conduct in the Treatment of Subjects: Reaction to the Draft Report of the Committee on Ethical Standards in Psychological Research. *American Psychologist, 26*(10): 887-96.   1975   Metaethical and Normative Considerations Covering the Treatment of Human Subjects in the Behavioral Sciences. In Eugene C. Kennedy (Ed.), *Human Rights and Psychological Research.* New York: Thomas Y. Crowell, Pp. 37-68.

BEALS, R. L.   1969   *The Politics of Social Research.* Chicago: Aldine.

BELL, E. H.   1959   Freedom and Responsibility in Research: Comments. *Human Organization, 18*(2): 49.

BENTHAM, J.   1789   *An Introduction to the Principles of Morals and Legislation.* Edinburgh: William Tait.

BERMANT, G., H. C. KELMAN, and D. P. WARWICK (Eds.)   1978   *The Ethics of Social Intervention.* New York: Wiley.

BERSCHEID, E., et al.   1973   Anticipating Informed Consent: An Empirical Approach. *American Psychologist, 28:* 913-25.

BLACK, H. C.   1968   *Black's Law Dictionary.* 4th ed., revised. St. Paul, Minn.: West Publishing Co.

BLASI, V.   1971   Press Subpoenas: An Empirical and Legal Analysis. *Michigan Law Review, 70:* 229-84.

BOK, S.   1974   The Ethics of Giving Placebos. *Scientific American, 231*(5): 17-23.

BONESS, F. and J. F. CORDES   1973   The Researcher-Subject Relationship: The Need for Protection and a Model Statute. *The Georgetown Law Journal, 62:* 243-72.

BORUCH, ROBERT F. and JOE S. CECIL   1979a   *Assuring the Confidentiality of Social Research.* Philadelphia: University of Pennsylvania Press.   1979b   On Solutions to Some Privacy Problems Engendered by Federal Regulations and Social Custom. In M. Wax and J. Cassell (Eds.), *Federal Regulations: Ethical Issues and Social Research.* Boulder, Colo.: Westview Press.

BOUCHARD, T. J., Jr.   1976   Unobtrusive Measures. An Inventory of Uses. *Sociological Methods and Research, 4*(3): 267-300.

BRADBURN, N. M., S. SUDMAN, et al.   1979   *Improving Interview Method and Questionnaire Design.* San Francisco: Jossey-Bass.

BRANDL, JOHN E.   1978   Evaluation and Politics. *Evaluation: A Forum for Human Service Decision-Makers.* Special Issue: 6-7.

BRANDT, R. M.   1972   *Studying Behavior in Natural Settings.* New York: Holt, Rinehart & Winston.

BREGER, M. J. 1976 Legal Aspects of Social Science Research. Presented during a symposium, "Ethical Issues in Social Science Research," at the University of Minnesota, Minneapolis.

BULMER, M. I. A. 1979 Parliament and the British Census Since 1920. Chapter 11 in M. Bulmer (Ed.), *Censuses, Surveys, and Privacy*. London: Macmillan. Pp. 158-69.

BURTON, R. V. 1976 Honesty and Dishonesty. Chapter 10 in T. Lickona (Ed.), *Moral Development and Behavior*. New York: Holt, Rinehart & Winston.

BUTCHER, J. N. and A. TELLEGEN 1966 Objections to MMPI Items. *Journal of Consulting Psychology*, *30*(6): 527-34.

CAIN, L. D., Jr. 1967 The AMA and the Gerontologists: Uses and Abuses of "A Profile of the Aging: USA." Chapter 4 in G. Sjoberg (Ed.), *Ethics, Politics, and Social Research*. Cambridge, Mass.: Schenkman Publishing Company, Inc. Pp. 78-114.

CAPRON, A. M. 1975 Social Experimentation and the Law. In A. M. Rivlin and P. M. Timpane (Eds.), *Ethical and Legal Issues of Social Experimentation*. Washington, D.C.: The Brookings Institution.

CARDON, P. V., F. W. DOMMEL, Jr., and R. R. TRUMBLE 1976 Injuries to Research Subjects: A Survey of Investigators. *New England Journal of Medicine*, 295: 650-54.

CARLSON, M. D. 1974 The 1972-73 Consumer Expenditure Survey. *Monthly Labor Review* (December): 16-23.

CARROLL, J. D. 1973 Confidentiality of Social Science Research and Data: The Popkin Case. *P. S., 6*(3): 268-80.

CARROLL, J. D. and C. R. KNERR 1976 The APSA Confidentiality in Social Sciences Research Project: A Final Report. *P. S.* (Fall): 416-19. 1977 Confidentiality and Criminological Research: The Evolving Body of Law. Submitted for publication.

CASSELL, JOAN 1978 Risk and Benefit to Subjects of Fieldwork. *The American Sociologist, 13:* 134-43.

CASSELL, J. and M. L. WAX (Eds.) 1980 Ethical Problems of Fieldwork. Special Issue of *Social Problems, 27*(3): 258-378.

CHALKLEY, D. T. 1975 Requirements for Compliance with Part 46 of Title 45 of the Code of Federal Regulations as Amended March 13, 1975, and the Secretary of Health, Education, and Welfare's Notice of May 20, 1975. Memorandum from the Director, Office for Protection from Research Risks, Office of the Director, NIH, DHEW, May 22, 1975.

CHRISTIE, R. M. 1976 Comment on Conflict Methodology: A Protagonist Position. *Sociological Quarterly, 17:* 513-19.

COOK, V. G. 1973 *Shield Laws: A Report on Freedom of the Press.* Lexington, Ky.: Council of State Governments.

COOLEY, T. M. 1888 *A Treatise on the Law of Torts, or the Wrongs Which Arise Independent of Contract.* 2nd ed. Chicago: Callaghan & Co.

CULLITON, R. J. 1976 Confidentiality: Court Declares Researcher Can Protect Sources. *Science, 193:* 467-69.

DAHLSTROM, W. G. 1969 Recurrent Issues in the Development of the MMPI. Chapter 1 in J. N. Butcher (Ed.), *MMPI: Research Developments and Clinical Applications*. New York: McGraw-Hill. Pp. 1-40.

DAHLSTROM, W. G., G. S. WELSH, and L. E. DAHLSTROM 1972 *An MMPI Handbook—Volume I: Clinical Interpretation*. Rev. ed. Minneapolis: University of Minnesota Press. 1975 *An MMPI Handbook—Volume II: Research Applications*. Rev. ed. Minneapolis: University of Minnesota Press.

DALTON, M. 1959 *Men Who Manage*. New York: Wiley.

"DECLARATION OF TOKYO" 1976 *World Medical Journal, 22*(6): 87-90.

DEUTSCHER, I. 1973 *What We Say/What We Do: Sentiments and Acts*. Glenview, Ill.: Scott, Foresman and Company.

DIENER, E. and R. CRANDALL 1978 *Ethics in Social and Behavioral Research*. Chicago: University of Chicago Press, 1978.

DILLMAN, D. A. 1978 *Mail and Telephone Surveys: The Total Design Method*. New York: Wiley.

DORNBUSCH, S. M. 1955 The Military Academy as an Assimilating Institution. *Social Forces, 33:* 316-21.

EDSALL, J. T. 1975 Scientific Freedom and Responsibility. *Science, 188:* 687-93.

EPSTEIN, L. C. and L. LASAGNA 1969 Obtaining Informed Consent: Form or Substance. *Archives of Internal Medicine, 123:* 682-88.

EPSTEIN, Y. M., D. SUDEFELD, and S. J. SILVERSTEIN 1973 The Experimental Contract: Subject's Expectations and Reactions to Some Behaviors of Experimenters. *American Psychologist, 28:* 212-21.

ERICKSON, M. 1968 The Inhumanity of Ordinary People. *International Journal of Psychiatry, 6:* 277-79.

ERRERA, P. 1972 Statement Based on Interviews with Forty "Worst Cases" in the Milgram Obedience Experiments. Reprinted in J. Katz, *Experimentation with Human Beings*. New York: Russell Sage Foundation. P. 400.

ETZIONI, A. 1968 A Model of Significant Research. *International Journal of Psychiatry, 6:* 279-80.

EYSENCK, H. J. 1961 The Effects of Psychotherapy. Chapter 18 in H. J. Eysenck (Ed.), *Handbook of Abnormal Psychology*. New York: Basic Books.

FARR, J. L. and W. B. SEAVER 1975 Stress and Discomfort in Psychological Research: Subject Perceptions of Experimental Procedures. *American Psychologist, 30*(7): 770-73.

FESTINGER, L., H. W. REICKEN, and S. SCHACHTER 1956 *When Prophecy Fails*. Minneapolis: University of Minnesota Press.

FEUILLAN, J. 1976 Every Man's Evidence Versus a Testimonial Privilege for Survey Researchers. *Public Opinion Quarterly, 40:* 39-50.

FISS, O. M. 1976 Groups and the Equal Protection Clause. *Philosophy and Public Affairs, 5*(2): 107-77.

FLETCHER, J. 1966 *Situation Ethics*. Philadelphia: Westminster Press. 1967 *Moral Responsibility: Situation Ethics at Work*. Philadelphia: Westminster Press.

FREEDMAN, J. L. and S. C. FRASER 1966 Compliance Without Pressure: The Foot-in-the-Door Technique. *Journal of Personality and Social Psychology, 4:* 195-202.

FRIED, C. 1978 *Right and Wrong*. Cambridge, Mass.: Harvard University Press.

GALLIHER, J. R. 1973 The Protection of Human Subjects: A Reexamination of the Professional Code of Ethics. *American Sociologist, 8:* 93-100. 1974 Professor Galliher Replies. *American Sociologist, 9:* 159-60.

GARD, S. A.   1972   *Jones on Evidence: Civil and Criminal.* 6th ed. Vol. 3. Rochester, N. Y.: Lawyers Co-Operative Publishing Co.

GELLHORN, A.   1978   Violations of Human Rights: Torture and the Medical Profession. *New England Journal of Medicine, 299*(7): 358-59.

GIBBONS, D. C.   1975   Unidentified Research Sites and Fictitious Names. *American Sociologist, 10*(1): 32-6.

GLYNN, K. L.   1978   Regulations Regarding the Use of Human Subjects in Research: Effect on Investigators's Ethical Sensitivity, Research Practices, and Research Priorities. Presented at the American Sociological Association annual meeting, San Francisco, Calif.

GOUGH, J. W.   1957   *The Social Contract.* 2nd ed. Oxford, Eng.: The Clarendon Press.

GRAY, BRADFORD H.   1980   Bills Support Confidentiality of Data. *ASA Footnotes,* (May) *8*(5): 9.

GRIFFIN, J. H.   1961   *Black Like Me.* Boston: Houghton Mifflin.

HATHAWAY, S. R.   1964   MMPI: Professional Use by Professional People. *American Psychologist, 19:* 204-10.

HENDEL, S. and R. BARD   1973   Should There Be a Researcher's Privilege? *AAUP Bulletin, 59:* 398-401.

HENDRICK, C. (Ed.)   1977   Role-playing as a Methodology for Social Research: A Symposium. *Personality and Social Psychology Bulletin, 3:* 454-523.

HESSLER, R. M., P. K. NEW, and J. T. MAY   1979   Power, Exchange, and the Research-Development Link. *Human Organization, 38*(4): 334-42.

HOLMES, D. S.   1976a   Debriefing after Psychological Experiments: I. Effectiveness of Postdeception Dehoaxing. *American Psychologist, 31:* 858-67. 1976b Debriefing after Psychological Experiments: II. Effectiveness of Postexperimental Desensitizing. *American Psychologist, 31:* 868-75.

HOMANS, G. C.   1946   The Small Warship. *American Sociological Review, 11:* 294-300.

HONIGFELD, G.   1964   Nonspecific Factors in Treatment: I. Review of Placebo Reactors; II. Review of Social-Psychological Factors. *Diseases of the Nervous System, 25:* 145-56; 225-39.

HUMPHREYS, L.   1970   *Tearoom Trade: Impersonal Sex in Public Places.* Chicago: Aldine. 1972 *Out of the Closets: The Sociology of Homosexual Liberation.* Englewood Cliffs, N.J.: Prentice-Hall.

INSTITUTE FOR SOCIAL RESEARCH   1976   Research Involving Human Subjects. A Report to the National Commission for the Protection of Human Subjects of Biomedical and Behavioral Research. Ann Arbor: University of Michigan.

JENSEN, A. R.   1969   How Much Can We Boost IQ and Scholastic Achievement? *Harvard Educational Review, 39*(1): 1-123.

JESSOR, S. L. and R. JESSOR   1975   Transition from Virginity to Nonvirginity Among Youth: A Social-Psychological Study over Time. *Developmental Psychology, 11:* 473-84.

JOSEPHSON, E.   1975   Notes on the Sociology of Privacy. *Humanitas, 11* (February): 25.

KANT, I.   1785   *The Fundamental Principles of the Metaphysics of Ethics.* O. Manthey-Zorn, trans. New York: Appleton-Century-Crofts, 1938.

KATZ, J.   1972   *Experimentation with Human Beings.* New York: Russell Sage Foundation.

KAUFMAN, H.   1967   The Price of Obedience and the Price of Knowledge. *American Psychologist, 22:* 321-22.

KELLING, G. L., et al.   1974   *The Kansas City Preventive Patrol Experiment: A Technical Report.* Washington, D.C.: The Police Foundation.

KERSHAW, D. N.   1972   A Negative-Income-Tax Experiment. *Scientific American, 227*(4): 19-25.

KERSHAW, D. N. and J. L. SMALL   1972   Data Confidentiality and Privacy: Lessons from the New Jersey Negative-Income-Tax Experiment. *Public Policy, 20*(2): 257-80.

KIPNIS, L.   1979   An Undergraduate's Experience with Human Subjects Review Committees. Chapter 13 in M. L. Wax and J. Cassell (Eds.), *Federal Regulations: Ethical Issues and Social Research.* Boulder, Colo.: Westview Press. Pp. 219-37.

KRASNER, L. and L. P. ULLMAN   1965   *Research in Behavior Modification: New Developments and Implications.* New York: Holt, Rinehart & Winston.

LAPIERE, R. T.   1935   Attitudes vs. Actions. *Social Forces, 13:* 230-37.

LATANÉ, B.   1970   Field Studies of Altruistic Compliance. *Representative Research in Social Psychology, 11:* 49-60.

LATANÉ, B. and J. M. DARLEY   1970   Social Determinants of Bystander Intervention in Emergencies. In J. Macaulay and L. Berkowitz (Eds.), *Altruism and Helping Behavior.* New York: Academic Press. Pp. 13-28.

LEVENDUSKY, P. and L. PANKRATZ   1975   Self-Control Techniques as an Alternative to Pain Medication. *Journal of Abnormal Psychology, 84:* 165-68.

LEWIS, O.   1961   *The Children of Sanchez: Autobiography of a Mexican Family.* New York: Random House.

LICHTENSTEIN, E.   1970   Please Don't Talk to Anyone about This Experiment: Disclosure of Deception by Debriefed Subjects. *Psycholgoical Reports, 26:* 485-86.

LISKA, A. E. (Ed.)   1975   *The Consistency Controversy.* New York: Halsted Press.

LOFLAND, J. R. and R. A. LEJEUNE   1960   Initial Interaction of Newcomers in Alcoholics Anonymous: A Field Experiment in Class Symbols and Socialization. *Social Problems, 8*(2): 102-11.

LUBORSKY, L. et al.   1971   Factors Influencing the Outcome of Psychotherapy. *Psychological Bulletin, 75*(3): 145-85.

LUEPTOW, L., S. A. MUELLER, R. R. HAMMES, and L. S. MASTER   1977   The Impact of Informed Consent Regulations on Response Rate and Response Bias. *Sociological Methods and Research, 6*(2): 183-204.

LUNDMAN, R. J. and P. T. McFARLANE   1976   Conflict Methodology: An Introduction and Preliminary Assessment. *Sociological Quarterly, 17:* 502-12.

LYKKEN, D. T.   1974   Psychology and the Lie-Detector Industry. *American Psychologist, 29:* 725-39. 1975a Lykken Replies. *American Psychologist, 30:* 711-12. 1975b The Right Way to Use a Lie Detector. *Psychology Today, 8*(10): 56-60.   1980   *A Tremor in the Blood: Uses and Abuses of the Lie Detector.* New York: McGraw-Hill.

MACALLUM, G. C., Jr.   1967   Negative and Positive Freedom. *Philosophical Review, 76:* 312-34.

MALAMUTH, N. M., S. FESHBACH, and M. HEIM   1980   Ethical Issues and Exposure to Rape Stimuli: A Reply to Sherif. *Journal of Personality and Social Psychology, 38*(3): 413-15.

MALAMUTH, N. M., M. HEIM, and S. FESHBACH   1980   Sexual Responsiveness of College Students to Rape Depictions: Inhibitory and Disinhibitory Effects. *Journal of Personality and Social Psychology, 38*(3): 399-408.

MARSHALL, E.   1980a   Psychotherapy Faces Test of Worth. *Science, 207:* 35-36.   1980b   Psychotherapy Works, but for Whom? *Science, 207:* 506-8.

MAUGER, P. A.   1972   The Test-Retest Reliability of Persons: An Empirical Investigation Utilizing the MMPI and the Personality Research Form. Doctoral dissertation, University of Minnesota (DAI, 33, 2816B).

MEAD, M.   1969   Research with Human Beings: A Model Derived from Anthropological Field Practice. *Daedalus, 98*(2): 361-86.

MEEHL, P. E.   1954   *Clinical versus Statistical Prediction: A Theoretical Analysis and a Review of the Evidence.* Minneapolis: University of Minnesota Press.   1969   Comments on the Invasion of Privacy Issue. Chapter 13 in J. N. Butcher (Ed.), MMPI: Research Developments and Clinical Applications. New York: McGraw-Hill. Pp. 273-78.

MEGLINO, B. M.   1976a   Human Participants in Research: A Methodology for Determining Risk Through Subject Perceptions. Unpublished report, University of South Carolina.   1976b   Human Participants in Research: Assessing Legal and Ethical Requirements Through Subject Perceptions. Unpublished report, College of Business Administration, University of South Carolina.

MENGES, R. J.   1973   Openness and Honesty Versus Coercion and Deception in Psychological Research. *American Psychologist, 28*(12): 1030-34.

MIDDLEMIST, R. D., E. S. KNOWLES and C. F. MATTER   1976   Personal Space Invasions in the Lavatory: Suggestive Evidence for Arousal. *Journal of Personality and Social Psychology, 33*(5): 541-46.

MILGRAM, S.   1963   Behavioral Study of Obedience. *Journal of Abnormal and Social Psychology, 67:* 371-78.   1964   Issues in the Study of Obedience: A Reply to Baumrind. *American Psychologist, 19:* 848-52.   1965   Some Conditions of Obedience and Disobedience to Authority. *Human Relations, 18*(1): 57-76.   1968   Reply to Critics. *International Journal of Psychiatry, 6:* 294-95.   1969   The Lost-Letter Technique. *Psychology Today, 3*(1): 30-33, 66, 68.   1970   The Experience of Living in Cities. *Science, 167:* 1461-68.   1972   Interpreting Obedience: Error and Evidence. In A. G. Miller (Ed.), *The Social Psychology of Psychological Research.* New York: Free Press.   1974   *Obedience to Authority.* New York: Harper Colophon Books.   1977   Subject Reaction: The Neglected Factor in the Ethics of Experimentation. *Hastings Center Report, 7*(5): 19-23.

MILGRAM, S. and P. HOLLANDER   1964   The Murder They Heard. *Nation, 198:* 602-4.

MILL, J. S.   1863   Utilitarianism. In S. Gorovitz (Ed.), *Utilitarianism: With Critical Essays.* Indianapolis, Ind.: Bobbs-Merrill, 1971.

MIXON, D.   1972   Instead of Deception. *Journal for the Theory of Social Behavior, 2:* 145-77.

MOSTELLER, F.   1980   Regulation of Social Research. *Science, 208:* 1219.

NATIONAL INSTITUTE OF HEALTH   1968   *Guide for Laboratory Annual*

Facilities and Care. (Public Health Service Publication No. 1029.) Washington, D.C.: U.S. Government Printing Office.

NEJELSKI, P. and K. FINSTERBUSCH 1973 The Prosecutor and the Researcher: Present and Prospective Variations in the Supreme Court's Bransburg Decision. *Social Problems, 21*(3): 3-21.

NEJELSKI, P. and L. M. LERMAN 1971 A Researcher-Subject Testimonial Privilege: What to Do Before the Subpoena Arrives. *Wisconsin Law Review, 1971*(4): 1085-1148.

NEJELSKI, P. and H. PEYSER 1975 A Researcher's Shield Statute: Guarding Against the Compulsory Disclosure of Research Data. Appendix B to *Protecting Individual Privacy in Evaluation Research.* Washington, D.C.: National Academy of Science.

NEW YORK TIMES, THE 1977 Ex-Lab Worker Convicted in Release of Two Dolphins. December 10, p. 12.

NORRIS, N. 1966 Impediments to Penal Reform. *University of Chicago Law Review, 33:* 646-53.

OLAFSON, F. A. (Ed.) 1961 *Society, Law, and Morality.* Englewood Cliffs, N.J.: Prentice-Hall.

ORNE, M. T. and C. C. HOLLAND 1968 On the Ecological Validity of Laboratory Deceptions. *International Journal of Psychiatry, 6*(4): 282-93.

PATTEN, S. C. 1977a The Case that Milgram Makes. *Philosophical Review, 88:* 350-64. 1977b Milgram's Shocking Experiments. *Philosophy, 52:* 425-40.

PILIAVIN, I. M., J. RODIN, and J. A. PILIAVIN 1969 Good Samaritanism: An Underground Phenomenon? *Journal of Personality and Social Psychology, 13*(4): 289-99.

PILIAVIN, J. A. and I. M. PILIAVIN 1972 Effect of Blood on Reactions to a Victim. *Journal of Personality and Social Psychology, 23:* 353-61.

PIUS XII, POPE 1958 Cited in O. M. Ruebhausen and O. G. Brim, Jr. Privacy and Behavioral Research. *American Psychologist, 21*(1966): 425.

POUND, R. 1957 *The Development of Constitutional Guarantees of Liberty.* New Haven, Conn.: Yale University Press.

PRICHARD, H. A. 1912 Does Moral Philosophy Rest on a Mistake? *Mind, 21* (81): 21-37.

RAINWATER, L. and D. J. PITTMAN 1967 Ethical Problems in Studying a Politically Sensitive and Deviant Community. *Social Problems, 14:* 357-66.

RATHJE, W. L. 1978 Le Project du Garbage 1975: Historic Trade-offs. Chapter 16 of C. L. Redman (Ed.), *Social Archaeology: Beyond Subsistence and Dating.* New York: Academic Press. Pp. 373-79. 1979a Archaeology Reconstructs the Present. *Mosaic, 10*(1): 30-37. 1979b Modern Material Culture Studies. *Advances in Archaeological Method and Theory, 2:* 1-37.

RAWLS, J. 1971 *A Theory of Justice.* Cambridge, Mass.: Harvard University Press.

REATIG, N. 1979 Confidentiality Certificates: A Measure of Privacy Protection. *IRB: A Review of Human Subjects Research, 1*(3): 1-4, 12.

REINHOLD, R. 1979 Seattle Experiment Provides Insight on Minimum Income. *Minneapolis Tribune* (New York Times Service), Sunday, February 18, p. 17f.

RESNICK, J. H. and T. SCHWARTZ 1973 Ethical Standards as an Independent Variable in Psychological Research. *American Psychologist, 28*(2): 134-39.

REYNOLDS, P. D. 1979 *Ethical Dilemmas and Social Science Research.* San Francisco: Jossey-Bass.

RING, K., K. WALLSTON, and M. COREY 1970 Mode of Debriefing as a Factor Affecting Subjective Reaction to a Milgram-Type Obedience Experiment: An Ethical Inquiry. *Representative Research in Social Psychology, 1*(1): 67-88.

RIVLIN, A. 1971 *Systematic Thinking for Social Action.* Washington, D.C.: The Brookings Institution.

ROBERTSON, J. A. 1978 The Scientist's Right to Research: A Constitutional Analysis. *Southern California Law Review, 51*(6): 1203-80. 1979 The Law of Institutional Review Boards. *UCLA Law Review, 26:* 544-49.

ROSENHAN, D. L. 1973 On Being Sane in Insane Places. *Science, 179:* 250-58.

ROTH, J. A. 1959 Dangerous and Difficult Enterprise? *American Sociological Review, 24*(3): 398.

RUBIN, Z. 1970 Jokers Wild in the Lab. *Psychology Today, 4*(7): 18-24.

RUSSELL SAGE FOUNDATION 1970 Guidelines for the Collection, Maintenance, and Dissemination of Public Records. New York: Russell Sage Foundation.

SAGAN, L. A. and A. JOSEN 1976 Medical Ethics and Torture. *New England Journal of Medicine, 294*(26): 1427-30.

SANDERS, J. R. 1979 Complaints Against Psychologists Adjudicated Informally by APA's Committee on Scientific and Professional Ethics and Conduct. *American Psychologist, 34*(12): 1139-44.

SANDERS, J. R. and P. KEITH-SPIEGEL 1980 Formal and Informal Adjudication of Ethics Complaints Against Psychologists. *American Psychologist, 35*(12): 1096-1105.

SAWYER, J. 1966 Measurement and Prediction: Clinical *and* Statistical. *Psychological Bulletin 66*(3):178-200.

SCHAPS, E. 1972 Cost, Dependency, and Helping. *Journal of Personality and Social Psychology, 21:* 74-8.

SCHULMAN, A. D. and H. J. BERMAN 1974 On Berscheid et al. *American Psychologist, 29:* 473-74.

SCOTT, J. 1978 Americans Enjoy Participating in Surveys, ISR Study Shows. *Institute for Social Research Newsletter, 6*(1): 7.

SEEMAN, J. 1969 Deception in Psychological Research. *American Psychologist, 24:* 1025-28.

SEILER, L. H. and J. M. MURTHA 1980 Federal Regulation of Social Research Using "Human Subjects": A Critical Assessment. *American Sociologist, 15* (August): 146-57.

SHAH, S. T. 1969 Privileged Communications, Confidentiality, and Privacy. *Professional Psychology, 1:* 56-69, 159-64, 241-52.

SHERIF, C. W. 1980 Comment on Ethical Issues in Malamuth, Heim, and Feshbach's "Sexual Responsiveness of College Students to Rape Depictions: Inhibitory and Disinhibitory Effects." *Journal of Personality and Social Psychology, 38*(3): 409-12.

SHILS, E. 1973 Muting the Social Sciences at Berkeley. *Minerva, 11*(3): 290-95.

SIMMONS, R. G., S. D. KLEIN, and R. L. SIMMONS 1977 *Gift of Life: The Social and Psychological Impact of Organ Transplantation.* New York: Wiley-Interscience.

SINGER, E. 1978 Informed Consent: Consequences for Response Rate and Response Quality in Social Surveys. *American Sociological Review, 43:* 144-62.

SINGER, P. 1975 *Animal Liberation.* New York: Random House.

SOBLE, A.   1978   Deception in Social Science Research: Is Informed Consent Possible? *Hastings Center Report, 8* (October): 40-6.

STRICKER, L. J.   1967   The True Deceiver. *Psychological Bulletin, 68:* 13-20.

SULLIVAN, D. S. and T. E. DEIKER   1973   Subject-Experimenter Perceptions of Ethical Issues in Human Research. *American Psychologist, 28*(7): 587-91.

SULLIVAN, M. A., Jr., S. A. QUEEN, and R. C. PATRICK   1958   Participant Observation as Employed in the Study of a Military Training Program. *American Sociological Review, 23:* 660-67.

TAPP, J. L. et al.   1974   Continuing Concerns in Cross-Cultural Ethics: A Report. *International Journal of Psychology, 9*(3): 231-49.

TURNBULL, C. M.   1972   *The Mountain People.* New York: Simon & Schuster. 1974   Reply. *Current Anthropology, 15*(1): 103.

VALPARAISO UNIVERSITY LAW REVIEW, 4   1970   Social Research and Privileged Data. Pp. 368-99.

VAN ALSTYNE, W.   1978   A Preliminary Report on the Bakke Case. *AAUP Bulletin, 64*(4): 286-97.

VASQUEZ, A. L. and R. RESCZCZYNSKI   1976   Ethical Questions to Psychologists: Techniques of Torture Used in Chile. Presented at the 21st International Congress of Psychology, Paris.

VAUGHAN, T. R.   1967   Governmental Interventions in Social Research: Political and Ethical Dimensions in the Wichita Jury Recordings. In G. Sjoberg (Ed.), *Ethics, Politics, and Social Research.* Cambridge, Mass.: Schenkman.

VEATCH, R. M.   1978   Three Theories of Informed Consent: Philosophical Foundations and Policy Implications. Chapter 26 of Appendix to *The Belmont Report: Ethical Principles and Guidelines for the Protection of Human Subjects.* Vol. II. (DHEW Publication No. [OS] 78-0014.) Washington, D.C.: U.S. Government Printing Office.

WALKER, C. E.   1967   The Effect of Eliminating Offensive Items on the Reliability and Validity of the MMPI. *Journal of Clinical Psychology, 23:* 363-66.

WALSH, W. B. and S. M. STILLMAN   1974   Disclosure of Deception by Debriefed Subjects. *Journal of Counseling Psychology, 21:* 315-19.

WARNER, S. L.   1965   Randomized Responses: A Survey Technique for Eliminating Error Answer Bias. *Journal of the American Statistical Association, 60:* 63-9.

WARREN, S. and L. D. BRANDEIS   1890   The Right to Privacy. *Harvard Law Review, 4:* 193-220.

WARWICK, D. P.   1973   Tearoom Trade: Means and Ends in Social Research. *Hastings Center Studies, 1*(1): 27-38.   1974   Who Deserves Protection? *The American Sociologist, 9:* 158-59.   1975   Social Scientists Ought to Stop Lying. *Psychology Today, 8* (February): 38, 40, 105-6.   1980   The Politics and Ethics of Cross-Cultural Research. In H. C. Triandis and W. W. Lambert (Eds.), *Handbook of Cross-Cultural Psychology: Perspectives.* Vol. 1. Boston: Allyn & Bacon. Pp. 319-71.

WATSON, P.   1978   *War on the Mind: The Military Uses and Abuses of Psychology.* New York: Basic Books.

WAX, M. L.   1972   Tenting with Malinowski. *American Sociological Review, 37* (1): 1-13.   1980   Paradoxes of "Consent" to the Practice of Fieldwork. *Social Problems, 27*(3): 272-83.

WEBB, E. J., D. T. CAMPBELL, R. D. SCHWARTZ, L. SECHREST, and J. B. GROVE   1981   *Nonreactive Measures in the Social Sciences.* 2d ed. Boston: Houghton Mifflin.

WEBB, T.   1980   Bathhouse Raids Moved Sex Behind Doors. *Minneapolis Tribune,* May 26, pp. 1B, 6B.

WESTIN, A. F.   1967   *Privacy and Freedom.* New York: Atheneum.

WHYTHE, W. F.   1955   *Street Corner Society: The Social Structure of an Italian Slum.* Rev. ed. Chicago: University of Chicago Press.

WICKER, A. W.   1969   Attitudes versus Actions: The Relationship of Verbal and Overt Behavioral Responses to Attitude Objects. *Journal of Social Issues,* 25(4): 41-78.

WOLF, E. and J. G. JORGENSEN   1970   Anthropology on the Warpath in Thailand. *New York Review of Books, 15*(9) (November 19): 26-35.

YOUNGER, K.   1972   *Report of the Committee on Privacy.* London: Her Majesty's Stationery Office.

ZIMBARDO, P. G.   1969   The Human Choice: Individuation, Reason, and Order versus Deindividuation, Impulse, and Chaos. In W. J. Arnold and D. Devine (Eds.), *Nebraska Symposium on Motivation.* Vol. 17. Lincoln: University of Nebraska Press. Pp. 282-93.   1973   The Mind is a Formidable Jailer: A Pirandellian Prison. *The New York Times Magazine* (April 8), Sec. 6. Pp. 38-60.

AUTHOR INDEX

SUBJECT INDEX